CARVED IN ROCK

Short Stories by Musicians

EDITED BY

GREG KIHN

THUNDER'S MOUTH PRESS
NEW YORK

CARVED IN ROCK: *Short Stories by Musicians*

Published by
Thunder's Mouth Press
161 William St., 16th Floor
New York, NY 10038

Library of Congress Cataloging-in-Publication Data is available.

ISBN 1-56025-453-X

9 8 7 6 5 4 3 2 1

Book design by Simon M. Sullivan
Printed in the United States of America
Distributed by Publishers Group West

CONTENTS

Introduction

GREG KIHN

A BOOK like this needs an introduction, but I'll be damned if I know what to say. First of all, I was blown out by how good it turned out. We're talking about musicians here, people who express themselves in a completely different way from ordinary writers. The creative process, however, is more or less the same. Just as the same three chords of life resonate through rock, blues, country, jazz, reggae, rhythm and blues, classical, and every other form of music, so do they resonate through the printed word. Three chords on paper.

In the great tradition of Woody Guthrie, all these musicians have their own *Bound for Glory* somewhere inside them. It was never a question of whether or not it could be done, just *when*.

I take no credit for any of this. The original idea for the anthology came from my very wonderful and endlessly creative literary agent, Lori Perkins.

She brought it to Neil Ortenberg at Thunder's Mouth Press, whose passion kept the idea alive while I slowly drove them all crazy. It took a million years and I missed countless deadlines. Neil's patience showed true elasticity. He assigned one editor after another to ride herd on me and my band of cutthroats, but it wasn't until Michael O'Connor became sheriff of Dodge that things started to happen. Without Neil, Lori, and Mike, you'd be holding air right now.

Some of the people in this book are accomplished writers with literary careers of their own. Others are testing their chops for the first time. The breadth of styles and subject matter varies greatly and, I think, is unique to an anthology like this. In here you'll find everything from sci-fi to comedy to straight narrative fiction. The honesty of the writing and the transparent nature of the prose allow you to see directly into the writer's mind, and hopefully catch a glimpse of who these musicians really are, as opposed to who you think they are. It's heady stuff. I think you'll know them all a little better as a result.

I hope you have as much fun reading this anthology as we had putting it together. To my knowledge it is the first of its kind, and certainly not the last.

Get ready for a hell of a ride.

Rock on.

GREG KIHN

CALIFORNIA, 2003

Don't Forget

(Inspired by a joke told by Willie Nelson)

KINKY FRIEDMAN

A MENTAL hospital is not always as romantic a place as it's sometimes cracked up to be. You always think of Ezra Pound or Vincent van Gogh or Zelda Fitzgerald or Emily Dickinson or Sylvia Plath or someone like that. Not that all the above-mentioned people resided in mental hospitals. All of them probably belonged there, but so do most people who don't reside in mental hospitals. I *know* Emily Dickinson never went to a mental hospital, but that's just because she never went out of her room except, of course, for brief walks in her garden with her dog, Austin. If she'd ever gone into a mental hospital and talked to the shrinks for a while, they never would have let her out. She might've done some good work there but that would've been her Zip Code for the rest of her life. Now you take van Gogh, for example. He lived in one with a cat and did some good work there. They put him in for wearing lighted candles on his hat while painting *Night Cafe*. Today, the arbiters of true greatness, Japanese insurance companies, have determined that his work is worth millions. Sylvia Plath I don't know too much about except that she wrote good prose and maybe some great poetry and then she put her head in an oven and killed herself but by then it was too late for her to reside in a mental hospital. Everybody thought she was crazy for many years until her husband's second wife also croaked herself and then people began to wonder if maybe Sylvia had been all right and it was her fucking husband who was crazy. I mean to have two wives conk on

you like that—I mean each one topping herself on your watch—
pretty well indicated to most people outside of mental hospitals that
if that husband wasn't crazy there was something wrong with him.
Now Ezra Pound I don't know a hell of a lot about except that he
hated Jews and still managed to do some pretty good work in wig
city. Hitler and Gandhi, both of whom probably belonged in wig
city, for different reasons, no doubt, somehow managed to avoid the
mental hospital circuit. They did, however, each spend a bit of time
in prison, which in some ways is not as bad as being in a mental hospital except that you come out with an asshole the size of a walnut.
In a sense both Hitler and Gandhi, who may well represent polar
opposites of the human spirit, found themselves in prison, where the
absence of freedom and the distance from their dreams may have
contributed to their achieving some pretty good work. Hitler, who
hated Jews almost as much as Ezra Pound, wrote *Mein Kampf,* which
was almost immediately translated into about fourteen languages and
would have made him quite a favorite at literary cocktail parties if
he'd been willing to stop there. Unfortunately, he couldn't hold a
candle to Anne Frank. Gandhi, who spent his time in prison listening
to a South African mob singing "We're going to hang ol' Gandhi
from a green apple tree," did some scribbling of his own but mostly
realized that he was tired of London yuppie lawyer drag and it was
time for visions and revisions both sartorially as well as spiritually.
But God only knows how Hitler and Gandhi, who were both interesting customers, would have fared had they been incarcerated in
mental hospitals instead of prisons. As it was, each man found himself in prison, something that almost never happens in a mental hospital because shrinks are constantly prescribing meds that keep you
invariably, perpetually, hopelessly lost. Speaking of lost, Zelda
Fitzgerald certainly qualifies in that category and technically, I suppose, she was confined to a "sanitarium," which was not truly a
mental hospital if you want to be a purist about it but no doubt still

probably had a sign in the lobby that read: THIS IS TUESDAY. THE NEXT MEAL IS LUNCH. She'd been drinking a lot of her meals evidently and so they'd put her in this sanitarium in Asheville, North Carolina, or maybe it was Asheville, South Carolina. I always get those two states mixed up. Where are the Wright Brothers when you need them? Anyway, the irony of the whole situation was that the sanitarium was in Asheville and the place burned down one night with Zelda and a fairly good-sized number of other no-hopers inside. I've wondered why God so often seems to send fires and other catastrophes to sanitariums and mental hospitals. It's kind of like swerving to hit a school bus. But all that being as it may, it's just ironic I thought that the sanitarium burned down and that it was in Asheville. But before Zelda came along to screw things up I was commenting on the fact that mental hospitals are far more sad and sordid places than you'd think, seeing as all these colorful, fragile, famous, ascetic people populate them. I mean it isn't all van Gogh and his cat. I mean there are men following you with their penises shouting, "Am I being rude, mother?" in frightening falsetto voices. People in mental hospitals are shrieking like mynah birds all the time. Or maturbating. Now Dylan Thomas was a good one. He used to masturbate a lot but I don't think they ever put him in a mental hospital, though God only knows he belonged there. And speaking of God only knows, Brian Wilson undoubtedly belongs there, too, except what would happen to the Beach Boys if you put Brian Wilson in wig city? I mean the only one of those guys who was really a surfer was Dennis Wilson. And you know what happened to him? He drowned. Ah well, the channel swimmer always drowns in the bathtub, they say. But I suppose I've come pretty far afield in this tawdry little tale, which the shrinks would assuredly call a rambling discourse. But if getting to the point is the determinant of whether or not you're crazy, then half the world's crazy. Unfortunately, it's the wrong half. I mean, whoever said anything important by merely getting to the point? Did guys like Yeats and Shelley and Keats who, by the way, all belonged in mental hospitals, ever bother getting to the point? I mean what's the point of getting to the point? To show some shrink with a three-inch dick that you're stable, coherent, well grounded? And I haven't even got to Jesus yet. Sooner or later everybody in a mental hospital gets around to Jesus and it's a good thing that they do because I'll let you in on a little secret: Jesus doesn't talk to high school football coaches or televangelists or Bible Belt politicians or good little church workers or Christian athletes or anybody else in this God-fearing, godforsaken world. The only people Jesus ever really talks to are people in mental hospitals. They try to tell us but we never believe them. Why don't we, for Christ's sake? Millions of people in mental hospitals who say they've talked to Jesus can't be wrong. It's the poor devils outside of mental hospitals who are usually wrong or at least full of shit and that's probably why Jesus never talks to them. Anyway, you can probably tell by the fact that I'm not employing any paragraphs and the fact that this little rambling discourse tends to run on interminably that this looks like a mental hospital letter itself. If that's what you think, you're right, because I am in a fucking mental hospital as I'm writing this tissue of horseshit and it's not one of those with green sloping lawns in that area between Germany and France that I always forget the name of. Hey, wait a minute. It's coming to me. Come baby come baby come baby come. Alsace-Lorraine! That's where the really soulful mental hospitals are. Unfortunately, I'm writing this from a mental hospital on the Mexican-Israeli border and they don't have any sloping green lawns. They don't even have any slopes. All they have is a lot of people who talk to Jesus, masturbate, and don't believe they belong in here. It's not a bad life, actually, once you get the hang of it, unless, of course, you hang yourself, which happens here occasionally, usually on a slow masturbation day. Anyway, the reason I'm telling you all this is that I really don't belong here. I've told the doctors. I've told the shrinks.

I've even told a guy who thinks he's Napoleon. The only one who agrees with me is the guy who thinks he's Napoleon. The guy's six feet tall, weighs two hundred and fifty pounds, and he's black, and he thinks he's Napoleon. I probably shouldn't have told him in the first place. But the funny thing is he's right. I don't belong here. The other day a woman reporter came in here from the local newspaper to do some kind of exposé on the place and she interviewed some of the patients and one of them was me. I told her I was perfectly sane and I didn't belong in here. She asked me some questions and we chatted for a while and then she said that I sounded really lucid and normal to her and she agreed that I really didn't belong in here. Then she asked me, since I seemed so normal, what I was doing here in the first place and I told her I didn't know, I just woke up one day and here I was and now the doctors won't let me out. She said for me not to worry. She said when she finished her exposé on my condition, these doctors would have to let me out. Then she shook my hand and headed for the door. About the time she turned to open it I took a Coke bottle and threw it real hard and hit her on the back of the head.

"Don't forget!" I shouted.

from Liverpool Fantasy

LARRY KIRWAN

NOVEMBER 26, 1962, ABBEY ROAD RECORDING STUDIOS, LONDON

"'Please Please Me' is a number one! You just get Parleyclone to put the bloody thing out and we'll be bigger than Elvis!" Lennon took a long drag on his Players, flicked away the butt, then ground it out beneath his boot.

Brian Epstein fingered his tie. That strip of carpet would cost at least forty pounds to replace.

"John!" To his horror, his voice modulated to an undignified falsetto. "How many times do I have to tell you? I think it's great, Mr. Martin thinks it's great, but the people upstairs at Parlaphone, well . . ." As he gathered himself, his pitch plunged, his accent shed all its northern flavor and in precise Etonian, he brayed: ". . . to put it quite bluntly, they would prefer to pursue 'Til There Was You.' I'm afraid it's a *fait accompli*."

Lennon was across the room in milliseconds flat; he stuck his long nose within inches of his manager's cologned face. "Keep yer froggy talk for yer little nancyboys, Eppy! It don't wash around here. Besides, I never even wanted to record that piece of shit in the first place, and now you have the nerve to tell me it's goin' to be our next single."

Epstein rifled his brain for a witty riposte but, as usual, that sullen Liverpool glare got the better of him, and he keened: "John, I just won't have you talk to me like that."

Lennon sneered and removed a piece of lint from Epstein's Saville Row suit. "I'll talk to you any bloody way I like, mate. That's what you're here for—to listen to what we want and then put it into action pronto."

He turned abruptly, winked at George Harrison, then tore off the opening bars of "Johnny B. Goode" on his Rickenbacker. George joined in but was left dangling on a suspended E seventh when Lennon choked the chord. Ringo Starr combed back his greasy hair and continued to keep time with a hefty four on the floor; finally, noticing the strained silence, he halted in mid-beat, and mumbled an unnoticed apology.

"I believe that if you read the terms of our contract," Epstein said, "you'll find that the contrary is quite the case. My duties are, and I quote: 'to advise you in all matters relating to your career.' And the choice of the next single, if I may be so bold, is absolutely crucial to the whole development of this endeavor."

"You can quote and be bold till you're blue in the face, it's all a one to me."

"Listen, you chaps." A megaphonic voice intruded from the control booth. George Martin straightened his silk tie and strode into the studio. In his corduroy pants, cashmere jumper and tan hush puppies, he appeared to float across the soundproofed room—a paragon of ease and detachment in this maelstrom of bruised egos, black leather, and sweat-stained guitars.

"Would it be at all possible," he ventured, "to try and approach this from a . . . well, less emotional point of view?"

Lennon unslung his Rick. With a sigh that would have done justice to St. Lawrence roasting on the spit, he grimaced at the lanky Harrison, who raised a nonchalant eyebrow while continuing to glide through his minor scales.

Lennon's look was not lost on Martin. "I have little doubt, John, that subsequent to the success of 'Til There Was You,' I can persuade my financial people to release 'Please Please Me' as a follow-up. Success breeds success, and . . ."

"Listen, wack, 'Love Me Do' got to number seventeen without any help from Parleyclone, and you know why?" Lennon jammed his index finger into Martin's cashmered chest. " 'Cause everybody and his aunt Fanny bought it up Merseyside. So put that in your pipe and smoke it, Mister Martin!"

But Mister Martin was made of sterner stuff than Mister Epstein and was not inclined to allow some trumped-up Liverpool teddy boy to get the one-up on him. He soaked up Lennon's scowl, then, cool as the other side of the pillow, said, "John, 'Love Me Do' was my product, too, remember? But I'm afraid the figures were too distinctly regional."

"Listen here, Georgie boy, we're not talkin' about sellin' cornflakes or Morris Minors. This is rock and roll . . . or is that a forbidden term around here?"

"On the contrary, I personally feel that you chaps have a wonderful future in the world of light entertainment; that's why I was thrilled when Paul suggested including 'A Taste of Honey' and 'Til There Was You.' "

Paul McCartney shrugged modestly and smiled. His meticulously tousled brown hair framed a round, boyish face, while his teeth gleamed in the soft glow of the overhead lights.

Lennon creased him with a glare. "It's a wonder we didn't have a go at 'Mary Had a Little Lamb.' Nursery crimes are all the go nowadays."

McCartney's smile dimmed to a troubled leer. He picked up his Hofner, bounced a couple of harmonics off the G string, and stared strategically off into the distance.

Lennon's guitar began to feedback, and he slapped angrily at the open strings. A burst of raw treble screeched through the studio but expired in mid-flight when he switched his amp to standby.

The red signal lights from the Vox AC-30s that had shimmered reassuringly through the session now seemed to cast a forlorn, eery glow. Ringo sniffled, then coughed in the troubled silence.

Epstein gazed in despair at his pride and joys. Even when they were at each other's throats, they could instantly coalesce and make him feel like the outsider he was. After all, he hadn't even heard of them back in the old days at the Jacaranda; nor had he speeded his brain off on prellies through eight-hour marathons in Hamburg. No, Johnny-Come-Lately Mister Manager, from toffee-nosed Childwall, had "discovered" them when they were already turning away scrubbers by the score from the Cavern—the hottest thing out of Liverpool since the Mersey Tunnel.

"Look here now, John," he said. " 'Til There Was You' is a marvelous song, and Peggy Lee herself has given it her personal seal of approval."

Lennon's guitar had begun sliding off his amp. Without taking his eyes off Epstein, he kicked back and shoved it in place. As he lit another cigarette, his upper lip quivered with rage. "When are you goin' to get it into your thick skull that you're managin' the Beatles, not bloody Acker Bilk! We're a rock and roll group; or, at least, we used to be until you came round and tried to deball us, you . . . !"

"John, please be reasonable." Epstein dabbed at his damp brow with a royal blue handkerchief.

"Reasonable! You know how you spell that word?" He jabbed his Players at Eppy's face. "S-E-L-L-O-U-bloody-T!"

The beleaguered manager retreated until his back was up against the window of the control booth.

"We used to be gear, mate," Lennon spewed forth bile that had been festering for months. "We used to get up on stage and play our balls off on anything that came into our heads. Then you said: 'You've got to be reasonable, John, you've got to write out a list of all the numbers you propose doing in a night.' As if I know what the hell I'm goin' to do till I get up there and do it."

He shook his head at the thought of such sacrilege; then, sucking in his cheeks, he pirouetted—hand on hip—and lisped, "After that, it was: 'Well, John, we've got to be reasonable, we can't have you goin' on stage like a crowd of teddy boys. So you get us to wear them silly collarless suits, like a crowd of bloody King's Road ponces. Well, let me tell you something, mate, this is the way I dress, 'cause this is the way I *feel*."

He jerked at his black leather jacket and blue jeans. "This is what we've always worn," he pointed at the other three, "and it did us right well till we had the misfortune to run into a wanker like you!"

The sweat was oozing from Epstein. He again reached for his handkerchief, but Lennon snatched it from him and loudly blew his nose in its laundered creases.

"John, this is outrageous! I really must protest."

"Ah, protest my bollocks!" Lennon said. "Once upon a time I could go anywhere Merseyside and hold me head high. Now I have to listen to Marsden, and the rest of 'em, sneerin' behind me back. 'Oh, there goes Little Lord Fauntleroy in his snazzy suit and his shiny boots, all paid for by Queenie Boy Epstein. Next thing you know he'll have 'em all wearin' silk knickers and bendin' for him into the bargain.'"

"Oh, for Christ sake, lay off him and for once in your life be reasonable," Paul pleaded, unaware that the hated adjective was ricocheting around the room—a red rag to a scouse bull.

Lennon flung a half-empty bottle of lager at the carpeted wall. Everyone ducked as beer sprayed the gleaming set of Ludwig drums. "Don't you know any other fucking word?" he roared, arms outstretched like a Merseyside Christ.

He grabbed for another half-filled bottle as band, producer, and management hit the deck; but instead, he took a long thirsty swig. "For Jaysus sake, Paul"—he belched and wiped off his mouth—"if it's got to be one of yours, why don't you do 'Long Tall Sally' or 'Tutti Frutti.' Somethin' that we can all be proud of. Right, George?"

"Yeah," the guitarist nodded, "my vote's for 'Please Please Me.' It's more us. It just bloody well is."

Lennon glowered triumphantly at Epstein and Martin. After some moments of dithering, they retreated to the safety of the control booth. But Lennon was relentless. He spun around, gave them the finger, and yelled into an open microphone, "This is a private conversation, if you don't mind!" His voice boomed through their monitors, and the two unmasked eavesdroppers quaked from the shock.

Satisfied, he turned to the others. "They backed down when we wouldn't do 'How Do You Do It.' All we have to do is stick to our guns, and they'll bloody well back down again."

Paul counted to a silent three and sighed. "Maybe we should go along with 'Til There Was You' and get them to put it in writin' that they'll release 'Please Please Me' next."

"If we back down on this, we'll be just another bunch of puppets and them two spastics in there'll be pullin' the strings. Next thing you know, we'll be dressed in tuxedos and singin' 'Moon bloody River' or the like."

Ringo was in like lightning—brushing along to a dead march version of the Johnny Mathis hit. Paul iced him. "No one's goin' to make us do anything! But Eppy does have a point! 'Til There was You' could do well across the pond."

"Oh, fuck America, and you, too, if that's all you can think of!"

"There's no need for that kind of talk, John, I want to do the right thing as much as the next one. It's just that we've all worked so hard for this break."

"Listen, this time there's no sittin' on the fence, lad. We have to go in there and tell 'em it's 'Please Please Me' or else they can stick their deal where the monkey stuck his nuts."

McCartney's lips hardened, and the baby fat seemed to drain from his face. "I'm not goin' back to Liverpool."

Lennon took another Players from the pack and tapped it against the heel of his hand. He frowned as he gathered his composure. "That's an odd kind of talk, lad."

"And no way am I goin' back to Hamburg to play all night for chip money!"

"Yeah, but at least back there we were our own bosses." Lennon tried to overwhelm him. "Not like on these bloody package tours with a crowd of dossers, wankin' around for twenty minutes a night."

"But that's progress, John! We're takin' home twenty-five quid a week each, and if we get a hit record, God knows . . ."

"Yeah, but if that hit is 'Til There Was Puke,' we'll be playin' the London Palladium to a houseful of geriatrics, openin' for Mel Torme or some other Yank wanker."

Paul paled somewhat at this scenario, and Lennon blazed on. "Listen! What's the worst that can happen? Even if I'm dead wrong, and they give us our papers? We'll make it one way or another, and on our own terms, too, right, lads?"

George strummed a diminished seventh and stepped on his vibrato foot-switch. While the chord swirled, he deadpanned: "I don't know, John, if your aunt Mimi ever hears you turned down a gig with Melly Tormented, you'll be for the high jump."

Paul was unconvinced but Lennon had a full head of steam. "Bugger the whole lot of them! We'll march out of here with our flags flyin', take the van back to Liverpool, and start all over again. And we don't have to go back to Hamburg neither; we've had a top-twenty hit in this country, and I bet we can get a new record company without Mister Big Shot Epstein. Where are we goin', Ringo?"

"Home, John?"

"No, you dumb bollocks! Where are we really goin'?"

"Oh yeah, to the top, mate." The drummer finally remembered the pre-gig drill.

"What top, George?"

"To the topper most?" George added somewhat more confidently.

"What topper most, Paul?"

"To the topper most of the . . . bloody popper most."

Lennon needled him. "I can't hear you, wack!"

"Oh, give over!" Paul pointed at the control room, where George Martin was talking on the phone. Epstein studied him, his chin cocked like a pointer. Once, he glanced out into the studio, his watery eyes darting ferally, but when he caught Lennon staring back, he looked away. They watched, fascinated, as Martin, urbane to the end, smiled, frowned, and silently coaxed.

"Me uncle looks like that when he's talkin' to his bookie," Ringo said, but no one paid him any heed.

The producer put down the phone and, solemn as a curate at a funeral, shook his head. Epstein dropped his forehead onto his palms and ran his fingers through his hair. He rubbed his eyes and nodded an unspoken assent. Then, taking a deep breath, he strode out of the control room.

Outside in the studio, they barely heard the insulated door open. However, to a man, they jumped and then squinted when Martin switched on the full lights that banished shadows and illusions, but not the gloom. John and Paul exchanged glances, each noting the pallor of the other. Epstein came right up to them, his face a study in despair. "It's no use, fellows. They're insisting on 'Til There Was You.' "

Lennon shrugged and switched off his amp. The red light on the Vox faded back into its tiny bulb. He unplugged his Rick and packed it in its case.

"Wait, John, I haven't told you the good part yet."

Lennon pulled his chord from the amp, deliberately wound it, and began to hum "Please Please Me."

"Will you please listen to me," Epstein implored. "Capitol has agreed to release 'Til There Was You' in the States, directly after Christmas. If it does anything, anything at all, we can be over there by Easter. I swear it, even if I have to pay for the whole trip myself."

But Lennon hummed on, and hung a blues interpretation on the bridge, stretching out the "rain" until it flowed like chiseled honey into "my heart."

George noted the stylistic change as he too packed his guitar. Ringo didn't care for it, but wiped off his drumsticks and stuck them in his jacket pocket.

"For God's sake, think of what you're throwing away," Epstein persisted.

But Lennon was already on his way to the door, busily deconstructing the last verse.

"John Lennon, don't you walk out on me!"

John Lennon didn't turn around. He threw open the door with a flourish and stalked off down the corridor, roaring the last chorus at the top of his lungs.

The slamming of a street door cut off the song in mid-syllable. For some seconds, a mortuary stillness gripped the studio, then George clicked his guitar case closed and flicked off his amp. Only one red light continued to glow. Epstein grabbed him as he walked past. "George, bring him back . . . please?"

"So long, Eppy. You're not as bad as they say you are."

"You're throwing away a fortune!"

The guitarist hesitated a moment, but then, ever conscious of his cool, turned up his jacket collar and countered, "Yeah, but I'm keepin' me integrity."

Ringo battened down his quiff against blustery November and scrupulously removed the ensuing dandruff from his shoulders. "Thanks for everything, Mister Epstein," he murmured.

Epstein didn't reply. He heard the street door slam behind George and, a moment later, close discreetly behind Ringo. Paul, meanwhile, gave a shrug and reached down for his Hofner. As he touched the steel strings, a small jolt of static darted up through his fingers. He recoiled, and a wave of rebellion surged through him. "He'll be back soon enough when his money runs out," he snapped and, firing up the volume, viciously dug into the intro of "Bring It on Home."

Epstein threw one last lingering look down the hallway. Then, with his heart coming apart at the seams, he closed the studio door. The red "recording in progress" light flashed on in the empty corridor.

Curtis's Charm

from FEAR OF DREAMING

JIM CARROLL

I RAN into my old friend Curtis yesterday, way uptown—the edges of Harlem. We'd been on a drug detox program together many years ago, long before they became fashionable and assumed the look of Ivy League campuses. We got fairly tight then . . . everyone did in those bleak surroundings.

Curtis had the same look as back then: long straggly goatee like some Chinese astrologer. A shaved head, giving him a remarkable resemblance to the boxer Marvin Hagler (though only about half his size).

I saw Curtis coming from a block away, heading downtown on Fifth with that cranked, purposeful walk of a purposeless man. He was cutting through the humidity with rocking elbows, auto-cruising on major fear and bad crack. Dangerously bad crack, speed-laced, dearly in want of sedative grace.

He was wearing the same hat he had on at our last chance meeting six years ago—a short-billed black beanie, leather. He told me that the blue zippered jacket and dark blue baggy trousers I was wearing made me look like I was on a work detail from Riker's Island. After asking about mutual colleagues from the old days and other musings, Curtis came up square on me with his eyes. Serious contact. Urgent. The whites of those eyes were as yellow as an old sheep's. I envied the man's teeth, however. He asked me if I was in any rush; said that he was involved in a situation which I might be able to help with. "You be just who I need talking to right now," he spoke, just above a whisper.

We crossed Fifth Avenue and walked down the stairs leading into one of the secret jewels of Central Park, the Conservatory Gardens. All the flowers were blooming full, all the benches were empty. Except for a suspicious park worker grooming the curve of a hedge with huge, brutal shears, it seemed we two were alone. We took a bench near the back gate, surrounded by high rows of pink mums, and surveyed the hordes of flora. I mentioned that these gardens were the place where Ben E. King came to get into the lyric of "Rose in Spanish Harlem" the morning before recording it.

"What ever happened to Joe Tex?" Curtis asked, by way of a non sequitur reply.

"No idea," I answered.

"See if you can find out," he said, almost as a command.

"You know," he went on, "I heard that James Brown once offered to pay for one of those sex change operations for Joe Tex, so that he could marry him as a bitch. He said he loved Joe's voice so damn much that he wanted to get down with him, but not like a faggot, dig? He wanted to marry him so as all be right in God's eyes and shit. You ever hear that?"

I hadn't, but I said that I had.

Then Curtis shot me another look that said it was time to cut through the chitchat. The guy with the giant shears was getting closer; the sound of his furious snipping getting loud and frightful in the silent, sweet-scented air.

Curtis is badly troubled. He's in a place where, for once, his street smarts and weaponry don't fit in nor do any good. As his tale tells, he's convinced that his new Caribbean mother-in-law, an adept of the dark tricks, is tagging him with sundry spells of heavy voodoo Ju-Ju. He claims he can feel the curse infiltrating his brain like flaming arrows through his ears.

His wife told him that because he's been seeing other women and spending the money designated for groceries and Pampers on crack, that now her mother is going to settle the score with various incantations and magic brews. He tells me that, right as we are speaking, there is a small brass crucible in the old hag's apartment with his name on it, and with his photo and some snippings from his privates resting within.

"And any hour now," he states, pacing back and forth (nearly trampling a row of peach hibiscus), "this old bitch's gonna take something from one of them voodoo supply jars she got all over the house and toss it onto my picture in that there bowl. My wife says that if it be some kinda herbs or shit tossed in, then I be all right that all it gonna do is straighten me out . . . you know, smarten up my ass and keep me in line.

"But if her moms wants to really get down to business, then she gonna take a scorpion, or some other creep poison bug, from them jars, and then I gonna be one sorry-ass black man hurting like a mo'fo' and there ain't nothin'—not a damn thing—that any straight-up doctor can do."

I was shifting all over the bench during Curtis's rant. His fear was genuine, his eyes widely palpitant with it. And I knew, now that he had opened the ventilation shaft, that I was in this problem for the long haul. It wasn't the type of day I wanted to spend disarming delusion either. It was only 10:30 A.M., but the grace period of cooler morning air had disappeared. The temperature was heading toward the mid-nineties again and the humidity was conjuring steam from the garden growth. The well-tended, even lines of flora suddenly seemed more like a virgin rain forest. The sweat from Curtis's black pores flowed free from his face as the porous neurons of madness, demons, and drugs fired through his mind. It seemed yellow-tinted, this sweat, as if from years of orange methadone biscuits and bad cocaine cut.

"Listen," he went on. "I know what you're thinking, but I know that this woman's shit be working on me already. Like, I been doing some weird stuff lately, or better said, some weird shit's been being done to me.

"The other week, I passed out smoking a plain old joint, and *two days later* I woke up in some rotten homeless men's shelter in *Queens!* In Queens, man, dig that! I ain't never been to Queens before that. Caused all sorts of problems. I missed my face-to-face down at Welfare and they held up my digit for eight damn days. Got in trouble at the methadone clinic, as well. They went and lowered my dose, so now each bottle I sell on the street be worth five dollars less than before.

"And when I get home and tell my wife what happened and why I was gone, she tells me, all nonchalant, that I just got hold of some bad grass . . . like it had been angel-dusted or some such nonsense. But I know, goddamn it, that it was her momma at work with her evil shit.

"But all that's chump stuff compared to what came next. Worse by far is what I've been *seeing* lately. Now, first of all, let me explain one thing. You see, I know that my wife's been stealing money out of my trouser pockets at night after I put on my house-shorts. So I been hiding the bread the last couple of weeks. But it don't do no good, because with her powers, my wife's old lady can see where it be hid, by rattling some beads and looking into this bowl of green water she got on her living room table. And she tells my wife. But even if I keep a twenty-four-hour eye on the bitch, I can't stop her from taking the money because—and don't you laugh man 'cause what I'm telling you be true; I saw it and I'm counting on you to help 'cause I figure you know about weird shit, and I can't talk about this to anyone else. You see, I can't stop her from stealing my stash because now she got the powers from her momma . . . or maybe it's the old lady herself coming over at night to my apartment . . . but one of them, somehow, *knows how to change into an animal.*

"And not just one kind of animal, but any kind of animal they want to be, no fucking lie. Because three days ago, only about eight blocks from right here, I saw this squirrel jump off a tree limb from Central Park onto the sidewalk on Fifth Avenue, and I'm sure, I'm positive, that little furry mo'fo' was following me down 108th Street, all the way to Third Avenue, while I was scoring some dimes of rock. Now when was the last time you saw a squirrel on Third Avenue, man? And the way that little sucker was looking at me, you know, sitting up on its hind legs like they do? You wouldn't believe it, man."

I didn't, but said nothing as Curtis paused in his astonishing rap. The guy with the shears was working much too hard for a city employee in high humidity. The *swish . . . clang* sound was so loud that Curtis almost had to yell the last part of his story.

We both stared at the guy; he sped up his act, staring straight back at us with a sick, defiant smile. Curtis freaked. He ran over to a trash can and loaded up with three or four empty soda cans, which he proceeded to wing at the guy in rapid succession. "He's one of them, man," Curtis yelled over to me as he continued to fling crushed aluminum. "He works for the old lady."

I grabbed Curtis while the besieged gardener ducked out of sight behind a hedge, and led him out the back gate. We ran up a hill and over some rocks, finally collapsing in totally-out-of-shape exhaustion on a grass patch beside a secluded path.

"Sorry man," Curtis spoke in half breaths. "It was just that I didn't like the way he smiled. It was evil."

"I think he was a cop, Curtis," my voice flared up. "He probably just thought we were getting high. You got to control yourself."

"You're most likely right." Curtis looked up, all settled in a crouch position now, wanting back my full attention. "Well, fuck that dude anyway . . . where was I?"

"You were being spied on, while purchasing drugs, by a squirrel," I answered.

"Right, but that was only the start." He took a look around, then continued.

"Last night was much stranger. Listen here: last night I was sitting at home in my good chair, feet up, watching a cowboy movie, and what do I see? On a bible, now, I'm swearing to this: right in my living room come this little black mouse—a shade of black the same as my wife, come to think of it—moving across the floor right beside the wall, *with a ten dollar bill in its mouth!*

"It was stopping after every ten feet or so, looking around all sneaky, just like a thief . . . *with a ten dollar bill in its mouth, man.* And it was coming straight from the direction of the loose plastic brick at the bottom of the phony fireplace where I been hiding my money. I looked over at the brick and could tell it had been moved just a tiny crack.

"So I got up to chase the little mo'fo' and it splits around the corner, then right under the bedroom door. I fling the door open and it's gone, nowhere in sight, and my wife is just laid out on the bed, all naked and chilled, with a big shit-eating grin on her face. I know she had that ten dollar bill stashed somewhere, and I know the only reason she be naked was because she'd just changed back from being the mouse and didn't have no time yet to put something on.

"So you tell me, man, can her momma, or anyone, have the power to change someone into a mouse, or a squirrel? You tell me, 'cause if the old bitch can do that, then I know any curse she wants to put on me is gonna work, and my butt be burning."

Curtis looked up at me in wounded-animal terror. The expression on his face was like that of an onlooker at a lynching in some gray turn-of-the-century photograph. I knew now that my old friend Curtis's fears were, in his mind, very real and, if anything, had become a perfect ally for the mother's sympathetic magic, real or imagined.

He asked again if I thought such powers of transmutation possible . . . if I'd read about that and these voodoo spells and curses. I told him how shape-shifting was big in the Middle Ages, but had pretty much petered out as of late, after making a short and abortive comeback in the late 1800s in France. I assured him that, even if her credentials were genuine, it was not at all likely his mother-in-law could turn his wife into either mouse or squirrel. Then I explained what I knew regarding homeopathic magic, breaking it down into its sub-sections of contagious and sympathetic magic. This was all pretty much out of *The Golden Bough,* and I realized halfway through it was a bit too academic for Curtis's benefit, under the circumstances. He just wanted to know if the old lady's curses were going to work, and, that being the case, what he could do in self-defense.

"See, that's just the point," I spoke up. "The worst thing you can do about any of this black magic shit is let yourself believe it works, and that you got no defense against it. Once you let that notion inside your head, then you're just gonna get paranoid and help it along. It's like they plant this seed of self-destruction inside you, and your sense of helplessness just waters the thing. The thing to do is think righteously and purify yourself, then any curse aimed at you will be thrown back off you and returned to the sender, working against her seven times stronger than when it was sent."

"How am I supposed to purify myself at this point, man? I mean, we're like two germs talking to each other."

He had a point, though I took umbrage at Curtis classifying me on an equal basis of "germ" as himself. I convinced him that I had made great strides since we first knew each other, as drug-infested microbes, toward "purifying" myself . . . at least to the degree where I could deal efficaciously against the forces of evil which he had incurred.

Whether or not this claim had any validity was irrelevant, and my reasons for putting the idea forth were not as petty as they might, at first, seem. The fact is that I had come up with a *plan,* and one of its essential aspects was gaining my man Curtis's unswerving belief that I had the power to carry it through.

The situation was clear. I had no chance of assuaging Curtis's terror by any psychobabble pep talks. He wasn't buying that shit, and who could blame him? He'd been tailed by a squirrel, and stood by helplessly as an Afro-mouse, who was his wife, raided his stash and made off with a ten dollar bill.

I was gonna fight Curtis's battle on a fire versus fire, or magic versus magic, basis. I'd match her spell for spell. In my sudden enthusiasm, I blocked out the possibility that his adversary might be horribly genuine, that my face, name, and address might be at this moment showing up clearly on the surface of her bowl of green water. *And what about* the dude with the loud gardening shears? Like I said before: no city worker works that fastidiously in that much heat.

No matter. I had, if not exactly purity, then stupidity and good intentions on my side. And a plan.

We started walking; I wanted to think on the move. Just as we were about to reach the large open meadow at 100th Street, however, we stumbled onto another frightful detour. At the base of a jagged boulder, its facade illuminated in red by some indecipherable glyphs, were three headless chickens. They didn't seem too old, though the open-neck cavities were being furiously traversed by about a dozen species of insects, busy and buzzing. Black candle stubs were scattered about, along with several half-smoked cigars. It was obviously the remnants of some ritual, a small oblation to some three-thousand-year-old Congolese river goddess. I suppose the old axiom holds true for elemental gods as well as old artists: If you continue to do anything long enough, people will begin to take you seriously.

All this dark synchronicity was becoming a bit tiresome. Was there any fucking glen or glade in this park without the vestiges of that old black magic?

I looked up at Curtis; he was gone. I saw him waving from a bench about two hundred yards away, on the edge of the meadow. Apparently the headless-chickens scene had inspired a dash out of Curtis that any world class sprinter could have envied. I sat down beside him on the bench, surveying the big, open field. It felt good seeing little wholesome kids playing whiffle ball with their dads, probably all divorced and out on their visitation day. Nothing spooky here.

I took out my mini-notepad and ripped out a blank page. I held it up in front of Curtis's face, that same strange sweat just moaning from his pores.

"Now we can take care of business, man. Putting aside all the bullshit of 'why' and 'how,' what you need is some magic of your own . . . some sort of protective charm or talisman, to block out this insinuating evil and neutralize it for good."

"That be exactly what I need!" Curtis perked up. "That's what I wanted all along, but can you do it?"

"Can I do it?" I sneered, my tone rebuking him for his doubts. "Of course I can do it. Man, you got to trust me." My main mission, at this point, was instilling total belief in the spiritual sleight of hand which I was winging.

"I've got a spell to match anything the dark force can toss your way, proven and powerful. I picked it up from this great holy man on the Island of Cyprus. They call him 'The Magus of Strovolos.' "

Curtis was visibly impressed by this arcane-sounding appellation. I had his attention and complete confidence. Actually, the Magus does indeed exist, as does the prescription for protection I was about to lay on Curtis. As for how legitimate its powers were, I could not really say since I'd only read about it in a book about the holy man. Certainly, it had the simplicity, precision, and elegance of a prayer—quite genuine, to both the heart and the mind. Naturally, whether I possessed any semblance of the purity of spirit essential to performing the task was another matter altogether.

I bent down on one knee and laid my notepaper across a day-old *New York Post*. I realized the moment I first laid my felt-tip down that I must have had more faith in the Magus than I realized, because I suddenly felt overwhelmed by a sense of blasphemy. Referring again to what I'd read in *The Magus of Strovolos*, I shut my eyes and pictured a ball of white light unwinding from my hand and surrounding my entire body. Still I heard the tiny voice in my head repeating the phrase: "*You kidding me?*"

I looked up at Curtis. I was now really pissed off that he had dragged me into this shit.

But I'd waved the blank paper as a promise in his face, and I had to deliver. I began forming the lines on the paper. First symbol was the Star of David, centered in the bottom half of the page. Then around it I drew four small crosses: north, south, east, west. Beneath each cross I printed the names of the four hierarchical archangels: Michael, Raphael, Ariel, and Gabriel. I confess that there was a specific clockwise order to these names—corresponding, I believe, to the four elements as well as the compass points—but I couldn't remember who went where, so I began with Michael on top and then continued randomly from there. That was the bottom half of the charm. It was sort of a preparatory incantation . . . a sort of spirit-battery. I held it up to Curtis. "This is the source of power. Now, above it, we address the evil that's challenging you."

I began on the upper half, Curtis scoping in tightly over my shoulder. The first designation here was a snake. Up until now, everything was straight lines and letters, but this required some slight ability of basic draughtsmanship, a gift which I have never possessed. Nevertheless, I got on with it, and the results seemed satisfactory enough to me. As I lifted the pen a moment, however, Curtis snatched the paper up and held it between us, hand trembling.

"What you doing drawing a picture of a *dick*, man?" he exclaimed vehemently. "I thought this be good magic . . . holy and good."

"That's a snake, not a damn dick," I sighed, lifting the paper out of his hand. "Here, let me fix it up a bit."

I embellished some rings around my snake rendering, then added a rattle on its tail and a long forked tongue darting all nasty from its mouth. I held it up again for Curtis's perusal.

"Still looks more like a dick than a snake," Curtis went on, "just got a fork coming out its tip now."

"Listen, man, it's just a *symbol*, you know," I shot back, peeved. "I ain't no photorealist, okay?" Besides, maybe that's what your dick looks like, but not mine."

I was down to the last sign. I drew a bolt of lightning, which started from the very top of the page and passed right through the snake's neck. It continued on to mid-page and ended. A righteous zapping of the serpentine evil archetypes by the Celestial Hierarchies.

I had Curtis sign the spell in the bottom corner, then I folded it in a series of elaborate angles. It was supposed to wind up as a neat, tiny pyramid of paper, but it came out more like some prehensile trapezoid. No matter, it was close enough. Curtis accepted it with a reverence and relief. "Now I got the mojo," he exclaimed, placing it in his pocket.

"Don't flaunt it, Curtis," I told him. "By the way, according to the Magus, you have to take it to church and sprinkle a little holy water over it. It's important . . . any Catholic church carries the stuff."

Whatever the real potency of the Magus's diagram, its effect on Curtis was exactly what I'd hoped for. His faith in the folded charm was absolute; his hands kept caressing the pocket which held it. I was wiped out . . . wanted to get away from there and soak my brain into something fresh and forgetful.

We came out of the park at 98th Street and Fifth. Curtis split uptown, turning around every twenty feet or so with some gesture of thanks. I stood watching him a short while, then headed down 98th Street over to Madison to pick up a paper.

Finally free of Curtis's presence and concerns, I was swamped with speedily vacillating thoughts and feelings during this one-block walk: the power of evil, the power of goodness, the extent of a joke's success. What if I was feeling some legitimate sense of faith, no matter how disarrayed? There was nothing wrong with that. The small voice again: "You kidding me?"

I reached the corner, fairly much neutralizing these rival, racing thoughts, which had all pulled up lame far before reaching the finish line.

Suddenly I thought of *The Tempest:*

But this rough magic I here abjure . . . .

I paid for the paper in one of those Korean combination newspaper- and tobacco/stationery/groceries/small-notions/and-salad-bar stores on the corner of Madison. What I saw as I exited the place just froze me on the spot. It actually felt like someone had smashed something rare and made of blue blown glass inside my brain. I did my first Manhattan double-take in about fifteen years.

Lying right there on the sidewalk, busy with lunchtime staffers from Mt. Sinai Hospital, was a snake. It was dead, of course, and only about nine inches long, but there it was. And how long could it have been there? Certainly no fastidious, eagle-eyed Korean merchant with a staff of fourteen relatives would allow a dead snake to linger very long right in front of his establishment.

Question: When was the last time you saw a snake in Manhattan? I grew up here, and I've never before seen a snake on a sidewalk, not in any borough (including Staten Island). I've never seen one in a park either. In all my years walking New York City, this was the first snake I'd seen.

At this point, I'm not buying any notion of coincidence: snake in Magus's instructions, snake in drawing, snake on sidewalk one block away.

I moved over and checked closer. Once again, the blue glass rattled in my brain, as I saw how it had been killed. Its body had been severed right at the neck . . . only a few strands of fiber and sinew held the head together with the remainder of its body: body of snake on sidewalk one block away sliced straight at neck . . . body of snake in talisman pierced at neck by lightning bolt of occult elemental righteousness. *"You kidding me?"*

I started to act hyper and strange. I wanted to catch up to Curtis and let him see this scene for himself. I needed corroboration. Apparently, I began thinking, I possess powers of some elect few, great gifts from the psycho-noetic realms. There could be money in it. I eyed an empty storefront across the street. I needed Curtis as witness, to pass the word on to others.

I grabbed a Korean stacking newspapers in front of the store. "Don't let anything happen to that snake . . . do you understand me? I'll be right back." He pulled away and ran inside. "Screw it," I yelled, running over and swiping up the filthy reptile from the sidewalk. I held it at arm's length before me with both hands, the head in one, the body in the other. It was essential the two sections didn't come apart now.

I ran over to Fifth Avenue and up to 103rd Street, fingers pointing at me from every direction. Finally, I realized there was no way I was going to find Curtis. Also, complete exhaustion from my run had sobered me considerably. I was a man holding a dead snake (with tenderish care) on a busy street lined with buses and their gawking passengers.

I went a few feet to the park wall and tossed the snake beneath a bush, once again abjuring the rough magic.

UPDATE

IT'S BEEN two months now since my adventure with Curtis in Central Park. I've been trying to find him, both to fill him in on the subsequent events of that strange day and to find out what his present situation is. I've had no success, however, and don't imagine I will. According to a mutual friend I saw two nights ago, Curtis has been seen by no one, having, a month before, fled the jurisdiction of New York City authorities and a charge of burning out the guts of the entire building in which his wife was, along with her mother, presently residing. Fortunately, nobody was injured in the blaze, though the mother-in-law's irreplaceable collection of Caribbean esoterica, as well as a small menagerie of reptiles, rodents, and insects, was completely destroyed. Whether Curtis ever took the time and effort to locate the prescribed holy water and sprinkle it on the talisman, I cannot say.

I, for one, would like to know the answer.

Bad Reputation

Joan Jett and Greg Kihn

VAMPIRES MAKE lousy lovers. They got no soul. That's why they want it so bad in others, so they can suck it out. Sucking is their whole world. Hunched over a nubile young thing, fangs inserted, lips clamped, sucking furiously, they can't exist any other way. Makes them kinda one-dimensional. I prefer a warm body, know what I mean?

Another thing—gender don't mean shit to a vampire. Once you're undead, what else matters? You're a predator, and you'd take man, woman, or child, to satisfy your craving. Shit, you'd take a dog, if need be. Or a rat or a raccoon. Being a vampire is a lot like being a junkie, when you think about it. Soul suckers one and all.

Which is not to say that vampires don't feel things. They do, just not remorse. They feel basic stuff, like hunger and greed.

Recently, though, something's happened. I noticed it first about a year ago.

In the black hearts of the undead, a craving for rock and roll nurtured itself, growing like a tumor on their endless angst. Once the pain and eternal agony found a voice, they started showing up at gigs.

Oh, great. Like I don't have enough shit to worry about.

I've seen them all over. Once you know what to look for, they're easy to spot. Pale, anemic-looking, exotic, otherworldly creatures. They float on the fringes of the rock movement where they can almost blend in. The Village, Jersey, Philly, D.C., Chicago, New Orleans, London, and most of all San Francisco. They love the fog. That, and all the lovely young souls who roam the streets with no place to go, all the pretty necks pulsing with rich red blood. Nothing turns a vampire on like corrupting the sweet and innocent, like mold growing on the ripest fruit.

That's how I came to know them.

A chick I knew crossed paths with a couple of bloodsuckers at an after-hours place in San Francisco. She showed up looking wan and ravaged at my hotel room at four in the morning, bleeding from puncture wounds all over her body. I called an ambulance, what else could I do? She needed a transfusion right away. She told me what happened.

"They sucked me. At first I liked it . . . kinda . . . then I started to get scared. They wouldn't stop. I fought but they held me down. Then I felt my life draining away and I just screamed and screamed. There were three of them, and they all fed on me at once, like suckling pigs."

"Like suckling pigs?" I said.

"Yeah, fuckin' suckling pigs."

"What are you saying?"

"Nothin'. I'm sayin' nothin'."

"Look," I said, "They could have followed you back here. It's still dark outside."

She sighed. I could hear the sirens outside. "Now . . . I might turn into one of them."

The ambulance arrived, and I rode with her to the hospital. All the way there she kept babbling about the lead vampire—a woman named Collum. "I think the other two were her slaves. At least, they acted like slaves. She even whipped them a couple of times while we were in the club, not like that got anyone's attention. People get whipped all the time in that place.

"They took me to a field and raped me with their mouths. After that, I don't know . . . When they suck you it's like a drug, you get kinda numb, like smack. I went all dreamy after a while. I musta screamed myself out."

I looked at one of the puncture wounds. It was raised and white, like a giant mosquito bite. They probably did excrete some type of blood-thinning anesthetic. I read somewhere that leeches do the same thing.

"They said they want to meet you."

I reared back. "Meet me? You told them you knew me?"

"They're huge fans."

"Oh, shit. I don't like where this is goin'. Listen, I got a gig tonight in San Jose. We're gonna drive down there around noon, do the soundcheck, get some food, relax, go do a radio interview, then play the gig. I think we're gonna drive back to the city after. Look for me when I get back. And don't bring any fuckin' vampires."

The next gig. There's always a next gig. And I love that. As long as there's a gig to go to, music to play, I'll keep doin' it. Fuck the vampires. Rock and roll is bigger than that.

I noticed them right away. They just appeared right in front of the stage in the middle of the second song. People were dancin' all around them, going crazy, but they stood stock still. They stared at me intently.

Every time we made eye contact, I felt like they were trying to mesmerize me. I felt like they were trying to pull me away from the music, to distract me and make me feel like I wasn't in control. But I got news for the bloodsuckers—I'm always in control. Onstage, I am made of steel.

I tuned them out. I gathered energy from the amps and shot right back at them. *Don't give me the evil eye, you soulless blood junkies.*

It must have made them uncomfortable, because they left after a couple of songs. Maybe the volume hurt the little dead eardrums.

I knew they'd try to get backstage later so I told the roadies to keep everybody out. I pointed out the bloodsuckers. "Especially them."

We had a great show. The sound was excellent. The crowd, except for the vampires, went bonkers. I changed quickly and jumped into a waiting limo with three bodyguards. My road manager pressed a tape of the gig into my hands. "Get her back to the hotel, pronto," he told the driver.

The limo rolled up 101 and I stared out the window. I looked at the reflection of my face, and noticed something disturbing. The bodyguard sitting next to me did not appear in the glass. I leaned forward and tried to view the other two bodyguards through the glass. They cast no reflection. I turned to look at them, and they were no longer the three big guys from security. Sitting next to me was Collum.

"You can't run away," she said.

"I wasn't trying to run away."

"Then, why did you leave so quickly?"

I frowned. "I'm a musician. I leave when I want. I don't need a reason."

Collum nodded. "Of course, of course. You're a musician. That's absolutely right."

I shouted to the limo driver. "Hey, driver! Pull over! These people are leaving."

Collum rolled her eyes. "Oh, please . . ."

"Get out of my limo."

Collum shook her head. "No."

"Get out now!" I screamed. The driver looked over his shoulder at me. He smiled and showed his fangs.

I turned to Collum. "You got to all of them?"

She nodded. "They're all dead—bodies sucked dry and stuffed under the stage. We assumed their identities. We can do that, you know, change appearances and whatnot."

"Am I supposed to be impressed? I'm not."

Collum smiled, showing a hint of fang. "Do you want immortality?"

"No."

"Stay young forever?"

"No."

"You could be the ultimate rock and roll rebel until the end of time. That doesn't interest you?"

I slumped back in my seat. "Listen, you unholy bitch. What I do takes a lot of soul. I put myself on the line every night. I squeeze everything I got for those people. If I didn't have soul, I couldn't do it. You think rock and roll is just going out there with a guitar and singing? Just posing and jumping around? That shows how little you know. The real connection takes place on a whole 'nother level. And you expect me to become one of you, and be some kind of undead superstar? Just spitting out the songs and prancing around? I don't think so."

Collum raised an eyebrow. "Feisty, aren't we? Now you listen, rock star. I am Collum, all-powerful leader of the undead. I command. I do not ask."

"What, you gonna force me?"

She looked away. "If I have to."

I reached out and grabbed Collum's chin and swung her face toward me. The move surprised her, I could tell. "You have to."

"Don't touch me," she said. Her slender white hand closed around mine like a pipe wrench.

I stared directly into her eyes, defiant and proud. My rock and roll blood pumped raw power through my veins. I felt like I was onstage, swirling in sound of my own making. I felt the righteous courage of twin hundred-watt Marshall stacks. I was not afraid.

I sensed that Collum felt all that when she held my hand. Nevertheless, she wouldn't let go.

Our wills locked in psychic combat, we raged at each other silently. I would not back down. I beamed my rebel soul like a laser.

"You think you can resist me?" Collum said.

"Yeah." My other hand slid into my pocket. I felt a cassette. *The tape of the gig.*

"With just your faith?"

"Yeah." The limo's tape player was next to me.

"Faith in what?"

"Rock and roll, you asshole." I rammed the cassette into the slot and a heartbeat later the car erupted with ear-shattering guitar tones. It was our opening song. Loud, fast, relentless. I sang along at the top of my lungs. I didn't care about anything except the music. I was completely in the moment.

Collum let go of my hand and shrank back into her seat.

"Come on!" I shouted. "Let's go! It's time to rock!"

The vampires looked at me, a confused expression on their pale faces. They didn't want me like this. They didn't want the real me. They were only interested in the rock star, not the heart that beats behind it. As long as the music played, I was safe. And in me, the music plays forever.

I closed my eyes and when I opened them again a moment later, they were gone. I drove the limo back to the hotel by myself and went to my room.

My friend called a few minutes later. "Did you see them?"

"Yeah, I saw 'em."

"Did they suck you?"

"Nah. My skin is too tough."

"What happened?"

I sighed. "They ran into something they couldn't control and it scared them, I think. The power of rock and roll. God, I love rock and roll."

"You're gonna have a bad reputation among the vampires now."

"I don't give a damn about my reputation."

Mirror Gazing with Brian Jones

GREG KIHN

THE HEAT in North Africa can be debilitating. It shimmers in the afternoon like ghosts hovering above the stones. I couldn't take it and told Brian so, but he just laughed that soulful laugh of his and pointed at the hookah. "That's what that's for."

"Oh . . ." I said. "In that case . . ."

Brian lit a big wooden match on the side of the table, and fired up the bowl of fragrant brown hashish. The smoke billowed across the room. Brian coughed violently.

"Steady there, kemo-sabe. Take it easy."

Brian smiled, his eyes watery and far away. "I shall never take it easy, Chas. It's not part of my code. Life is too bloody short for that kind of thinking."

I leaned forward, took a short pull on the pipe, and sat back, my head spinning. I let the smoke drift from my mouth, a lazy blue cloud. Nothing tastes quite like hash—pungent and mysterious, stinking of dreams, the very essence of Morocco. A waiter brought us more room-temperature wine, and we sipped it to cool our throats. Brian shook his head. "This is the first place I came after Keith stole Anita from me. The rotten bastard took half the dope and half the records too."

"It could have been worse, he could have taken it all."

The bags under Brian's eyes quivered. "He must have had a rare attack of conscience. But the fact remains, he might have taken only half the stash, but he took *all* of Anita. And that's what hurts."

I said nothing. I'd learned when to shut up around Brian when the topic strayed to his love life. He was an emotional train wreck following the first trip, and I knew that those wounds were still fresh. The complex relationships that swirled around the Stones and their women made for a kind of decadent rock and roll soap opera. You could never be sure who was sleeping with what. Being a hired hand, I stayed clear of the whole circus. It made no difference to me anyway.

I'd worked for the Stones at Olympic Studios. Being an American with experience recording blues guitarists, I guess they trusted me. Maybe trust is the wrong word—the Stones didn't really trust anybody. If they liked you, you might find yourself a member of the inner circle for a while, but that didn't mean they trusted you. I guess you could say they respected me. At least I didn't want anything from them, like those other slackers did. I was an employee, a recording engineer. An honest bloke.

When Brian asked me to go to Morocco with him and record the Master Musicians of Jajouka, I said yes. I liked Brian, and I worried about him. He was so damn vulnerable. And the rest of the band seemed to tolerate him less with every passing week. Mick and Keith had taken over the group, and Brian had become the odd man out. He wasn't driven the way they were. He wasn't as obsessed with keeping up with the Beatles as they were. He reacted to Mick and Keith's musical activism by staying zonked out on drugs most of the time. I could see their point. The Stones were a business, one of the two great bands of their era, and they had to deliver every time out. Brian had become a liability. The fact that he was a brilliant musician didn't seem to matter anymore.

I thought getting out of London was just the ticket for him. So now we sat in a café in Tangiers, waiting for writer/artist Brion Gysin, a friend of Brian's. We'd been here two days and Brian was anxious to get out in the field. I'd brought a pair of portable battery-powered Uher tape recorders, the best money could buy, and a selection of microphones, to make sure we got every note. It was only two tracks, but Brian assured me there would be no overdubs. "These guys play live, all-in, one take. You gotta be ready, man."

I would be, if the equipment worked. I'd have to lug it on my back across the barren landscape, which is the true reason I think Brian brought me along. Still, it would be a grand adventure. And I'd never seen Brian happier.

"This place is magical. You can smoke dope right out in the open. I love it."

"Do you know where we're going?"

Brian shook his head. "Brion Gysin actually knows these Jajouka guys, he hangs out with them in their little village up in the mountains. He'll take us there. Without him, we would never find them."

Brian busied himself with another match, another toke. This time I shook my head when the pipe was offered. "Not just yet, I'm still dizzy from that last one."

While Brian smoked, Brion Gysin entered the café, looking like something out of a Hollywood biblical epic. He was dressed in a long white robe and sandals.

"Going native?" Brian said as they shook hands. "You look more Moroccan than the Moroccans."

Gysin was deeply tanned and wore a small fez on the crown of his head. His piercing blue eyes sparkled. "When in Rome, dear boy . . ."

"This is Chas Sumner, from Muscle Shoals, Alabama, USA."

"This is Mahmoud, my houseboy."

We shook hands. Gysin and Mahmoud pulled up chairs. Brian ordered some coffee and pastries. The hash pipe came to life again, and the air turned thick and lazy.

Gysin said, "I am prepared to take you to record the Master Musicians of Jajouka. You're in fantastic luck, because the Pipes of Pan Festival starts today."

Brian gave the thumbs-up. "Groovy. I've got portable recording equipment, and a capable recording engineer who, by the way, doubles as photographer. We're ready to rock, man. Now, just exactly where is Jajouka?"

The way Gysin looked directly into your eyes when he spoke was somewhat disconcerting, and I could see Brian squirm under his unblinking gaze. "In the Rif mountains, one hundred kilometers south of here. Deep in the country, my friend. I took William Burroughs there and it blew his mind. And Bill's mind is hard to blow. It's like going back four thousand years."

"And the music?"

"Trance-like. Passionate. Extraordinary. The pieces rise and fall, reaching crescendo after crescendo. Sometimes one song can last several hours."

I snapped to attention. "That could be a problem. You can't fit that much music on one reel of tape."

"I have a way," Brian said quietly. "We've got two recorders, right? We stagger the start of each tape so when one rolls out, the other is still going."

I didn't want to deflate Brian's thought-balloon by pointing out the nightmare such a plan would present in editing, so I shrugged, and smiled, and accepted the pipe when it came to me. "Interesting theory."

"The Master Musicians of Jajouka all come from one incredibly huge, ancient family. Their music has been handed down for thousands of years, from father to son. It's amazing, when you think about it. Bill Burroughs called them the world's only four-thousand-year-old rock band."

Brian sniffed. "Kinda makes the Stones and the Beatles seem somehow . . . insignificant."

"A man named Hadj Abdessalam Attar is their leader. I know him. He's a good person. I'm sure he will cooperate with your recording."

A disturbance in the streets outside caused us to look out the window. An old man beat a young boy with a cane. I had no idea what they were saying but Mahmoud thought the kid had stolen a piece of fruit. "That's a serious crime if the both the boy and shopkeeper are Moslem."

By now a crowd had gathered and the kid was being dragged away by the wrists. The boy fought violently. Excessive force subdued him.

"What are they gonna do, cut off his hands?" I asked, half-jokingly. The somber expressions of Gysin and Mahmoud silenced me.

Brian turned away from the window and swatted a fly off his glass. "What kind of place is this?"

Gysin used his hands when he spoke, illustrating the sentences with elaborate gestures. "Tangiers? It's a beautiful anarchy, my friend. There are three official languages; French, Spanish, and Arabic, but most people speak a little English. Two official currencies; the peseta and the franc, but dollars and pounds are welcome too. Almost everything is legal; drugs, prostitution, homosexuality. Legend has it that Hercules killed the giant Antaeus and buried him here. Apparently he had the hots for Antaeus's wife, and she for him. Antaeus is the god of losers. Tangiers has always been an open city. Matisse lived here for several years."

Brian raised an eyebrow. "I had no idea."

"This is a very old town. For instance, the foundation of the building you're sitting in dates back to the time the Romans occupied Morocco."

I looked at the floor. "Jeez . . ."

Gysin was just getting warmed up. "The music goes back to ancient Egypt. These people still worship the great goat-god Pan, whose minions stretch back into the dawn of antiquity, centuries before Christ."

The crowd outside dispersed, the heat pressed down on me. "That's some old shit . . ."

Gysin laughed. "Yes, some very old shit."

Brian cleared his throat. "Will we be able to communicate with them? Can we jam? What language do they speak?"

"Even though there are three official languages, Morocco actually has eleven languages, two of them extinct. In that section of the Rif mountains, they speak Ghomara. Luckily Mahmoud speaks Tarifit, which is quite similar to Ghomara. Hadj speaks a little English, plus some standard Arabic, so we'll get along just fine. Besides, once the music starts, there is only one language."

I thought of Brian's dulcimer solo on "Lady Jane," and how I marveled at his ability to play any instrument he picked up. "It's all the same," he said. "All of it: guitar, sitar, dulcimer, piano, cello, marimbas, fucking kazoo, whatever. It's all the same three chords. The three chords of life." Here in the furnace of heat and passion, I imagined Brian would get a chance to prove his theory.

Gysin grinned. "A Rolling Stone and the Pipes of Pan. This I'd like to see."

"What are your plans for the rest of the afternoon?" Brian said.

"I'm going to an auction. Would you like to come along?"

"What kind of auction?"

"A local shaman has died, the last of a very old family. His estate is being auctioned to pay creditors. I think there might be some rather esoteric items available. Care to view the merchandise with me?"

Brian started laughing, and certain frequencies within the sound of it seemed to vibrate in my head like a tuning fork. Something about it filled me with dread.

One hour later we were at the auction house—a huge, smoky room full of sweaty men of all nationalities. A large water stain on the ceiling resembled a map of Ceylon. Business was conducted in rapid-fire French, and moved quickly. Items we had viewed earlier were brought out and placed upon a table where a one-armed auctioneer presided.

Brion Gysin bid on several ornamental boxes and some tapestries, purchasing all of them. Brian, on the other hand, seemed bored. He wasn't really keen on any of the stuff, and acted indifferently

throughout. That is, until an odd little mirror was brought out. I'd
noticed it before, at the viewing. It was about the size of a standard,
eight-by-ten, glossy promo pic. The frame was black, polished stone,
carved with tiny hieroglyphics. The glass in the mirror was uneven.
When I looked into it, the reflected image seemed slightly distorted.

"That's that weird little mirror you were looking at," Brian said.
"Might be a valuable antique."

Gysin gripped Brian's arm. "That's a special mirror. Buy it."

Brian raised his hand and the auctioneer began babbling incom-
prehensible phrases at warp speed. The veins on his neck stuck out
like vermicelli. Brian, with Gysin's help, outbid three other guys and
bought the mirror.

"What did you mean, special?"

"Magic," Gysin whispered. "Ancient, beautiful, actual magic. That
mirror is for gazing, *scrying* some call it. It's a form of meditation.
Mirror gazing. It's said to open the third eye, and cause the gazer to
see . . . things. Some believe that Nostradamus was a mirror gazer,
and wrote many of his quatrains after gazing into the future. Mirrors
like that have been found in tombs centuries old."

Brian beamed. "And now it's mine. All the posh birds of London
will powder their noses in it. Maybe we'll use it to snort coke off of.
It's a trip, man. Dig it, I own a magic mirror."

Gysin's voice modulated down a half-step. "Don't make light of it,
my friend. You, of all people, should be receptive."

I watched Brian with bloodshot eyes. We'd been smoking hash all
day, and drinking wine, and I knew he had to be pretty whacked by
now. I was suddenly worried. Maybe that mirror was fucked up, maybe
buying it was a bad idea. Maybe, in the light of day, he'd regret it.

"That thing gives me the creeps, man," I said. "I don't want anything to do with it."

Brian seemed genuinely amused. "Chas, I'm surprised at you. The
devil's mirror you say? Evil? Afraid of it, are you?"

I tried to laugh but produced only a dry, gurgling sound, like low water pressure through old plumbing. Brian sensed my stoned-out paranoia and used it like mustard gas against me.

"You *are* afraid, aren't you? You bloody wimp. You're looking at a man who just recorded a song called 'Sympathy for the Devil,' whose last album was called *Her Satanic Majesty's Request.* Come on, man. I wrote the book on all that black magic crap. I've been to the edge and looked over the rim, and you're afraid of a fucking mirror?"

"I'm just sayin' . . . if this was a horror movie . . . you buying that mirror would be Act One."

The next day we set out for the Rif Mountains. Brian had the mirror with him, I could feel it's unnatural weight when I loaded his bags into the back of the Land Cruiser. Mahmoud drove south through the sun-baked towns and Bedouin camps. Outside Tangiers, the road simply vanished beneath our tires, and the desert surrounded us. Off to the south I could see the blue ridge of foothills to the Rif Mountains. They looked ominous. Brian put me to work taking pictures of the scenery. "I want to document everything," he said.

Hours passed, the mountains drew closer, and the land changed from arid desert to rolling hills. Mahmoud proved to be an excellent driver and navigated us through the valleys until the terrain became impassable. "We'll have to go on foot from here. The village is not far, just a few kilometers."

I climbed a mountain pass with the tape recorders on my back and cameras swinging from my neck. Mahmoud carried a knapsack full of blank tape and film canisters. The mirror was in there, among Brian's toiletries. Glad I wasn't carrying it.

We walked into the village of Jajouka at dusk. The festival was already in full swing. I realized at once how far from Western civilization we had come. All the creature comforts I took for granted were absent: electricity, phone service, plumbing, paved roads. None of it fazed Brian. He was in a state of euphoria. "Oh my God, we're missing all this great music! Quick, Chas, get the equipment set up as soon as you can."

Gysin calmed him down. "It's OK, the festival goes on for days and there will be lots of music to record. Why don't we secure lodging for the night and have some dinner first?"

Brian's face sagged. "But . . ."

"Things happen here at their own pace. Your job is to adjust to it, not fight against it. Tonight the real ceremonies get under way."

Mahmoud had relatives in Jajouka and arranged for us to stay in the house of an uncle. The uncle killed a goat and cooked the meat on skewers over an open fire. We dined like sheiks as darkness fell.

The people of Jajouka were quite taken with Brian's appearance. The man with the long golden hair and colorful clothes drew a crowd wherever he went. They had never seen anything like it. Brian, a mystical shaman in his own right, one of the Master Musicians of London, seeker of truth, had come all this way to see them. And they treated him like royalty.

As the sun set, I placed my microphones on boom stands around a hilltop, bordered on one side by a high stone wall, which I figured would act as a big resonator. The musicians gathered for their first evening performance. Gysin cautioned me not to be surprised by some of the aspects of the Pan Festival, namely the dancing, which he said could become quite frenzied. Nothing could have prepared me for what I witnessed, photographed, and recorded over the next ten hours.

Fifteen rhaita players blew a shrill fanfare on their oboe-like double-reed horns, a line of drummers pounded a rumbling, complex beat. I listened through my headphones, adjusting the levels to capture all the instruments. Just as I arrived at a workable mix, my attention was distracted by a naked old man, standing between the drummers and the horn players. At first he just seemed like one of the throng, another pilgrim here to see the festival. As he began to move, I realized he was much more than an onlooker; he had to be part of the ceremony. He started to dance, and within minutes he was jumping around like a twenty-year-old London mod on speed. His wrinkled skin shook and shivered as he stomped, testicles bouncing like burlap hemorrhoids.

The music seemed to drive him insane. Something gleamed in the firelight. A large knife appeared in his hand. The band played louder and faster, the old man whirled like a dervish.

I looked at Brian and Gysin, who were enthralled by the music and didn't seemed to notice the old man. How could they not? A naked old man with a bowie knife is hard to miss. The knife flashed, and, for a fraction of a second, our eyes met. I've never seen eyes like that; completely crazed, without fear, capable of anything. The eyes of a maniac. I wanted to look away, to scream, but the old man held me in his gaze. Then, he stuck his tongue out at me and spun away. *What the fuck?*

All the while the amazing music pulsed and swirled. The band seemed to have doubled in size while I wasn't looking, because now there were fifty or so musicians going great guns. I remembered Gysin saying that once the music started, everything else stopped. He said it would be hard to concentrate, that the trance-like music sucked you in, that to fight it would make you insane. I believed him. The horns cried and wailed, like thousands of grieving Arab women, shrieking above the cacophonous wall of sound. The lack of anything resembling a standard Western melody was disconcerting. And suddenly I was afraid. The old man was on the move now, the knife between his teeth.

Someone released a terrified goat into the crowd. The people moved back, forming a circle, the trapped goat ran from side to side, frantic to escape. After much dancing, the old man jumped on the goat and pretended to hump it. He reached around with the knife, and with one practiced motion, slit the belly of the goat wide open. Blood and entrails spilled out onto the ground. The music hit another crescendo. The goat bucked one last time, then died twitching in the old man's arms. The music was so loud it was impossible to think, louder than a rock band, louder than the Stones themselves. But it wasn't just volume of sound, it was psychically loud, broadcasting into your soul at fifty thousand watts on the astral plane.

The old man laid the goat on the ground and began to remove its internal organs. I gagged more than once, but the tapes kept rolling and the band kept playing. While I watched, the old man picked up the freshly skinned goat and got inside the carcass. it draped over his shoulders, the goat's head above his head, the hooves hanging use-lessly, dripping blood. He began to dance again. Gysin looked at me and mouthed the words "master of skins."

Brian pointed at the camera and indicated I should be taking pic-tures of all this. Reluctantly, I began to shoot.

The old man in the goat skin danced for hours. When, at last, he threw it off, he was covered in blood mixed with his own sweat. At one point during a frenzied moment of particularly intense music, the old man danced over to Brian. He writhed before Brian like an eel with an arrow in its head. Brian looked on, a bemused expression on his face. He'd been smoking various forms of hash, kif, and pot all day, and his eyes were red slits. The old man keyed on Brian for a while, then moved on. The Golden Stone never flinched.

The music lasted until dawn. I used up most of the tape and half of the film I had. I was exhausted and my head throbbed. I took some aspirin with a swallow of brackish water, and trudged back to our host's house. We crashed on the floor, too tired to move. Conversa-tion evaporated. The Pipes of Pan had drained us

The next day, Brian was up early. "Wake up, Chas. A new day has begun. There's much to do."

I rubbed my eyes and tried to compute how many hours of sleep I'd managed. "What the hell time is it? My watch has stopped."

Brian shrugged. "I don't wear a watch, man. Time is a bummer."

Time is a bummer? "Is there any food around? I'm starving."

"Yeah, Gysin's gone to fetch some breakfast. I suppose it would be too much to ask for some bacon butties."

I laughed. "I don't think that's going to happen, but I hear the goat's good."

Brian lit a cigarette and squinted at me through the smoke. "Could you believe that old man last night?"

I shook my head. "That was insane."

"Did you take pictures?"

I sniffed my fingers. The aroma of goat turned my stomach. "I got everything: sight, sound . . . and, unfortunately, smell."

Gysin and Mahmoud entered with bowls of rice. "Breakfast is served."

Brian said, "What was all that last night about the master of skins?"

Gysin settled next to Brian. "That was the reenactment of the legend of Boujeloud. The master of skins is supposed to be the god Pan himself, half-man half-goat. It goes way back to the time when Saint Sidi Sherk introduced Islam to this region around eight hundred A.D. He gave moral authority to the Master Musicians of Jajouka. Since then, they've been venerated. A sacred link to the Holy One. There's nothing else like it in the world."

"I'm sure the goat didn't appreciate it," I said.

Gysin raised an eyebrow. "The goat is chosen. It is a great honor."

Brian raised his hand, as if in school. "Question? Will there be more music to record today?"

"Oh, absolutely."

Brian looked at me. "How much tape is left?"

"I used most of it last night, plus several rolls of film. My guess is we'll be able to record another three reels, say, ninety minutes of music, if we conserve."

"Good. That's settled, then." Brian clapped his hands together. He turned to Gysin. "All right, man. Let's talk about mirror gazing."

Gysin smiled. "Yes, of course. That intrigues you, doesn't it? The mirror you bought is very powerful. You want to try it out. I can understand that. Well, today is the last day of music. Why don't we stay tomorrow, and I'll show you the technique."

We spent the day recording music. The old man did not make an appearance. I used every inch of tape I had, filling each with the weird, hypnotic keening of the horns and the raging cadence of the drums. If you listened to it, it drove you crazy, if you didn't listen to it, it drove you crazy. It was impossible to tune out. When the second night of music was over, I felt relieved. I'd done my job. Brian seemed satisfied.

Gysin acted as tour guide through the ancient stones of Jajouka, answering our questions and pointing out sacred sights. It seemed that almost everyone in the village was a musician related to the Attar family.

Brian Jones walked through the town like a holy man. People wanted to touch him, to be near him, to gaze upon him. He smiled and waved, blond hair radiating light.

Then, at dusk, the mirror gazing began. After eating a few of Mahmoud's hash cookies, Brian was anxious to try it. In a room lit by candles, Gysin explained the technique. He sat Brian on some pillows on the floor and placed the mirror in front of him so his face filled the glass. "Look past the mirror. Concentrate just beyond the plane of the glass. Remember, this is a form of meditation, so complete relaxation is essential. After we leave the room, take a moment to clear your mind. Focus on your breathing. Try not to think any thoughts, just keep your mind blank. The third eye will open only after the mind shuts down."

I listened to Gysin speak, but, for me, all that third-eye jazz was a little too esoteric. Besides, something about the mirror upset me, and I felt uncomfortable with the whole experiment. Brian was keen on it, though, so after making my feelings known once, at the outset, I remained silent. I didn't want to be a party pooper.

Brian pulled me aside. "Hey, man, I want you to photograph this."

I looked at him like a confused Irish setter. "What? But . . . you'll be alone. I mean . . . if I come back into the room, I'll distract you, and break your concentration."

Brian grinned. "I know, but I've found a way around that." He pointed to an open window behind him. "You'll be out there, using the zoom lens. You can shoot over my shoulder and still get the entire mirror in view. If something appears in the glass, get a picture of it."

"But, Brian, that's impossible."

The weight of Brian's hand on my shoulder surprised me. He wasn't a very physical person. "Nothing's impossible. If there's one thing I've learned from being a Rolling Stone, it's that nothing, absolutely nothing, is impossible. It may be difficult, it may be hard as shit, but not impossible. I would only expect you to try your best." The worried look on my face must have troubled Brian. "It's all right, man. Nothing bad will happen. Why are you so spooked by this thing?"

My voice quivered slightly. "I don't like supernatural stuff. Never have. Gives me the creeps."

"Hey, man. It's all part of nature."

"Nature, my ass. It's evil."

Brian rolled his eyes. "Yeah, but . . . Will you do it?"

I sighed. "Aw. shit, Bri— All right, I'll do it."

"Great! OK! Let's rock!"

"What if nothing appears in the glass? I mean, what if you're the only one that can see it?"

The Golden Stone shrugged. "Then shoot a picture of the blank glass every ten minutes. We'll examine the film later."

"I don't know, Brian . . ."

"It would mean a lot to me, man. Look, I'll pay you extra."

"Money's not the issue."

"Humor me, Chas. Just sneak up and snap off a picture every once in a while. Easy as pie."

Gysin called Brian to the mirror. "Sit so that your head fills the mirror."

Brian glanced at me conspiratorially. I looked away, not wanting to egg him on. He'd succeeded in getting me to do something I didn't want to do again. Brian seemed to have that talent. Gysin adjusted Brian's position. "Stay here for as long as you can. It could take many hours. Remember, keep your mind blank."

We exited the room, leaving Brian Jones alone, staring into that strange little mirror. I glanced back over my shoulder at him. He sat like a child, an expectant, curious look on his face. Candles flickered as the disturbed air rushed past. I could see their reflection in the dark glass from the corner of my eye.

Gysin and Mahmoud went to get something to eat, leaving me skulking around the back window of the house with my camera. Feeling like a voyeur, I watched Brian through the window. He sat very still, his glorious blond hair hanging down around his shoulders. I noticed that his breathing had slowed. It was barely perceptible now by the slight rising and falling of his back. I checked my camera. I had the right film and lens for the job, allowing for the lowest light. All I could do now was wait.

Twenty minutes passed. I decided to take some pictures. As quietly as I could, I snuck up to the window, aimed the camera over Brian's shoulder, and focused on the mirror. Its surface seemed as black and liquid as oil. I took three exposures. For the next several hours, I took pictures every ten minutes. No change in the mirror.

I felt silly carrying out Brian's request, and was about to sod the whole thing, when something happened.

I was preparing to take another set of photos, and I had aimed and focused the camera exactly as I had before, but now the mirror looked different. Instead of reflecting Brian's face, it seemed lighter. I thought I could discern a cloudy image coalescing behind the glass.

The camera whirred and clicked, and I felt an involuntary chill. *Brian's doin' it, man. He's actually doin' it. That cat is amazing.* Whatever it was, I was getting it on film. But it was like trying to photograph smoke.

The image faded and I stood ready to photograph the next. But none came. I stayed there for another hour, sweating as if I were in a sauna, waiting for some change. The image had not returned. I took a few pictures anyway, just for the hell of it. I had the camera aimed the same way, about to depress the shutter release, when suddenly Brian's head turned. His face loomed in the camera's viewfinder, eyes glazed, looking utterly mad. He reminded me of the old naked man, he had that same manic look. It startled me and I pressed my finger down, taking a rapid burst of pictures. Brian's pale face, with bags under his eyes, nostrils flared, upper lip quivering, seemed to glare at me through the lens. I captured it all on film.

"I'm . . . leaving the group," he croaked. "The Stones . . . go on . . . without me . . ."

I didn't know how to respond. Was Brian hallucinating? He certainly looked like he was tripping.

"Brian?"

"Huh?"

"Brian? You OK?"

Brian blinked. "What's going on?"

"You were mirror gazing. Then you turned around said something to me. Do you remember what you said?"

Brian shook his head. "I don't know." He looked dazed.

"Let's get some sleep, man. We'll talk about it in the morning."

"Did you take the pictures?"

"Yes," I said. "I took lots of pictures."

"Was there something there?"

"Yes," I said. "I think there was something there."

I flew to Paris two days later. A producer friend of mine offered me another job recording a French pop singer, and, needing the money, I happily agreed. Brian went back to London. We stayed in touch by phone. I'd promised to develop the film as soon as I had time.

Brian Jones parted ways with the Rolling Stones that weekend, amid a media hurricane. He retreated to his Cotchford estate. I prayed that Brian would land on his feet, so I rang him up a few weeks later. "Brian? I've developed the film."

Brian's excitement leaped across the phone line. "Fantastic! What does it show?"

I tried to be succinct. "One group of pictures show a cloudy image . . . I'm not sure what it is. It's indistinct."

"Come on, Chas. What's your best guess?"

I cleared my throat. "It looks like you, and you're flying."

Brian gasped. "That's exactly what I saw. Me, with my arms above my head, flying through the sky like Superman."

"Your hair was blowing."

"Yes! My hair was blowing all around. That's bloody amazing. And you caught these images on film?"

"Yes. I'll send you a complete set."

Brian told me his plan to form a new blues group and start recording as soon as possible. He offered me a job engineering the sessions. I agreed, of course, and thought no more about it. Brian said he'd call when they were ready.

The next day I stopped at my usual café for coffee and pastries. Across the street was a newsstand carried international papers. The headline on the kiosk screamed at me through the traffic.

BRIAN JONES MORT!

Brian Jones dead? Oh, my God! I ran across the street and grabbed the *International Tribune.* The story was page one. "Brian Jones, recently departed guitarist from the Rolling Stones, was found dead yesterday. He apparently drowned in his swimming pool."

Goose bumps prickled my neck, and my mouth went suddenly and completely dry. I let the paper drift from my hand and stared across the street, into oblivion. My mind flashed on the photo from the mirror gazing. *It wasn't Brian flying, that wasn't it at all.*

It was Brian floating, facedown, in his pool, looking up from below. I was sure of it now, and the revelation shook me to the core. Brian had seen his own death, and had misinterpreted it.

The tragedy of Brian's passing weighed on me for months. I had nightmares about the mirror. Part of me wanted to go to Cotchford and find the damn thing and destroy it. Part of me wanted to just quit and go home, to get out of the music business altogether. In the end I stayed in London, working pickup gigs when I could. I became known as the guy who went to Morocco with Brian Jones. People kept asking me questions, but I never told them about the mirror. As far as I know, Gysin never mentioned it either. The secret died with Brian.

Maybe, in a way, he was right. He *was* flying. Flying right off this planet, into another dimension somewhere behind the glass.

RICHARD HELL

.I.

IT WAS March and the weather was like a pornographic high-fashion magazine. But Raw's Drink was a gutter derelict in it. The room was see-through brown broken by a debris of battered tables and cluttered walls. There was a little clearing in the far corner where a stalk of microphone stood leaning thinly.

David felt affection for the poor poets, his family. He thought he probably liked them more than anyone else did. He was popular for that.

Tonight's reader was Tom Bennett. Tom was a filthy drug addict who was too smart for his own good. His face was like a monkey's carved from a blond wood doorstop wedge, he was going bald, and he wore reddish whiskers that looked like pond scum. He never stopped talking and he considered himself a Buddhist. Whatever, he was in his element at Raw's this night, and it was heartening. He was a messenger and David was mentally gorging on it. "God made everything from nothing, but the nothing shows through."

David played a favorite mental trick for enjoying poetry readings and imagined the reader had died long ago.

The reading ended and everyone drank on and the room got noisier. People went out into the air and smoked grass together and came back. David saw the kid. He planned to find him but hadn't gotten around to it when he sensed the attention shifting in the crowd. The kid'd gone up to three different poets in the room and told each what he thought of him. He told Bill Miller, "I read your latest book and all I can say is that your only virtue is its own punishment." He told someone else that he'd "ruined frivolity for a generation." Then he gave each of the poets hand-copied examples of a new poem and told them that they could suck his cock for twenty dollars. He arrived at David, and just as David realized who he was the kid introduced himself. He was the boy who'd sent him a letter a few weeks before. The letter had read:

Mr. Parsons! Sir!

I write to you most humbly, most presumptuously. I am no one except that I am a poet. And it is because I am a poet that I eat up your books. And that is why I write and enclose the pages you find here. I hope that you will respond to them.

I'm going nuts in this nowhere. Used to be I could twist in my misery and big time lusts, sweating, and the breezes of these suburban streets would cool me a little, the fruity sunsets would bring me something, as would old literature, but now I know too much! One must always move on. (It is not important to live.) I'm rotting here! I will come to New York. Especially since I know of you.

Do you know what I mean that I am no one except that I am a poet? I will explain so that you cannot misunderstand. I do not want to be anyone. I have nothing to protect! I want to see and be seen through. I am given to see and I see aloud. It is necessary that "I," that cowardly imposition, be discarded, in order that nothing interfere, that nothing interrupt, that nothing pollute what speaks. It isn't pretty! But it is poetry and all we know of—of——. I know you know what I mean.

Have mercy on me.

Your admiring little bro,
T.

David had written back and told the kid he should come to New York and to call him when he got there.

"I am drunk," the boy said.

"You are?"

He lowered his voice again. "Come outside and walk with me."

They left the party behind and the air outside was a nice surprise. The presents kept coming, piling up around them as they walked. David got breathless and aroused.

T. told him his big ideas. He said honestly there were only two or three poets and that he himself was first among the living, with the possible exception of David himself, though he was in danger of going slack. He talked of how the literary was sacred but the literary was shit. That the poets' poor knowledge must be *advanced in life* for poetry to be worthy of its name. That the poem is everything, but incidental—it's shit and come, it's tracks and mirrors, hair, snot, ricocheting beams. It's nothing, but it's all we get and if we will be receptive it's the thing itself, the nothing itself, and what else is there to desire, want, have, be, and it only follows from delirium, which is just ordinary life. "No big deal," he said, and it was true—David'd heard it before (though he hadn't seen it). "You want to kiss me, don't you." He reached for David's crotch.

They'd stopped and T. was shuffling David back toward a dark building wall on East 3rd Street. David's heartbeat was out of control. David was taller than him and he grabbed T.'s ruffled head and bumped his mouth on his. They almost fell over but the wall got there just in time. The mouth was a scooped-out thing that felt unreal; David couldn't adjust, he was still too apart from him, but he wanted to feel his cock through his pants and when he did that it went really real for a moment before they separated again.

David just wanted to run his finger along the crack of his ass, and T. let him turn him to the wall and do that. He reached under and T.'s cock had gotten harder and he squeezed its base through his pants. T. gave him charge of himself there for a moment, and he took advantage of it by pulling his shoulder to turn him, kissing him once again, and it felt closer to a kiss. He started them walking back along the the street. David wasn't going to hurry or let T. think he was at his mercy. It was better to stretch it out anyway.

"So how does it feel to be a faggot?" T. asked.

"What? . . . Uh . . . So far, so good."

They stumbled into David's rooms on Bank Street at about 4:00 A.M. In the house everything was stagnant and half-size, defensively smug. When the pregnant wife came in T. threw up. She screamed and stuttered.

"What a stink," T. said, "That stuff smells . . . Let's try to go to sleep." He looked at David and suggested, "Why don't you slap that thing."

David lurched toward his wife and she fled. David turned and grinned as if he'd just scored a goal, started back to T., and slipped in the vomit and fell to his hands and knees. He laughed. "Ugh." It wasn't too bad. T. sat down in an armchair as David got up and put one foot in front of the other toward the kitchen around the corner. When David came back with a large wet terrycloth, T. in the chair had his penis out and was playing with it with one hand. As David knelt over the pool of vomit he looked at the penis and then at T.'s face. He put his own hand down inside his pants, but no, he wanted to wipe up the mess. The smell stung, but for a second he liked it: scent of death rot, home, was the sticky inside of his own asshole when he stuck a finger in it masturbating. He was getting a kind of hard-on, but he threw the towel over the vomit and tried to wrap it up. His wife scurried into the room holding a soft little overstuffed bag, no dignity, though when she saw them she recovered it for a moment in amazement, and for that moment David sank and groaned inside but T. was tougher and she retired from the house.

David crawled over and pulled T.'s cock in between his lips. He filled his mouth with it most gratefully and T. gazed at him with contempt that was tremendous and delicious. David was still a little bit ashamed and that's what made the cruelty right and the perfection of it melded them together. After all, T. was David's admirer, and T. was the grateful one, for being allowed to be mean with love. The world was young.

And in the morning the sun found them out on the floor of the little parlor entangled and gritty, the faint death-smell of the half-digested food and alcohol mixing with the brute light; bodies God's idle graffitto.

.II.

WHEN THEY awoke they started drinking again right away. It was a hot day. T. put on an Albert Ayler record and started pulling books off the shelves. He took a Bill Knott, a Borges, a Frank O'Hara, and a Ron Padgett and put them in his knapsack. Every once in a while he would oddly kiss David like a father. David cried once.

T. said, "Today the theme will be time, work, and sex among men. Sex among men is like using your wood to make a violin."

They walked up Seventh Avenue toward David's bank on Sheridan Square like corporeal beings among the ghosts, or melodic rustling in the silence. It was another cloudy day, but duller, the sky a bruised white that shone too hard to look at. Below it, buildings and streets were pounded from dead hard matter that felt like a headache, with all those quaint and obnoxious announcements posted in their determined efforts to infiltrate and influence people. It occurred to David that T. was speaking to him that way: proclaiming himself and trying to enter and take his mind. But he knew he'd been raised a level, and the puke-flecked boy was all the sweeter-seeming for having his behavior seen through unbeknownst.

David withdrew a little money at the bank and then nudged T. through the angular small streets in the direction of Washington Square.

"Look," said T., "What do you think of that?" There before them was a garbage can with a glossy damaged issue of a *New Yorker* magazine topping the pile of trash. It was open to a picture of a sparkling braceletted wrist and an impossibly elegant woman's face. The scripture said "Diamonds Are Forever."

"This is the hotel I was thinking of."

In the tiny room they lay in the narrow bed. It had started raining outside and the smell of it came in puffs under the doubly dirty open window.

David said, "Your program sounds like a lot of work. The good life is lazy," his arm under T.'s head. T. had his elbow bone in David's ribs.

"Indolence has a highly valued place in my system."

"Uh."

"I think we're through, Parsons. You're uptight or something or we're in different places and it's hopeless. Maybe we should get someone else in here to improve our marriage."

"How about that desk clerk?"

"Yeah, I bet he knows where the drugs are too. I'd suck him off . . . So what's this big idea?"

"It's kind of the opposite of yours . . . or the other side of the coin . . ."

"What we need is a coin with one side."

"You're a coin with one side."

"And all of us are merely players."

"That's stupid. You're ridiculous."

"I knew what you were going to say. Aw, I'm sorry. Go ahead and tell me."

"Nothing."

"Don't pout now—"

Just then there was a knock at the door. David and T. looked at each other, their noses too close.

"Who's that," called T.

Through the door, "It's Terry, the desk clerk."

David's eyes had started to water as he looked back at T. T. asked, "Should I open the door naked?" For a second David felt like he was losing his mind.

"I don't know."

"I want to."

"Do it then."

And he did and before long they were all having sex.

So David woke up with T. again. The sunlight this second morning was gray again, undone, through the narrow airshaft. David had work he had to handle, and a wife and an unborn son. There was a half-smoked joint right in arm's reach and a bottle of wine. He saw a tuft of T's armpit hair. He had to decide whether to drink or think.

He drank, but he got up to leave anyway. He wrote to T. "Here's ten bucks. I have to go check on things. Thanks. Soon, Later, Love, David."

On the way out the door he saw a scrap of paper on the floor. It could be deciphered:

see the light look into the hole
cheap hotel room wall to the
next room past
the hole in the crack

of the desk clerk's bent rear
end he's shown us
the hole damn catalog
cheap hole tea-room

hair-lined butt like a private
eye out in the saliva
to see the light
look into the hole

and then you eat it
I know the taste of light
Red: cock head, Blue: asshole
(clean), Green: eyeball, White: blood

all sweet, all key fund as glances
in an icy tub and I swill it, drenched
in the gushing seen m, the big pissing
over broken head suppository of it

the wack, the tang, the brassiere
the poop eye candle-flame
slick and cold banana popsicle fuck
in the face the eye the prick slit of it

come next May flowered China haunches
flush to fan rhapsodic array
toe carrot pressed further doe
person of a cartoon persuasion bursting too of it

flowers

What! He cracked a syllable of laugh out loud. T. must've written it
the night before. What a night. The writing brought it back. And it
blew him away, this poem by his sixteen-year-old boyfriend.

He thought of the sight of T.'s penis, and how it was shocking, like
the exhibition of a person's internal things, but quite great.

Everything was changed now, though inevitable (as things will be once they've happened). Maybe he shouldn't leave. But he wanted to be out in the morning, and not altogether dependent on T., and he needed to do something about his wife.

He went, descending the smelly back staircase the flight down. A different desk clerk was on duty. Outside the day was brilliant by Washington Square Park. He felt himself turning in the cold fiery cranks and mechanisms of the new day, like something from a Blake poem or Dante. "Scent of garbage and patchouli and carbon monoxide . . ."

They call me the Chinese Monkey. Smear me like icing. "Oh fuck what do I do now?"

Um . . .

Take a breath now . . .

I'm a little confused about those days.

My memory's not the best, and I don't trust memory anyway. T.'s dead and my wife'll have nothing to do with me.

Pink and blue smear. How do people do that (believe in their memories—it's like believing in art)? I remember the feelings, I think. But I'm not who I was in 1971—I have to imagine that person.

Nothing wrong with that. One's "personality" is continuously being modeled by the, the things that happen. Isn't that right? (It's not like we're instruments that are played, we're like dogs that are trained. Or hairdos. ((*I, hairdo.*))) Plus one tends to get more selfish and conservative, if maybe less judgmental, upon coming with age to realize one will actually be dying. And I guess I do have an advantage across near-thirty years for having the same genes and experience . . .

Then again, maybe there's destiny ("Character is fate"). ("Tomorrow is another day, but then so was yesterday.") Maybe I'm just too fastidious (yeah, right)—but be that as it may, I wouldn't presume to call it "nonfiction." It's all true though! If the truth be told, I'd rather think about Liv Tyler right now. She's such a distraction! I wonder is her glow subliminally tinged by her name's hint of "Liz Taylor"? Nah—that's pretty far-fetched. Her coltishness—velvety—and (star-)crossed eyes, her overbite, so lovely it makes my room change color ("teeth to hurt"). That's what we want from a star. How will *she* age I can't help but wonder. Imagine her with a dick! Wow! (Anyway I've never been so impressed by Liz Taylor. She's for real faggots. I'm not really a faggot. I just have a queer streak. A nice strong queer streak.)

I still do things that I absorbed from Him. Where are the dead? Piled up in me like a log jam? Is that why my chest is dry and hurts, why it's hard to talk? Don't be overdramatic. It's true they (the dead) can take care of themselves, whereas we need to take care of ourselves (each other). Maudlin (word derived from "Mary Magdelene"!). As Pasternak said, one's soul is in other people.

Yes I'm over fifty now!

> *and mentally skipping*
> *around the hospital room*
> *surprised to be alive*
> *(don't ask)*
> *but here-and-now so pleased*
> *to be that suddenly I break*
> *into song like Anna Karina!*

Sorry. Good grief. This anesthetic or painkiller (same thing, isn't it: no-pain=numb) they have me on is nice, but it has me lulled (and riddled, shuddering, with parentheses)—woozy, giddy, and well-ventilated. I am fond of freesias. I close my eyes and go to the most marvelous places. Opiation. Opiated freesia places. And the universally concupiscent M. Jean-Luc! He's the poster boy for getting old (and making things more and more beautiful and wild, not to say funny, less to say sad (((I don't want to say "deep" at all, as you can imagine))). The window and the freesias are where the eye goes (when not inward). Freesias Where the Eye Goes. Freesias: those Picabian mechanoerotic clusters like the unlikely so-fragrant flesh-pockets of the air itself (revealed by some colorful method of scientific staining). God, *what* am I talking about? It is a flower like an old-time movie star (Claudette Colbert, Norma Shearer) with those stunning and elaborate, bright butter-yellow, deceptively delicate, heads on those swaying bent thin stalks. But aren't they all? The "stars" altogether more like flowers than stars . . . As penises are . . .

It's funny, I liked the least the other week that picture of Schiele's in the show at the Modern that depicted bare winter branches, like insect legs—legs with legs—in a crackling dry web or network across the canvas, sky—it looked to me like a motel-room abstraction—but somehow now it has me finding the same freezing view from this window so pleasing, which I would have hated before. Viva art.

About writing as acting—but how you can't err (*Individuum est inefabile.*—Goethe)—how we wondered and worried and gossiped re T.

See you later (or earlier I mean).

David found himself wandering in the direction of his old friend Paul's apartment and so he called him up. Paul asked him to pick up some Lucky Strikes and come on over.

Paul, large in a smudgy white T-shirt and unshaven, was squeezing the blankets up to his neck as he lay in the bed that took up most of the apartment's only real room. There was a narrow pathway between the bed edge and the exposed-brick wall, a tiny table with a typewriter in the lower corner by the window, and a few small overstuffed bookcases and some papers and ashtrays beside it and cornerwise at the foot of the bed. A smoking filterless butt hung and bobbed in the right corner of his mouth, forcing him to squint his eyes.

"Hi buddy, I just made a new poem and it got me thinking. I want to wash your brain, OK? Try this, and I bet you can—now I know

I'm not a pretty picture, though I have my partisans—but imagine you'd just come from viewing a totally great painting that did things in a way you'd never seen in a picture before, that isolated this class of look you'd never really noticed, or at least appreciated the greatness of, before, and to which I, here, am closely enough related in my magnitude and general vista as to thereby reveal to you my own heretofore overlooked and unfairly neglected beauty . . ."

"Not necessary, Paul."

"Great. You knew all along. I'm glad you see it my way. And you, you too are beautiful . . ."

"What's the pill situation?"

"Horrific."

"Oh."

"And that's the least of it."

"I'm glad you admit that."

"I admit it, son . . ."

David's eyes focused on a piece of notebook paper that was taped to the wall. Scrawled in a big baby-handed script onto it were the words "so-called piercing glory" and David felt a little dizzy, he felt as if a larger reality was just beyond his comprehension, though possibly reachable. It was trippy. A ringing sound swelled from one ear through his skull to the other. He shuddered, his whole body's position-sense vibrated, and he was momentarily deeply, nicely smeared. He staggered slightly. Paul laughed and asked if he was all right.

"I had a crazy night last night—wait—days actually, well . . . two nights and a day . . ."

"Tell Paul."

He hadn't realized how worn out he was. Grateful for a little kindness. He sat down in a wooden kitchen chair against the brick wall. "I've been with this boy and he has me completely turned around . . ."

"A boy, huh . . ."

"It sure is going to make a mess of things."

"What do you mean he has you 'turned around,' exactly? Your butt in his face?"

"Ha ha."

"He makes you dizzy?"

" . . . Yeah, yeah, yeah," said David nasally.

"Yeah, but you are fucking—or whatever you homosexuals call it—him . . . ?"

"Well, what am I talking about?"

"That's exciting, or suspenseful anyway. He's the kid at the reading, at the party, right?"

"You know about him?"

"Yeah. I was there, I got there late. People were talking about him. I actually saw you leave with him. . . . I wondered how long it would take once you got married."

"I know, goddamn it. What the hell does it mean? Shit. He already has me half pulled into his psycho way of looking at things. I need a little perspective. On the other hand . . ."

"What I've got is yours, pal."

"Do you have a drink?"

"A drink? Nope. Sorry."

"What the hell do you have?"

"Me. It. And . . . But no butt!"

"Uh . . . Ah . . . It's all so weird. . . . Why don't we go to a bar right now. Do you want to go sit at a bar? Like the Blarney Stone on 14th Street?"

"Sure!"

.III.

Gee I almost want to start making up a book about Paul. Well, he's in this one.

He's dead too of course. It's so unlikely that I'm alive.

The dead take you with them though. If I don't write about us, it will disappear into nothing forever. (When you think about it, in a way there is no "past" except nothing: complete empty darkness: it's what's actually forgotten, unrecorded, unknown to anyone. The rest of the past is really the present.) Half of it is already gone with those who died (one's "better half").

What a line is "it's so unlikely I'm alive" for obvious reasons, but that's why we like it I guess and have now written it twice! It's some kind of odd luck (and luck that will come to an end soon enough).

> *The whole city seemed to*
> *optically snap with the*
> *cool bright*
> *ness of the just moist*
> *light and air ricocheting*
> *in pings and flapping planes*
> *widely below the sky, in*
> *to which, later, like chairs*
> *broken over heads, giant*
> *graphically depicted*
> *pins and needles, with*
> *splintered breaks like*
> *kindling, the*
> *pretty light and air*
> *rises lightly back up, leaving*
> *nothing but this [ominous] sucking [inhaling] chill.*

Jeez, that's a sad poem. But not, because it kind of works.

At dusk the light returns to the sky as your vision will rise up the skirt of a girl as far as possible.

In a way, "art" is just "making the best of things."

Time the entertainment. "Compelling!" "Irresistible!" "Fascinating!" "Suspenseful!" It is fascinating: that from there one has gotten to this. No, give me pussy and . . . "Yesterday I saw a man / In front of a hotel / Calling, 'Dick, Dick.' / How many times have I / Wanted to stand / On a street corner / And yell for dick?"

These young poets and even some journalists come around to see me or try to. The ones I welcome, of course, are the ones who bring me things, gossip included. It'll get them through the door anyway. Sex'll get them furthest of course. And they want gossip from me too, gossip of the old days. It's almost like I'm the last surviving member of a big-time rock group. They most want stories of Him, though the best are least likely to ask (except the very best, who don't give a damn what they say). As I'm writing the book I tend to bring him up anyway. After all I wonder too.

I lived and he didn't. There's no virtue in surviving, as war veterans know (and it messes them up).

Tim brought me this book of Godard interviews. Gee, J.-L. makes it feel worthwhile. (I know it is anyway.)

Could I talk about death for a moment? I'll try to keep it short. I scared myself about it a few days ago. I'd forgotten that could happen (get scared about it) until it did and I realized it'd happened before. I always think of myself as pretty OK with death, but . . . it is infuriating, disrespectful, humiliating, lonely. It takes the breath out of you. Everything you've gone to any trouble for, all the ins and outs—swept away, blown away, no meaning or purpose, no friend or companion—zip: taken. And no appeal heard. One time all my books got stolen and that was traumatic.

Then again maybe one could just be completely brave and casual about it. Obviously that'd be the smart thing. Dying's milk that got spilt a lot of generations ago. But then we are "wired" to consider it the enemy, right?

And the night sky falls into your heart. Which is some kind of ice cream. The heart in flames of dark ice cream. Licked by death.

Why do I try to preserve? There's that theory too isn't there. I'm making my contribution to the meme-complex, the culture. Maybe I'm singing like a bird. ("I lift my voice in song.") ("I'm just like that bird, singing this song to you.")* I remember crooning to T. (and many others). Drunk, too.

I was a sheet of gold that he hammered.

The answer to a toe that asks the lilac sky-flow ties:
(remains to be seen)

The magic of intensest poetry-snot penetrating literature

the numbered-times-in-a-lifetime sudden too-late knowledge that you
can be seen by the unseen from the dark because you're in the light

* Bob Dylan, "You're a Big Girl Now."

A Little Bit of Abuse
from WATERLOO SUNSET

RAY DAVIES

DONNA WENT past the park bench where the bag lady sat. She confided in the woman about how after all the anger she still loved Les. The ducks were hanging around like scavengers waiting for a tramp to fall asleep so they could steal crumbs from his sandwich. A jogger ran past and the birds scattered; their angry protestations echoed around the park. The old bag lady didn't even blink.

Donna left the park and made her way to the antique shop where Fox had been painting and went around the back to a small courtyard, then climbed the fire escape up to an attic room.

Fox had done his best to make his little single room half respectable, but his years as a prison inmate showed. Newspapers and magazines were meticulously stacked in piles on the floor. Nothing was wasted or thrown out. Every inch of space was reserved for something particular. His few personal belongings were stored in a wooden chest next to his single bed. The room had one window in the center of the wall. The floor was covered in cheap linoleum, with a slightly garish flower design, but a tiny Persian rug bought in a junk shop gave him some comfort, some respite perhaps from the memories of a cold prison cell. Modern conveniences were minimal: a portable gas stove with two burners; a small refrigerator that looked as though it used to be a hotel mini-bar; and an old office lamp with a red bulb, which gave the room a hint of seediness once the sunlight had gone. Fox heard the church bell chime. Donna was supposed to be here now. He looked around anxiously to see if there were any last-minute adjustments to be made, and there was a gentle knock on the door. Fox received few visitors and Donna was the first woman to cross the threshold. He took a deep breath and sat on the bed with a pad, pretending to finish a sketch.

"Come in, the door's not locked."

Donna entered wearing a fawn-colored Burberry raincoat. He did a double take. She was wearing a black wig along with black high heels and no stockings. It was a little chilly outside, and he could see the goose bumps on her legs.

Fox thought it best not to comment on her hair, and tried to make her feel welcome.

"The kettle's on. Would you like a cup of tea?"

Donna smiled gratefully.

"That's okay. I'd rather get started, if you don't mind. Where do you want me to sit?"

Fox looked around, in a panic. He was unprepared and slightly nervous.

"Oh, on the chair by the window, to get the natural light."

Donna didn't comment, and sat down in the chair. She took out a pack of cigarettes and slid off her high heels as Fox set up his easel. She looked around the room.

"D'you mind if I smoke?" Donna had already opened the packet. Fox didn't even answer.

Donna put down the pack and looked out the window. As the light hit the left side of her face, Fox noticed a fading bruise, and found the position he wanted.

"There. Just there. Don't move. That's great."

Donna didn't reply; she just kept on staring out the window.

Fox tried his best to be professional, but he had never painted a woman before—let alone a real woman, and in his bedroom. He was just about to sketch an outline when Donna startled him with a request.

"Do you mind if I take my raincoat off?"

Fox didn't mind.

She slipped off her coat, and her voice took on a slightly amoral tinge.

"I'm not wearing much underneath. In fact, nothing."

Fox's hands started to shake, but he tried to stay calm, doing his best not to look at Donna.

"Just as you like, love."

He looked at her. Her beautiful pale skin. Tiny, hard breasts, long body with just a hint of loose fat around the waist. Then her legs. Still covered in goose bumps and a few bruises along the shins.

"Get those playing football?"

"Just picked them up. You know how it is."

"No, love. Don't know how it is. That one on your cheek is a real beauty."

Then Donna took off her black wig.

"Excuse the disguise. It's a chance for me to be somebody else."

Her short blond hair seemed to transform her from a Latin tart into a Byzantine angel.

"My boyfriend thinks I look like Joan of Arc with attitude."

Fox smiled. "Oh, he means Jean Seberg. The actress who played her. She was a goddess. My era."

Donna smiled and suggested that Fox concentrate on her body. She parted her legs slightly, but Fox could only think about the gorgeous images projected on her luminous skin by those bruises. Donna asked questions. Where was he from? How long had he been in prison? The only question he hesitated to answer was why he had been sent there.

During a tea break, he did tell her—a crime of passion.

"Caught my woman with someone else and beat them both to a pulp with a cricket bat."

Donna laughed. Half in disbelief, half in terror. Fox went on to describe the incident, graphically. The more it shocked her, the more lurid the details became. Eventually, he tried to justify his actions.

"I'd been inside for armed robbery. A couple of years and was let out on parole for good behavior. I came home. There they were. Together. I just snapped, I suppose. The judge wanted me put away forever, but they lived. I only rated GBH, so I got off light. I would have settled for double homicide, though. I wanted to do them both in. Still, I'm lucky to be out."

Fox took a long, hard look at Donna and asked about Les. She started telling him, but her own story sounded trivial in comparison. Fox had borrowed a book on art from the prison library. When he talked about painting he seemed different, almost scholarly. Then he told her how he had used art as therapy, to channel his anger into something beautiful rather than letting it use him to destroy and inflict suffering.

"I was looking at the religious paintings. This bloke, Della Francesca. The pictures were so calm and exact. All the perspective clinically worked out so you felt detached from the suffering going on. Never related to that kind of thing before. When I first went to prison and got separated from the wife and kid, it wrenched me in two. Only violence and aggression moved me—van Gogh's manic brush strokes, Goya's execution paintings. Then I read in a book that explained about how to appreciate the delicacy of a curve or intricate shading, and perspective. It calmed me down. But nobody can ever get it quite right. I read somewhere that no artist is perfect, but most artists search for perfection in their work."

Donna was taken aback. She had no idea that Fox had so much feeling, let alone the ability to articulate it. She found herself talking about the violence in her and Les's relationship. With Les, how the fighting was almost an accompaniment to their lovemaking. Fox smiled and told Donna to enjoy her relationship while it lasted; eventually something would snap, passion that strong would envelop and eventually destroy. He also held out little hope for Les's kids.

"I had a kid with that woman I bashed up. There was no way an ex-con could ever get custody, so I just let it go. Your fella's doing nobody any favors waiting around all week for Sunday to come so he can pretend to be happy with his daughter for a couple of hours. He's just waiting for a kick in the balls. Kids can see through all those pre-tend smiles and that nervous laughter." Fox thought it would eventu-ally push Les over the edge.

The session didn't last much longer; Fox explained that he could now complete the painting from memory. Donna felt she was being dismissed, but still there was relief when she put on her Burberry and left his room. There was a strange clarity to Fox's thinking. So unsen-timentally practical. Cut and dried, no frills. His cynicism had the opposite effect on her, though. She determined to make a real effort the next time Les's kids were down. She went into the bakery and ordered a cake so they could celebrate Les's birthday with his daugh-ters that following Sunday.

Back at the squat, Donna replaced a print that had been knocked off the piano. She rehung the framed poster from the cubist exhibi-tion at the Tate that covered up the crumbling plaster of the wall where she had smashed Les's Fender Stratocaster. Maybe they could take the children to an art gallery. Maybe they'd all find it soothing.

Sunday morning, and Les walked through Regent's Park. There was a spring in his step, as if he was entering into a new phase. He'd come to an agreement with his wife—he could see his daughter when it was convenient for her. He'd play the game and abide by the rules, take the judgment with a smile and accept that she had the upper hand.

He stopped by the flower stall outside the Episcopalian church and bought Donna some flowers. He ran down the road, up the stairs, and burst into the squat to find Donna crouched on the floor. Her eyes were welling up with tears, anticipating the worst. Then she broke the news.

"Your wife phoned again. Your daughters ain't coming. She must have heard something about us. All the fighting."

They both sat down, too sad to be angry. Donna told Les about Fox's imprisonment and his rehabilitation through art. She didn't dare tell Les about posing naked. Or about her disguise. Les was thinking about the ex-con too. Even in this crisis, Les was managing to string some ideas for a song together, using Fox as a subject. A song about how art had helped him cope. Les's daughter was like a painting in a gallery. He could look at her sometimes, but she would never be his. And then there was his own art. Always angry. But the violence in his work had begun to take over his life. Feeding off his anger, invading his and Donna's life. When work and love got that entwined, the end was twice as bitter. Les sat down at the broken piano and picked out a gentle melody with one finger. All the anger had been punched out of him.

Scenes from New Europe

GRAHAM PARKER

SCENE I

HERR TODAY

We enter a comfortable, unpretentious brasserie on the outskirts of Knippsbatan, Germany. The proprietor, during recent weeks, has informed the locals that on this particular day the premises will be closed to the general public. For on this particular day, a meeting is to be held within the walls of this very establishment. A meeting between some of the most self-important minds in all of New Europe. A meeting to decide the fate of one of the most self-important plans ever proposed in this now coalesced state, and whether such a plan should be thrust into action, or returned, where many contend it belongs, to the wasteland of obscurity from whence so many bold and innovative ideas languish.

2:00 P.M. SHARP.

In bustles Herr Lipp, his enormous countenance draped with an aggressive black cape trimmed with fake ermine, his girth held in check by a red silk cummerbund. Grunts issue from beneath Lipp's hedge-like mustaches as the former Conservative MP, Sir Bob O'Dowd Booth, now restaurant owner/maitre'd of Toutes le Main Brace, this very establishment where our portentous meeting is about to get under way, seats him with a mincing flourish.

"Porter!" orders Herr Lipp as he crashes into the proffered chair, not even glancing at O'Dowd Booth.

"You have some baggage, Herr Lipp?" Inquires O'Dowd Booth, immediately playing with fire, but at least succeeding in getting Lipp's attention.

"Porter—a dark brown, heavy English malt liquor resembling ale, you idiot!" spits Herr Lipp, in no mood for O'Dowd Booth's waggish humor.

"Ah ha, touts suite, monsieur," O'Dowd Booth assures him. "And I'll bring a spittoon with it," he mutters under his breath as he makes for the bar.

The jousting has indeed begun, and so far only one of our important men are here—but wait . . . outside can be heard the crude splutter of an ostentatiously ancient motorbike: a 48 Beezer to be precise. This can only mean one thing—Herr Do has arrived.

His entrance, more snooty than dramatic, is acknowledged by a phlegmish grunt from Herr Lipp, for it is well known that these two rarely see eye to eye on anything, and here they are, about to go toe to toe on a very ticklish subject indeed. What these two, and the other distinguished gentlemen we await, are going to decide, is whether or not my plan to feed the homeless should be implemented and passed into law.

I have worked for the Bureau of Brilliant New Ideas since its formation, two years after the final coalition of the New Europe government, and have finally, due to hard work, rapacious networking, and a good measure of luck, begun to have my imaginative and often provocative schemes recognized.

The plan is complex yet beautiful, and since the runaway success of my toad implants and my diet pamphlet, "The Porker Method," men of great importance are listening to what I have to say.

The plan, cunningly dubbed "Do You Want All That Kebab, Mate?" involves giving diners at every legal restaurant in New Europe—and eventually one hopes, in the United States—a choice as to the amount of food actually served to them. Simply put, an example of the dish each customer has ordered will be shown to him or her, probably in the form of those plastic models often seen on display in the windows of Japanese restaurants, or perhaps depicted in photographs, laminated and neatly arranged in glossy albums. Under pressure of law (and, one hopes, charity) the customer will be forced to decide on a lesser portion (a guideline maximum will be implemented) than would normally be served, the remainder of which would later be transported to centers jammed full of ungrateful starving homeless street people.

And now, back to our learned Herrs . . .

"Afternoon, Herr Lipp," says Herr Do, in a voice suggesting a man well in touch with his feminine side. "Or is it morning for you?"

"It's morning in Tokyo, Do," counters Lipp, without missing a beat. "Well prepared with a bucket load of liberal nonsense today, are we?" continues Lipp, glancing at Do's copious notes.

"Just a few ideas, Lipp, just a few ideas . . . ah! Do I hear the waffle of familiar voices?"

Just then, the rich mahogany doors of the brasserie swing open and there stand two further infamous debatees. Both of them, to Herr Upp's instant irritation, already two sheets to wind.

"Mine's a pint!" bellows Herr E'ass, a man who likes to get to the pint before getting to the point.

"Schnapps!" hollers Herr' O'Th'Dog, and O'Dowd Booth floats off to get the gentlemen their drinks, already hoping that this "meeting" will collapse in a sea of alcoholic indignation and aggression so that perhaps the police can be summoned to remove the whole lot of them, well before the evenings regular clientele arrive.

"Got a head start on us then, eh Lipp?" slurs O'Th'Dog, almost knocking over Lipp's porter as he wedges himself past to get a seat nearer to the wall.

"I hope you are familiar with the territory we are about to navigate, gentlemen," says Lipp mechanically, ignoring O'Th'Dog's flip comment. "Because if you are as ill-prepared as you were the last time we found ourselves around a table—a little matter of whether we should press Mercedes-Benz into the production of three-door cars for sale exclusively to fat American drivers, if my memory serves me—then Herr Do and I would like to know now, before we've wasted the entire afternoon."

"This is a meeting about whether or not people who don't clean up after their dogs should be shot on sight, or whether they should be given at least a pretense of a trial, correct?" offers Herr E'ass, looking genuinely confused.

"No no no!" is the high-pitched reply from Do. "We had that one two weeks ago. Really Lipp, we're not going through this again . . ." he says imploringly, then spins on his heels and stalks over to the bar where O'Dowd Booth, with a knowing weaselly grin on his face, has prepared Do a noxious-looking green drink in which slices of fruit jostle among ice cubes and a paper umbrella swirls jauntily.

"Really?" questions E'ass, just barely keeping a straight face. "I wondered why that old woman was lying facedown with a poodle yapping in her ear outside on the corner. So we decided to administer instant punishment then?" E'ass can now barely hold in a guffaw, building in his gut.

"Of course we did!" shouts a steaming Lipp. "Your mistress was one of the first to get her comeuppance, surely you remember that, you Styrofoam clown?"

"So that's why she's been so unresponsive lately . . ."

At this point, the tidal wave of tittering finally breaks through E'ass's hand, which he has brought up to his mouth in a vain attempt to stem it.

"Oh Christ. This is too much," mutters Herr Do, making a hand movement as if flipping a feather boa over his shoulder.

"Don't worry, don't worry gentlemen," offers O'Th'Dog spreading his mottled hands before him in a pacifying gesture. "E'ass and myself are well briefed on this matter. Something about feeding the homeless rich peoples' puke, isn't it?"

Both jokers are now chortling violently into their drinks, having of course arranged this little wind-up previously in the Naughty Nineties bar, just across the street.

"All right," hisses Lipp. "Let's get on with it."

The learned men are at last ensconced around the table, ready, one hopes, for an immense display of self-importance.

"Now," broaches Lipp, clicking fingers for a second porter. "This . . . this plan we have before us . . . briefly, involves—by dint of law, no less— giving half of one's meal away before it has even reached the plate to . . . to complete strangers!" At the very mention of this outline, Lipp's voice rises with indignation and incredulity. O'Dowd Booth gingerly places a frothy glass of porter in front of him and makes a hasty retreat. Lipp continues with widening eyes.

"To actually stare into a facsimile meal and say in all seriousness to the waiter, 'No, I'll just have half the amount! Send the rest to those peons who can't be bothered to put in a decent day's work to pay for a meal themselves! Go on, off with you, take my food away!' "

There is a brief silence now as Lipp spreads his hands on the table around his porter glass, a look of outraged incomprehension building on his florid face. Can it be that he will be a prime opponent of my brilliant plan?

There is a moment's silence as the men gulp at their drinks.

"I find it rather . . . rather a brilliant plan," says Do slowly in a whiny voice, pulling a small red tassel out of the pocket of his mock-caftan and twiddling it between his fingers. From beneath his beetling brows, Lipp affixes him with a gimlet eye.

"You may summon the gimlet eye," says Herr E'ass, suddenly appearing quite sober and rushing to Do's defense. "But I feel Do has made a very good point."

"He hasn't made a point!" hollers Lipp. "He has merely disagreed with my obvious distaste for this ridiculous proposal."

"Even so," counters E'ass with a huff of self-importance, "I read volumes in it."

"You what!" Blurts Lipp, already almost unable to contain himself as Herr O'Th'Dog, slacker that he is, leans back a little too far in his chair and crashes to the floor, his quince schnapps miraculously unspilled in his hand.

"As I see it," says O'Th'Dog, acrobatically flipping to his feet even though like all these men he is a good deal overweight, "this is an extremely dangerous proposition that may well begin with a simple arrangement—which at present still allows a choice as to how much of your own good food you donate to complete strangers—but in time gentlemen," he says, raising a finger and stifling a belch, "that simple choice may well slowly, slowly be drawn away from us as the starving homeless increase and their reliance and expectation become the norm. Soon, gentlemen, could they not be sitting here, in our very seats? Eating our very meals instead of us? And why for heaven's sake can't they just have what's left over on our plates? Why must this determination be made before we tuck in?"

"Sanitation Department," announces Lipp flatly, rifling through his papers. They've been over this plan already, as per government regs."

"But I must say 'Here Here,'" says Lipp, surprised at O'Th'Dog's allegiance. "Here bloody here."

"Bugger it," mumbles Herr E'ass, "two agin two agin, tch."

Lipp begins to speak, "I am absolute—"

"Absolut?" Interrupts E'ass. Make that two! No cranberry juice for me O'Dowd Booth!"

"I am not ordering drinks!" booms Lipp.

"Oh sorry, thought my luck was in," says E'ass, the grin welling up again.

Lipp continues undeterred. "I am absolutely against the idea of encouraging layabouts and wastrels to expect free—and in many cases free gourmet!—handouts, as if it were their God-given right," says Lipp quickly before the tittering prompted by E'ass's drinks ruse rises to actual laughter.

Just then, the doors swing open and another large, self-important gentleman strides in wearing a garish red tuxedo. He snaps his fingers at

O'Dowd Booth, who rolls his eyes and begins fixing a gooseberry schnapps with a sliver of raw garlic.

"Oh no," moans Herr Do quietly, "Herr Bagg."

"Thank you, O'Dowd Booth," says Herr Bagg, accepting the schnapps and tossing it back in one gulp. He releases a small belch and chews on the garlic sliver, eyeing the meeting from a few feet away.

"Got a problem, Herr Do?" he asks, raising his patchy graying eyebrows.

"What are you doing here?" responds Lipp, as Do assumes a sulky posture.

"I'm across town, meeting with Net and Style—we're deciding whether birching should be allowed in comprehensive schools, or whether we should just go right back to the cat-o'-nine-tails."

"So," says Lipp impatiently. "Why are you here?"

"Herr Style and Herr Net have broken into a serious arm-wrestling competition and will not concentrate on this most important issue. Personally, I'm for the cat—I'd be happy to know that those blasted vandals and sodomites currently filling our educational institutions were having the skin ripped right off their spotty behinds."

"You're sick, Bagg," states Herr Do flatly, not looking up.

"I love you too, Do," counters Bagg sarcastically. "How's it going here?"

"It was going somewhere at least," says Lipp, sensing the focus of the meeting drifting.

"All right, all right, I'm going!" snaps Herr Bagg. He turns and strides toward the exit. "Nice drink O'Dowd Booth," he shouts as he pushes through the door. "Put it on Lipp's bill!"

Cool air, laced with the tang of diesel gasoline, rushes into the brasserie. The gentlemen look toward the entrance as one, staring with interest at the afternoon shoppers on the cobblestone street outside.

Herr Lipp ignores Bagg's comment, collects himself, and glances around the table authoritatively, swiftly marshaling the attention of the others before their concentration is lost.

"Can you imagine gentlemen," he says, spitting out the words like a bad clam. "Can you imagine, decent hardworking gourmands, sitting down innocently, a good quaff in the right hand whilst the left pours over a fine leatherbound menu in 'La Poive du More,' and selecting, for example, canard à la juniper with wild rice and those delightful little pommes miniature from Donegal, and then"—his voice now rises in indignation—"and then forced perhaps by some namby-pamby commie pinko!"—here, the veins in his forehead bulge ominously as his outrage volcanoes—"paisley-shirted pooftah—" Herr Do draws a breath through his nose and rolls his eyes up and slightly anticlockwise. "—pouncy agitprop vegetarian wishy-washy twat, to give half of it away, because—and mark my words gentlemen—if this does indeed become a fashion we will be expected to forfeit not only half our well-earned meals, but probably half our bottle of Lafite Rothschild as well!"

"I agree with Herr Lipp," adds O'Th'Dog quickly. "It's one thing this nonsense becoming law—a law of this nature may well turn out to be largely unenforceable—but for it to become . . . *de rigueur* . . . ouch."

At this point, Herr Do and Herr E'ass exchange little glances at one another as obvious light bulbs of realization flicker across their eyes.

"You mean," ventures E'ass, a sudden image of filthy, good-for-nothing homeless welfare pampered scum, swigging his own order of '89 Meursault or '66 Chateauneuf du Pape flitting through his suddenly one-track mind. "You mean we might have to give away half our beverage, too?"

"Of course!" booms Lipp, seizing upon this propitious moment. "Why should drink be omitted from this ghastly travesty?" He flips through the papers. "It states it here: 'This proposal may include, subject to further review, beverages of . . . blah blah blah . . . an *alcoholic nature*'! You see? Here, in black and white!"

"Then . . ." creeps in Do, sensing a shrinking wallet, "one would probably have to order two bottles of wine at each meal . . . one in fact, to give away!"

"Precisely," says Lipp, already checking his watch, smelling an early exit.

"Well, gentlemen, this um . . . throws an entirely new light on the matter—O'Dowd Booth!" shouts E'ass, suddenly buoyant. "Schnapps all around! But give half of mine and Do's away to the homeless truck out back!"

At this the men applaud loudly and exchange slaps and whistles, realizing that they can get to the nearest sports bar in time for the second half.

O'Dowd Booth meanwhile is on the phone accepting a call from the local constabulary. "No, officer. No, everything is fine." He glances over at our happy Herrs as Do is pulling his rug back to show the others his new toad implant—a nifty striped number—and telling of his forthcoming Caribbean Ital-tasting tour.

"No, I won't need the force in today. They seem to have reached an agreement, if any fighting is to take place it'll probably be in the Naughty Nineties Sports Bar over the game, I think they have bets on," says O'Dowd Booth to the constable. "Okay. Thanks. Good-bye."

As O'Dowd Booth hangs up, Lipp, with an arm around O'Th'Dog's shoulder, is saying as they head for the door: "Thank God for that, eh? Still, I don't stop working till six. After the match I am meeting Herr Transplant to discuss a Homeless Termination Plan he has devised. Better than giving them our food, eh? Ha ha ha."

"Transplant?" inquires Do as they blunder through the doors. "Still living with Cut is he?"

"Jealous sod!" laughs Lipp as a blast of cool air from outside leaves O'Dowd Booth whistling merrily, preparing the tables for the evening— O'Dowd Booth, a balding man, for once glad to be short a few Herrs.

SCENE 2

THUGS DE FOIE GRAS

Due to his terminal unpopularity in the United States, Jerry Lewis, the comedian, has moved to France, where he is held in God-like status and was once awarded its highest honor—le Crosse Futile—for his contribution to the arts. He is revered here as a true genius and cannot walk down the streets without people shouting out, "Oui, La Jerry Lewis, La Jerry Lewis. Très funny!" as those wacky humor-loving French pull contorted faces à la *The Nutty Professor.*

It was Jerry's bitterness toward the American critics, whom he refers to as "morons," and the apathy of his homeland's cinema-going public, that drove him to New Europe. Here, he enjoys not only public idolatry, but also critical acclaim, and every time he employs the bandy-legged rolling-eyed spastic routine (his stock in trade) that any ten-year-old schoolboy can routinely muster, the French fall about laughing until their sides hurt.

Jerry's only role in the latter half of the twentieth century that the American critics had a good word for was his portrayal of an aging, bitter comedic talk show host in Martin Scorcese's *The King of Comedy*, a role that presumably the critics saw as being closer to the truth than the zany, buck-toothed fellow he usually portrays. The French, however, find his over-wrought physical brand of comedy an unremitting howl, and they will jam the cinemas to capacity whenever a Jerry Lewis movie is being shown.

So Jerry then, understandably, has moved to the country that truly appreciates his talents and is ready to grovel at the feet of his every pratfall.

What is not so widely known is that Jerry *Lee* Lewis, the rock and roll singer/pianist, has also moved to France. His motives are somewhat different—he owes the IRS about seven million dollars. Jerry "The Killer" Lee Lewis, known for his wild antics offstage and on, his consumption of massive amounts of "medication," his half a stomach due to a recent surgical procedure, and his many wives who have "died" under strange and suspicious circumstances, is also held in high esteem on the continent. For although the French have no idea as to what actually constitutes great rock and roll, they do know a legend when one lands with a drunken splat on the Champs Elysée.

So there are two Jerry Lewises in Paris, and this fortuitous coincidence has not gone unnoticed among the many "bright minds" in the French entertainment world; hence the new weekly musical/comedy/game show: "Les Deux Jerry Lewis."

The show has run only three times, but already its success is astronomical. It has the largest viewership of any TV show in the history of the country, and has the population alternatively rocking like dervishes, or convulsed in side-splitting laughter.

The format is simple: each episode has lots of music, lots of laughs, and a good old-fashioned game show section that soundly abuses it's participants who for the most part take it in good spirits. And so you would expect them to: they are French and very lucky to have these two great men on one show, in their country.

Of the three programs thus far aired, the format and content have been virtually identical, and there seems no indication that the show's writers will change this winning arrangement. It starts with a closeup of two gnarly, be-ringed hands thumping out barroom rock and roll on an old upright piano. The voice-over announces in thrilled tones: "Welcome once again to—*Les Deux Jerry Lewis!*"

Massive applause both real and canned booms out and the camera pans from the pianist's hands upward. Presumably a cut is made in the film here, for when we get to the face, we see the other Jerry Lewis, his hair stuck up in spikes, his eyes crossed, and a madcap expression upon his face.

The applause cascades into crazed, deafening roars of laughter, and before we can catch our breath, the high-speed editing crew treat us to a shot of the two Jerry Lewises standing on a white studio floor with a gaudy shimmering blue curtain behind them. One of the Jerry Lewises pulls out a gun and pretends to shoot the other Jerry Lewis. This scene is couched in absolute howls of mirth as the Jerry Lewis who has been shot executes a very professional pratfall and writhes around in mock agony on the studio floor while the Jerry Lewis with the gun spins around and starts hammering at the piano, firing the occasional shot into the air. He shakes his unruly forelocks, and close-ups of his face, with a maniacal sneer plastered across it, are again followed by huge waves of laughter. Shots of the audience are interspersed; some of them are in tears, overwhelmed with jollity.

Then we see one of the Jerry Lewises take two bottles of colored capsules from his suit pocket. He opens the bottles and begins stuffing the capsules into his mouth and washes them down with slugs from a whiskey bottle. The studio audience goes into an absolute frenzy as we see the *other* Jerry Lewis begin to pull distorted faces to indicate that the pills are taking effect. The lights go dim and eerie background music plays as the first Jerry Lewis, his crazy face lit from below, hollers: "Bring me a wife!" More howls and applause as a blond woman in a cowboy outfit enters the scene. She stands between the two Jerry Lewises, who then appear to punch and kick her until she lies, blood pouring from her mouth (from a blood capsule?), on the studio floor as if dead. The two Jerry Lewises then shake hands and slap each other around a bit. The cameras scan the audience, some of whom are red-faced and almost prostrate with hysterics. Then it's time for a commercial break that features Citroën, Pernod, and Gauloises advertisements.

Backstage in the green room, the two Jerrys take their brief break. Vast amounts of alcohol in a tempting array cover a long narrow table that is bolted against one wall. Another table, draped with a white tablecloth and boasting a fine selection of niblets, stands in the center of the room flanked by two dun-colored foldout metal chairs. As the two Jerrys enter, an assistant, fiddling with the first tier of bottles, quickly leaves the room with her head down, as if expecting blows.

Jerry Lee Lewis grunts and pours himself a glass of champagne. Jerry Lewis waits for him to sit, splashes champagne into a glass, then sits down also. They drink silently, neither acknowledging the other. Between slugs, both stare moodily at a white clock that hangs on the wall above the table of drink. After a few moments, Jerry Lee Lewis gets up with a heavy sigh and pours more champagne into his glass. He returns to his seat and downs the drink in one gulp. Jerry Lewis follows Jerry Lee Lewis's move almost exactly.

The door opens and a slim blond woman in a rumpled black suit enters. "Costume," she says nervously in an Irish accent. "Five minutes left."

The action returns:

One of the Jerry Lewises is hammering out "Whole Lotta Shakin' " on the piano while the other, dressed as a schoolboy, convulses and shakes in a lunatic manner, the camera flashing between his twitching body and his head, which exhibits a startling array of facial gymnastics. After this extravagant display, the two change places and the piano-thumping Jerry Lewis does an excellent impersonation of the erratic twitching Jerry Lewis and the erratic twitching Jerry Lewis does an excellent impersonation of the piano-thumping Jerry Lewis. As the show continues, the audience finds it harder and harder to distinguish one Jerry Lewis from the other, and some laugh so hard that they have to be removed from the studio for medical treatment.

After another commercial break, we come to the game show segment. In this, the two Jerry Lewises stand at podiums on opposite sides of the screen and, one by one, various audience members are brought up before them. The two Jerry Lewises wear paper bags over their heads and the hapless "volunteer" has to guess correctly which one is which. If they guess incorrectly—which is now a definite possibility since the lines of identity have been blurred considerably as the show has progressed—the two Jerry Lewises step down from their podiums amid whoops and hollers from the crowd, and soundly abuse the contestant. The contestant is then led off and another one brought on. There is much relieved laughter from the audience members who are not selected because the prize for guessing incorrectly is either a good punching, a bucket of duck liver poured over the head, hot mushroom sauce tipped down the trousers or skirt, or raw frogs legs forced down the loser's throat. (Thickset men dressed in leopard-skin loincloths are standing by to assist the two Jerrys in their task.) The prize for correctly guessing which Jerry is the comedian and which is the musician is a safe return to the studio floor. Between turns, the two Jerry Lewises step behind a curtain and re-enter, still wearing the paper bags over their heads and sporting discreet changes of garb in order to further confuse the next competitor.

This jolly madcap game goes on for roughly fifteen minutes, and then we come to the finale. The two Jerry Lewises announce—one in a bleating childish voice, the other in a deranged southern psychopathic slur—that they in fact have grown sons, both named Jerry Lewis Jr., and would like to introduce them to the viewers. The audience goes into a frenzy of screaming laughter at this, and with the French National Anthem playing as a backdrop, the young Jerry Lewises are brought out. Two of the Jerry Lewises thump the upright piano and sing, "Drinkin' wine spodey odey drinkin' wine," as the other two Jerry Lewises gyrate across the stage, running through the complete repertoire of pratfalls, silly walks, and facial tics. And here, to deafening laughter and applause, the nearly hysterical female voice-over yells, "Monsieur, madam—Les Quatre Jerry Lewis!"

This incredible performance ends with the original two Jerry Lewises looking into the camera and announcing (each Jerry Lewis taking consecutive words and delivering them in his own inimitable style, which produces a macabre ping-pong effect),

"We'll-be-back-next-week-with"—and they holler this next bit together—"Les Deux Jerry Lewis!!!"

And so, as this cultural coupe winds to a close, the French go back to their business in this brave New Europe with lighter, more laugh-filled hearts. Various organizations of artistic endeavors—of which there are many in France—hold earnest meetings in which to decide upon the many awards the show will receive, and bohemians of every pretension pack the cafés and bars to discuss the multilayered subconscious subtext of each week's episode.

What, one wonders, would Monsieur Hulot have thought of it all?

The Bukowski Brothers
A Small Tale of Big Things

Eric Burdon

We came off stage in Berlin's Columbia Hall to a crowd almost out of control. "One more time! One more time!" Did we have anything else to give?

No. Leave 'em hanging for more. Besides, we had an overnight bus ride of hundreds of klicks to Lake Constance near the Swiss border.

Christian, the tour manager, reminded us that we had to break down our PA, etc., load out and get on the Autobahn as quickly as possible. Our bus driver had slept all day, so he'd be ready for the long trek. But our kitchen crew had not forgotten our need for overnight meals. Neatly arranged in small cardboard take-aways. Heida, our kitchen chief, laughing at the ridiculous expression she'd learned from one of the band . . . "doggie bag." She thought it had sexual implications. "Doggie bag, here, whoof! Whoof! is your doggie bag!" Plus a gift, the true gift from our Berlin fans was a small cellophane packet of the very best home grown the city had to offer. Also a small yellow plastic container, egg size with a miniature animal inside . . . different animal for each band member. Mine was a bull, the sign for Taurus.

"How nice, thank you very much." A kiss on both cheeks. "See you in Lake C." We climbed on the bus after signing shirts and photos for the gathering of hardcore fans. Guitarist Dean Restum yelled out, "We've been saving Das Boot for this long haul." As the video rolls, it's in its original German language, making it all the more authentic. The bus becomes the U-boat and the German crew members and the

Yanks and me all hurling jokes and friendly insults at each other. The Merlot flows and the bus rolls into the night toward Lake Constance. The movie is epic, even better in its original-language version. I use some of the quieter moments to take apart the plastic container, remove the small bull and put him on the headboard of my bunk . . . and transfer the small packet of green grass into the egg-like container before rolling one up. As I climbed into the sack, one of the crew yells, "Ya! Mein captain Swiss border six hundred meters and closing . . . torpedoes loose!"

The next morning around eleven we pull up outside our hotel. Bleary-eyed and somewhat hungover from Berlin. The hotel is upon a hillside overlooking the massive freshwater lake that is German on one side and Swiss on the other.

It is a massive lake, almost an inland sea, and in the hotel lobby we find tourist information about the Zeppelin Museum. The location of the zeppelin works has been here since the Great War. Of course the perfect location because if one of the monster craft should explode over the test area there would be minimal loss of life. So we have a day off and band members decide to go in search of the Zeppelin Museum as soon as we awoke the next day. Breakfast, big German breakfast . . . the "John Mayall Food Drive," as it was referred to in the band.

So we were directed to the museum which is about 30 km due west following the lake shoreline. Turns out to be a big disappointment. For sure, it was great to see the fantastic workmanship that went into the superstructure of the massive machines . . . but . . . the photographs alone with the giant red-black-white colors of the Nazi swastikas airbrushed out on the tail plain as the beast cruised over the New York skyline . . . looking like one of Jayne Mansfield's breasts. Without the evil tattoo, was just too much of self-denial, like the airbrush-out of Robert Johnson's spliff on the U.S. postal stamps, thus in the case of the zeppelin turning it into a giant sex toy rather than a political terror machine, which is what it really was. I was really getting fed up with all this politically correct stuff. I wanted the real thing.

Why did I find this so disturbing? Well, there's a family tale that in 1928 the Baron Von Zeppelin did a tour of Britain, making peaceful appeasing speeches to the Brits, trying to rekindle the flame of brotherhood twix England and Germany. When he arrived in my hometown, well known for its production of war machines for Britain's attempt at worldwide conquest . . . he chose the main gate of Vickers Armstrong shipyards, Lord Armstrong being the Brit equal of the Krups. My granny on my father's side had a second-story abode within spitting distance of the works entrance. When the Baron in halting English explained that this was really not his first visit to Britain, that he'd seen it before but from the air during one of the zeppelin bombing raids in the Great War . . . the family tale goes that my granny, from her kitchen window, tossed a vase full of dirty dishwater down upon the Baron's head. I came away recalling this family legend with pride in my heart.

Next day, the band took off in the opposite direction toward the enchanting cobblestone streets of Meersburg. Myself, Martin G. (he's German), and bass player Dave Meros walked into a small pension to take a local brew. As we entered the small café we knew the local girls eating ice cream would smell the road upon us . . . we gloated over them as they licked their ice cream cones . . . I myself ordered grappa and coffee, talk of the zeppelins continued from the previous day, brought on by the low-cut dresses of two of the local frauleins.

Martin engaged them in his good German native tongue. He said they were happy to accept invitations to the show that night. They gave us the news that just next door was the secret family collection of the great Baron Von Zeppelin. I was elated at this hot tip from locals, for it was just at the top of some stone stairs a small sign read "Zeppelin Family Museum" and a green door was leading to the Zeppelins' own family collection.

I pushed open the door, a bell rang as if to disturb the dead. The place seemed empty, but in a flash a rather plump lady, blue eyes, a bright red dress floated across the room.

"Weekomme Bitte!"

There could not have been anyone better than this fine German specimen to represent the Baron and his treasures. She looked and sounded like she was filled with helium. As round as she was she floated from glass box display case to the next and she showed the case containing the Baron's sextant, map case, and Luger .9mm. We knew we'd struck the Zeppelin comstock, then there was the Baron's personal tea set. Perfectly preserved, not a crack or scratch. And for sure the famous photo of the dirigible dominating the skyline of New York, including the damned swastika on the tailfin, seemed to be saying, "Hands up, New York!"

Martin handled the translations, which weren't really needed. I was fascinated this was the real thing.

The plump sweet-faced lady was overjoyed that we took so much interest and as the tour wound down and we stood in the doorway trying to make our exit . . . one can have too much of anything, even Baron Von Zeppelin. She was now almost frothing at the mouth and I could well imagine that the little gold breast pin she wore, in another time and place, could have been a party pin. Anyway my perverse sense of humor got the best of me. I couldn't resist giving the old party salute . . . not full-fledged arm in the air, but old lazy one, you know, the palm outward shoulder high. She looked at me and blushed.

I followed through with a click of the heels and bowed slightly. The guys didn't see this—their eyes were elsewhere, but she reacted, she blushed, her blue eyes flashed, she said something to Martin. As we climbed down the stairs I asked what she'd said. "She wanted to know if you, my friend, had any military service in the past."

It was time to head back to the hotel and get ready for soundcheck.

As we arrived at the bus terminal, I observed a ferry way out on the horizon heading swiftly toward the port, which, in turn, connects to the bus depot. A city bus rolled in and awaited the arrival of travelers from Zurich, soon the ferry docked and the landing, swarming with travelers, cars arrived to pick up people, and vans and trucks offloaded people. Soon the city bus would also pick us up and get us back to the hotel for five o'clock soundcheck. The three of us were making small talk, mainly about the probability of recording when we returned to L.A.

It was then that I saw him. He reminded me of Forrest Whitaker. A face spent between two or more emotions, one eye laughing inquisitive, the other crying or dead; he seemed to be leaning on something but he was nothing there, just air. He half turned his head, I looked his way, he turned back again . . . this happened a couple of times. "Yes," I thought to myself . . . I have this guy nailed, he's a junkie . . . looks old but is not . . . again, I repeated in my head, he's a junkie returning from Zurich where it's easy to score and he's on his way back to Germany with a stash. Then as he turned toward us standing there in the bus shelter he reminded me of the Hunchback of Notre Dame.

He spoke.

"L.A. You guys from L.A.?"

"Yeah," in unison we answered.

"Where you from?" I inquired.

"Ho Chi Minn City, Vietnam" came the answer. I was shocked because I was dead wrong. I'm usually good at nailing people's place of origin, plus the only people connected with Vietnam were people I'd met that were Americans who still, even now, had the red mud of 'Nam clinging to their boots and minds.

But rarely Vietnamese, most certainly from the north, I figured his age to be twenty. He smiled, shuffled toward us.

"Yeah, L.A. man, great." There was a lonely breath of stunned silence.

"I hate my communist face man, my family spread all over the planet, I want to go to America, learn to fuck and drink like Charles Bukowski."

I said, "San Pedro."

"What's that?"

"San Pedro—that's where he lives," I said.

He slowly says "Saannn Peeddroo."

"Yeah, I was once at a party there at his house, with a German movie director who wanted to cast him in a film, told us to "fuck off."

He smiled. "Yeah, Charles Bukowski. Fuck! Fuck! Fuck! Drink like Charles Bukowski!"

I chanted back at him, "Ho! Ho! Ho Chi Minn!"

He chants "Charles Bukowski! Charles Bukowski! Fuck! Fuck! Fuck! Drink! Drink! Drink!"

The bus arrives. We climb aboard and move to the back. I guess he's exhausted his English because he repeats "Fuck! Fuck! Fuck! Drink! Drink! Drink!" And we all come back with "Ho! Ho! Ho Chi Minn!"

The bus pulls up at the first stop. Soon filled with dozens of schoolgirls all carrying backpacks and uniformed in green. The bus rolls on down the road.

"Charles Bukowski! Charles Bukowski! Fuck! Fuck! Fuck! Drink! Drink! Drink!"

Suddenly, I'm not in Germany. I'm on a bus driving through East L.A. transported mentally half a world away, but our stop looms up ahead; back to reality.

As we leave our Vietnamese friend lost in a sea of high-pitched chatter from the schoolgirls, the doors open and we step down onto the sidewalk. Martin and Dave jog across the road toward the hotel. I stay, allowing the city bus to pass. I see his head among the kids. He moves forward to the window. The bus passes, picking up speed. I put my clenched fist up to my chest and with the other, a two-fingered peace sign . . . he returns the same salute . . . the bus disappears.

Later that night, I'm backstage after our final encore. I'm lathered in sweat . . . a towel wrapped around my head . . . soaking, I reach toward my overnight bag. A clean fresh T-shirt. Aynsley Dunbar, sitting next to me, is also toweling off . . . then, I hear a voice.

"Bukowski! Fuck! Fuck! Fuck!"

It's him . . . from Ho Chi Minn City. We laugh in each other's faces. I reach into the bottom of my bag and retrieve the little yellow egg containing the buds from Berlin.

He reaches into his deep pocket and smiles a big friendly grin. His egg is red . . . also contains green buds, and so it was that the Brothers Bukowski went outside into the cool night to share a smoke and have a good-hearted stupid laugh at each other.

I never saw him again. But I am sure I will. There's hope for the youth of the world yet, I thought, as I climbed on board the bus off to our next stop along the road. A final farewell, a salute to the Brothers Bukowski.

Pearlywhite

Marc Laidlaw and John Shirley

THE BOY they called Inchy was on his way to meet his friend Clyde for breakfast down at the City Shelter, when Pearlywhite appeared on his shoulder like a wisp of ivory smoke. "Stop. Go back. Around the block." He'd found his own shelter from last night's rain and fog beneath the thrown-back lid of a dumpster in Longtree Alley, where half a dozen Asian restaurants cast out their scraps and he could usually find something to eat for dinner. Breakfast was a different story though.

Pearlywhite's sudden appearance, in the strong gray light of morning, was startlingly out of place: a small but powerful-looking dragon made of white mist that fairly shone in this light; twisting its body as smoke twists; the smoke writhing as Inchy supposed dragons do.

Usually the smokedragon didn't show itself any earlier than twilight— and then only on the darkest days, when three o'clock felt more like dinnertime than it usually did. He wasn't used to talking to Pearlywhite when other people were around. He didn't want to look crazy, but right now no one was looking.

For the first time he noticed the tail end of a prowlcar pulled into the alley up ahead, Naiad Lane, and a muttering gathering of people crowded around the spot. Yellow police tape held them back, aided by a lady cop the kids called Officer Cat (from Catlett). "Everyone get back," she told the crowd, menacingly. It was a different tone of voice than she used on Inchy when she talked to him about getting off the street, into a program. He was always nice to her and pretended to consider her advice, but he always managed to slip away.

She hadn't seen him yet. Pearlywhite's warning had kept him from walking into her view.

"Be very careful, Inchy," said the infinitely soft voice, softer yet more penetrating than the constant rushing noise of traffic. "I want you to go back the way you came, around the block to the corner of Mawkin and Lydell."

"Whuh—" he started to say, and then noticed a pouch-faced man in a business suit staring at him as he walked up the street, away from the crowd. He didn't want to look crazy even in front of this suit-guy. " 'kay." He stepped back into the entryway of an apartment building, a little stoop reeking of cigarettes and urine, lined with mailbox slots, and waited till the man went by: a businessman passing through the dingy part of town, on his way to buildings where the lobbies smelled of fresh-cut flowers.

Inchy dreamed of someday entering those buildings on real errands. His dream was to be a courier—on bike, skates, or scooter, he didn't care. He would wear a helmet and a leather jacket and a scarf thrown round his neck; he'd wear new high-top sneakers and carry important parcels from one office to another, delivering them in person to men like this one, who gave him a chilly blue-eyed look that made Inchy even more determined to accomplish his dream.

Inchy spent some time looking after the man, waiting to see if he'd look back, but he never did.

"Go," Pearlywhite insisted, and Inchy went.

Around the corner and up one block, then down Mawkin to the boarded-up back end of Naiad Lane.

"Now stop here and duck down," Pearly ordered. "There's a loose board. Go through it."

He crouched down, not even daring to see if anyone was looking, for fear that would bring on more attention. Often he hated feeling invisible to the people who passed by, but right now he wished he could have made himself completely transparent. Pretending to stoop for a dropped coin, he reached out a hand and touched the boards until one of them swung aside. There was room to squeeze through, but the cops in Naiad Lane would surely see him.

On the other hand, Pearlywhite had never steered him wrong, and this was no place for an argument. He scrunched through the splintered gap, thankful that Pearly was insubstantial, and came out in a small pile of junk. He was in the alley's blind end now: Trash cans and giant dumpsters were shoved back here, heaped with wooden pallets and tangles of wire.

He checked his pocket to see if the string of pearls was still there. Once they'd fallen out, when he'd bent over to climb through something, and he'd almost lost them forever. Since then, he checked them constantly. His Mom's pearls. There were seven and one more on the string. He counted them: one-two-three-four-five-six-seven and one more. He could only count to seven; he couldn't remember the name of the next number, if he'd ever known it.

He stroked the pearls, wondering what now. A police radio crackled nearby. If he went any farther they'd catch sight of him, and you knew where that could lead. Some of the places they put homeless kids—especially ones without families—were no better than prisons.

"Pearly," he said, slipping the pearls back in his pocket, "Clyde's waiting on me. He's gonna go nuts if I don't get down there soon. You know how he gets when he's starving."

"Quiet, Inchy. We have to see this. We have to be sure."

"We?" he said. "Whatever this is, it's your idea."

"You're doing this for all of us. Now sneak through those bins and put your head out. Not far. Just enough to peek. We have to be sure."

"Sure of what?"

But Pearlywhite wouldn't answer. He could be maddening that way—never answering the most basic questions, leaving Inchy to work things out for himself. Inchy sighed, resigned to it, and got down on all fours. The pavement was oily and cold, as if it had sweated all night in a fever; he could smell fish and rotten vegetables and automotive grease, along with the odor of brewing coffee, which was always everywhere on cold mornings. He put his head down and crept under a snag of wire, between two crumpled metal drums. When he lifted his head again he was staring at a cop. Two cops. Three. Two had their backs to him and the other, the one he'd seen first, was crouching down examining a shape crumpled on the asphalt. What mostly stood out was a pair of small feet, white beneath grime they shared with the pavement.

Two small feet, and one of them, the left one, was missing its little toe.

That was all the detail he noticed. That was enough. His mind stopped after that. He just kept thinking one thing: *Clyde.*

"Get back now," Pearlywhite said. "Inchy, get back."

He wasn't sure how long Pearlywhite had been talking to him. For once the smoky voice didn't reach him—couldn't cut through what he was feeling. What finally prompted him to move was fear that the cops might spot him.

The crouching cop was pointing out things around the body— Inchy couldn't exactly see what. But one of the things started to move. It looked like a ball of ragged bits of string, all different colors collected and tied together and rolled up in a tangle, the sort of thing you'd find in a kid's pocket. And without any of the cops noticing (so far), the ball came rolling slowly down the alley toward Inchy. Maybe one of them had kicked it. All Inchy knew was that it was coming straight at him. Eventually one of the cops was going to notice it out of the corner of an eye and turn and see the ball of string—and beyond it Inchy himself. And then there would be questions and confinement, and he couldn't have that. Not ever again.

He started to scramble back, but he'd only gotten a few inches when Pearlywhite said, "Wait."

"Nooooo." A thin whine.

But Pearlywhite had never been more insistent. Inchy had the feeling Pearly was actually capable of physically stopping him, although the smokedragon never had before. He'd never felt a hint of this much power. This must be important. He stopped. He trusted Pearlywhite and knew Pearlywhite would never do anything to harm or endanger him, unless . . .

Well, he'd never known there was an "unless" until now.

What had changed?

The ball of string touched his fingers. He opened his eyes, not having realized they were shut. His hands closed around the ball.

"Okay," Pearlywhite whispered. "Let's go."

He backed into the cans, bumping them in his anxiety to be away. A piece of crumpled tin came clamoring down, and suddenly there were shouts and whistles blowing, and a whoop of sirens at the far end of the alley. Inchy threw himself free of the garbage, slammed into the board that swung by one nail, and was out on the far side, diving into traffic that somehow couldn't touch him. And not noticing at first that in slamming past the board he'd driven the nail into his arm . . . He felt as if he were made of the same stuff as Pearlywhite. Wispy, weird and insubstantial, flowing between the cars. And then there were more alleys, more streets, on and on until he came to the invisible edge of his world, the border beyond which he wasn't really welcome, where he was always the opposite of invisible. Even if he passed beyond, into those broader, brighter streets, he carried the barrier with him. He was forever something out of place, out there.

He needed to be invisible now. He needed to blend in. He backed up, thinking of places where he would be safe, where he could think for a while. Pearlywhite was gone now. And he had this ball of twine in his hand. He had a feeling nothing was going to get any clearer until nightfall, when Pearlywhite would certainly return and they could talk openly in the dark. He would just have to hole up and wait it out. And he was used to that.

He barely took notice of the small, perfectly round red-oozing hole punched into his left upper arm.

Inchy sat on the floor of a big circular room—the Thinking Tank—with a high ceiling, under blinking Christmas lights, eating half a stale egg muffin from a dumpster bag. The lights were plugged into a much-taped cord that ran across two roofs to a light socket on the roof of a building that still had electricity.

The nighttime has two personalities; there are two spirits abroad in it, or so it always seemed to Inchy. There was the nighttime that protected, that was like a comforting mother swathed in shadow; there was the nighttime that hunted you. One nighttime tried to protect you from the other.

Right now, Inchy felt he was safe in the arms of night the protector; he knew that Pearlywhite was coiled up in the pearls in his pocket, and the night was curled up around the tank. The Thinking Tank was a dry, busted-open water tank that stood on metal poles atop the defunct Mesmer Brewery. By common agreement, the kids didn't use it for a home—you only slept there in emergencies. Be there too much, and someone would notice. But they met in the tank when they needed advice, or when they just needed to meet up with each other; if you couldn't figure out what to do by yourself, you went to the Tank and waited for someone else who also needed help to come. Answers came more easily when you could talk things over.

The mostly empty, rat-haunted factory below still smelled of moldy hops and grain, though no beer had been made there for as long as any of the kids remembered.

Inchy thought about Clyde as he chewed meditatively on the rubbery remnant of fried egg white within the hard crust of the English muffin: Clyde and Inchy at the river, fishing with other people's broken fishing lines, rusty old hooks; Clyde pretending he was going somewhere to piss where he wouldn't drive off the fish, actually crossing the rotting old wharf and climbing down to the support beams below, where he grabbed Inchy's line and tugged on it, in the shadows. "*Clyde—I got a huge one! It's something monster big!*" Then hearing the fish laugh—but recognizing that laugh. Inchy had been annoyed, but now he smiled at the memory.

He scratched at the tingling wound in his arm, and remembered when Clyde had found some arcade tokens, and taken him into the Flashpoint Arcade to play the games—the greatest moment of their lives, until they got chased out by the fat guy with that drippy wad of smokeless in his mouth.

He remembered when Clyde had been attacked by that wild dog in the bushes of the park, and he'd lost a toe to it—how Clyde, once he'd gotten away, had actually laughed, seeing the dog snapping and gulping the toe down. "Wild dog got to eat too," he said. But then he'd turned white and fainted, and Inchy—acting on a suggestion of Clyde's Invisible, Koil—had to drag him to shelter.

And sometimes, when they slept in the cardboard fort under a bridge near one another, they awakened late at night to hear their Invisibles whispering to one another . . .

"Yes," Pearlywhite said, issuing from his pocket, drifting upward. "It's good to remember lost friends. It's their real funeral, remembering them; it's the real way to say goodbye."

"What really happened, Pearly?" For the first time since Clyde died, Inchy felt his eyes burning with tears.

Pearlywhite took up his place on Inchy's shoulder, nestled against his ear. Inchy could feel the gentle pressure, just a hint of warm cotton. "I don't know," Pearlywhite said. He was changing colors with the Christmas tree lights. A red Pearly; a blue one. "But there might be enough left of Koil to ask."

Inchy's eyes widened. "I thought he was . . . gone!"

"Let's see. He was homebased in that ball of string."

"He was?" Clyde had never told him what object Koil was homebased in. You didn't usually see them go in and out of their homebases, and most of the kids were secretive about it.

Inchy took the grubby ball of string, a little smaller than a baseball, out of the paper sack and hefted it in his hand. It felt *less* than it looked. Not lighter, but . . . *less.*

He set it on the floor between his outstretched legs, beside his scabbed knees.

Pearlywhite said something in the language of the Invisibles, which sounded like a breeze whistling through a broken bottle. The ball didn't move. Pearlywhite spoke again. The ball rolled—ever so slightly—a quarter-inch one way, then back. Just rocking in place. Then the end of the string lifted up, and from it issued a smoky bluish shape—more like a sea horse than a dragon—made out of strings of mist; the foggy tendrils stretched up and twined, and turned, and coiled, back and forth, looping in the air to make the outline of Koil's body, like a sculpture made entirely of a single strand of wire.

But this time, the living string of mist was broken, here and there—stretched thin and missing in places, fraying to nothingness at the edges. Fading.

"He's weak!" Inchy said in alarm.

"What happened to Clyde?" Pearlywhite asked Koil; in Inchy's language, so he could understand.

Inchy heard Clyde's voice faint and far away in his head, through a crackliness like the song on the scratched record his dad had played for him, when he was little; before the police took his dad away, and his mom died.

"Killed . . . too strong . . . no . . . experience with . . . teeth like the blade of all suffering . . . with what sorrow, he . . . glass three . . . hunter hunted by his hunting . . ."

"His weakness is even in his speech," Pearlywhite said. He whistled another question in his own language.

But a gust of wind seemed to answer from the two-foot-high gap in the rusted metal of the wall, its sharp edges curled back by the kids—and the wind reached into the Thinking Tank to push Koil out of shape, so that he blew into wisps—and then into nowhere.

"Koil!" Inchy shouted, grabbing the ball. There seemed to be a fading bluish light deep in the ball of twine, but then even that ebbed and went out without answering.

"Something's taken them both," Pearlywhite said.

They heard a crunch in the broken glass outside. And Inchy knew from the slightness of the crunch that he didn't have to worry about bolting.

In came Garvey, a black kid who was older and stronger than his small limbs and legs suggested. He wore a brown suit jacket, brown cor- duroy pants with a seam so sharp it looked like he had just picked it up from the dry cleaner. His shoes were shiny brown, freshly polished and buffed. Beneath the suit jacket, the neck of a frayed yellow T-shirt was just visible. He wore a ring he'd found in the train station bathroom, missing its jewel; there was just a shiny socket. And in the jacket's breast pocket, the pointed tip of a neatly folded bright red handkerchief, vivid as a rose—clean and crisp in appearance, although the kerchief was older than Garvey and had belonged to his father. The kerchief was the one unchanging element of his attire. Garvey had the uncanny ability to delve into masses of dingy rags at the clothing banks and emerge with an outfit that looked as if it had been tailored for him. His father, a Caribbean immigrant who'd sold flowers on street corners, had taken similar pride in his appearance. And even though he'd hardly known his father, Garvey spoke with a hint of the older man's Island accent.

"Good," Garvey said, not at all surprised to see him. "You got word of the meeting."

Inchy shook his head. "I've been here all day."

"That's not smart."

"I had—I had to hide."

"Let me in," came a small cracked voice from outside.

Garvey turned and held the ragged metal open behind him, and Mina put her head through, pausing when she saw Inchy getting to his feet. Her eyes slid around, looking scratched and blurred behind her thick eyeglasses. She had hair cut just below her ears, dyed turquoise at the ends, a look at odds with her shyness, since it meant that you couldn't help but look at her, and that always made her nervous. She stood with her back to the curved metal wall, wiping her nose on the thick tattered sweater several sizes too large for her, and pulling on the blue ends of her hair, looking away every time Inchy glanced at her.

After Mina came Vick, a tall boy with wild white hair and skin so white it seemed to be powdered and eyes of cold blue crystal. Vick stood next to Mina, a few feet away, his back to the wall. Then came the twins, Rosalie and Junebug, and they took their positions. Inchy got up as Cassandra came in, and she was the last one for now. He leaned against the chill metal until it boomed beneath his weight. They all jumped at the sound, and Garvey gave him an irritated look.

"You shouldn't have come so early. We were looking for you." And to the others: "Inchy's been here since daylight."

"Stupid," said Vick, who always had some reason not to like anyone.

"Shut up," Inchy said. "I had to come. They saw me seeing Clyde . . . the cops did."

"You saw him?" Mina said, holding him in the regard of her blemished spectacles. "After . . . ?"

"Pearlywhite sent me to look at him. Yeah, it was after."

"What happened to him, then?" Cassandra asked. She was a plump, unsmiling girl with stringy brown hair; Clyde had tried many times to make her laugh, even for a moment, and failed. Her face looked broken from inside, more than usual; and Inchy found himself wondering if she had maybe hoped that Clyde would make her really laugh some day . . . and now that far-off hope was gone.

"I don't know. He was on the ground . . . just lying there in Naiad Lane."

"We know where," Vick said. "They took him away and we scouted the place. But we don't know what happened."

"And the cops or somebody got his charm," said Rosalie. "His homebase."

"No," said Inchy. "That's why Pearly sent me. See." He put out his hand. The ball of string lay there, unmoving. "Koil came out. Pearlywhite called him and he came out and said something I couldn't hardly understand, but . . . but whoever hurt Clyde, they got Koil too."

"Clyde's not *hurt*," Vick said savagely. "He's dead."

"K-killed," Inchy said. "I know."

"But . . . but that's impossible," Mina said softly, and they all turned to look at her because she spoke so rarely. "The Invisibles are . . . they can't die. Nothing can hurt them."

"Maybe if they kill *you*, your *Invisible* goes away," Inchy said.

"The hell with maybes," Garvey said. "Why don't we just up and ask 'em?"

They looked from one to the other, there in the gently twinkling light, and reached silent agreement. One by one, each of the children standing ringed around the wall of the tank put out a hand holding his or her homebase, whatever precious object their Invisible had chosen to inhabit.

Inchy pulled the remainders of his mother's pearl necklace from his pocket; the beads dangled from his fingers, in the same hand that held Koil's ragged ball. He felt Pearlywhite stirring. Smoke seeped from the pearls and pooled in the palm of his hand, and the wise dragon eyes blinked open to stare at the other kids.

Next to him, Garvey slowly drew the red handkerchief from his pocket and draped it across his hand. A dark stain muddied the middle of the cloth. It never went away, no matter how often Garvey washed it. That was his father's blood, from the chest wound where the bullet went in, when the cop who shot Garvey's father had mistaken a black iris for a gun.

The kerchief seemed to stir, something rising up from the stain, then subsiding. Garvey looked impatient and he took the cloth by a corner and snapped it, then settled it again on his palm. "Come on, Slink!" His Invisible was slow to wake tonight.

Mina took off her glasses, which weren't hers after all, but had belonged to her lost brother. *Her* eyes were 20/20. She wore the thick lenses despite the blurred vision they gave her, the dizzying headaches. They had all stopped trying to talk her out of wearing the things; Garvey sometimes said she ought to at least smash out the lenses, but she would never do that, nor would any of them. Mina's Invisible lived in there somewhere, and now came out in a subtle warping of the ambient light, as if the air itself had turned into a thick lens. This was Glimmish. It flickered up into the air before Mina's eyes, and Inchy gladdened to see her clear-eyed, knowing that for once she was able to see him as well as he saw her. He wished she would look at him the way she looked at Glimmish. But Glimmish, really, was the only thing she trusted anymore.

So it went around the circle. Vick's Invisible, Catseye, sprang from a red and white marble, and it was a thing like a mottled glass eye that spun and stared and sang when it spoke, which was rarely. The twins carried two halves of a golden locket, each half with its own chain, and their Invisible was likewise twinned, so that two shapes sprang from the locket-halves and twisted around each other until the seething shape settled into one form with two faces peering in opposite directions with eyes of emerald and ever-murmuring mouths. Cassandra was the last of them to put out her hand; she did it with a sigh, slowly straightening her fingers until they could see the crucifix with the shortest bit broken off so it now resembled a T. Hers was the only somewhat humanoid Invisible: A luminous, ethereal Christ, dripping crusted blood from hands and feet and brow. The little bearded man, glowing like a night-light, stood erect on her palm with a pained expression that mirrored Cassandra's. She called him Jessie.

By then, finally, Slink had taken up the task of animating Garvey's handkerchief. The red cloth sat on his hand like a wrinkled four-legged doll, its legs drawn from the corners of the kerchief, its central body a bunched mass marked with the dark bloodstain. The crumpled red doll wriggled and dropped to the floor, freeing itself from

Garvey's fingers, then stumped out into the middle of the Thinking Tank. It walked with a scaled-down version of Garvey's swagger.

Pearlywhite swirled down to meet Slink. Catseye whirled toward them, giving off a sound like singing crystal. The other Invisibles joined them, making their own smaller circle at the center of the Tank, taking up positions between the kids.

"Koil no longer manifests," Pearlywhite said. "I tried . . ." Pearly's speech dissolved into sussuration, and the other Invisibles merged their comments into the hiss. After a few minutes the sounds became something the children could understand again, mostly.

"One stalks," said Glimmish, in words that flashed along the inner walls of the tank. "Stalks children."

"Children?" said Cassandra. The horror Inchy felt struck all of them; even Vick and Garvey, too tough to show fear in their different ways, seemed to take the news badly. Cassandra clenched tight to the glowing figure in her hand, and they heard it gasp in a smallish voice: "Calm down, Cass!"

"But . . . but why?" she said.

"I got another question," Garvey said. "One we could maybe answer. Where's Niall? Where's Leafjacket?"

The kids began to murmur. Niall was missing . . . the only other kid aside from Clyde who had failed to reach the Thinking Tank tonight. He was usually down at the Library, hidden in the darkest reaches of the stacks, reading some big old book of useless knowledge. And Leafjacket was his Invisible, a papery rustling thing that lived inside a waterlogged, yellowed paperback with pages thoroughly stuck together that Niall himself didn't know what was written inside.

The Invisibles began to murmur. The mouths of the Twins' Invisible contorted in something like fear, and Inchy realized he had never known them to show anything of the sort. What could frighten Invisibles?

But then again, they had all thought Invisibles were immortals and apparently that was not the case.

"I thought you were gonna tell Niall about the meeting," Vick told Garvey.

"I was," he said. "Then I ran into the Twins and they were headed toward the Library, and they said they'd tell him."

"We did," said Rosalie.

"He said he'd be here," Junebug agreed.

"Then something's happened . . ."

"Yesssssss," sang Catseye. "Happening now. Leafjacket—"

Slink suddenly stiffened. "Leafjacket! Something . . . something . . . !"

They feel it, Inchy thought. They're in touch with Leafjacket. And if something's happening to the Invisible, it's happening to his boy. Niall's in trouble too.

"We gotta find him!" Inchy said. "Where are they? Where's Leafjacket, can you tell us that?"

But even as he threw out the question, the Invisibles were slipping away. The red handkerchief settled to the floor. Catseye dropped and rolled back toward Vick's feet. Pearlywhite leapt catlike back into the string of pearls. All the kids fell quiet, their sense of panic perfectly preserved, and listened to the night.

Something out there—night the stalker now, night with a predator's hunger, sniffing for them.

A footstep on the rooftop, just outside the Tank; a heavier than usual crunch in the glass. And then the soft creak of the metal flap pulling open. Inchy smiled, thinking it must be Niall at last, joining up with them, late as always.

But the Invisibles wouldn't have fled then.

And the person who ducked and came into the Tank was not Niall at all.

"I thought I'd find you here," said Officer Cat.

She straightened up, smiling around at the blinking Christmas lights. She was Chinese—she'd married a white guy and taken his name—but she had no accent, she'd lived here all her life. She had a round face and small eyes and a wide flexible mouth; when she smiled, her whole face moved.

Garvey and Inchy looked at each other; a flicker of mutual understanding. They went to stand in front of Officer Cat, their backs close to the curved, rusty metal wall, to keep her attention focused on them so the others could get away.

"How long you know about this place?" Garvey asked.

"A little while. I looked in once when you guys weren't here." Officer Cat amiably rested a hand on the butt of her gun. Her belt radio crackled and talked to itself. Some numbers and a description of someone on foot on East Third. She didn't seem to pay it any attention; she was absorbed in looking at Garvey and Inchy. "I had a feeling you'd be meeting here tonight. You guys tired of living on the streets yet?"

Inchy glanced past her and saw Mina slip through the door. Vick and the others were going, one by one.

Officer Cat turned her head a little at the sound of their going, but she didn't try to stop them. She probably figured she could only get one or two kids at a time, if that's what she was here for.

"Who's livin' on the streets?" Garvey asked, offended, one hand clasping the lapel of his coat like a politician. "I live with my cousins."

Officer Cat shook her head. "Far as I can find out, you live in that car in Old Mule's Pit, most of the time. Aren't you tired of it? I know the system is a drag for a while but if you're patient they'll eventually find you either an adoption or foster care—"

"Nobody's going to adopt us. They like babies," Inchy said.

"I *done* foster homes. No thanks. That's why I'm—I'm living with my cousins. Don't tell me where I'm living, Officer Cat, I got to have my props."

"Uh huh. Well. I think you might be in danger on these streets, more than usual. There's a guy out there killing kids, we think. We don't think Clyde was the first one. We don't want one of you to be next."

Inchy nodded gravely, but he had no intention of going with her.

He knew Pearlywhite wouldn't follow him to any foster home. Like Garvey, he remembered what being in the system was like.

"Is that supposed to be some kind of threat?" Garvey said.

"We can't protect you out here, and you boys are way overdue for . . . Whoa, hold on there now—"

She spread her arms as the two boys started to move away from each other, circling her, in opposite directions, to make a dash for the doorway. "Inchy, Garvey—I mean it! Don't take another step!"

She reached for her walkie-talkie, to call for someone to help her round them up, Inchy guessed. As she pulled the radio out of its belt loop, Garvey slapped it from her hand.

"Damn it, Garvey!" she yelled, as the radio tumbled to bounce low on the wall. Instinctively, she bent to retrieve it, giving the boys the moment they needed to dart past her.

Garvey was hunkered over, scurrying through the crude door, Inchy crowding after—but she caught Inchy by the ankle and held on as she followed onto the roof, dragging him back into her grip.

"Inchy, shit, hold still! I'm trying to save your life, here! Come on!"

He stopped struggling—he didn't want her to put cuffs on him. He might get his chance later, if she didn't do that. Garvey had gotten away, anyhow.

"Okay," she said, turning him to face her. "How about if we get something to eat?"

He shrugged. "I'm not hungry."

"Oh *really?*" She didn't believe him for an instant. "I remember you like fresh hot pizza slices, right? I'll buy you one, any kind you like, and we'll figure out how to get you to someplace safe and warm. And a bath. You could definitely use a bath."

She kept a good strong grip on him down the fire escape, to the street, muttering to herself about what a death trap the fire escape was, with its bolts grinding loose in the powdering concrete sockets as they passed.

He pretended to be eager for the pizza. He would've liked it, too;

but if he accepted a slice and then ran away after eating it, he'd feel bad about that, somehow. Pearlywhite wouldn't approve, he knew. Pearly believed in living by a code of honor.

When they got to the sidewalk-service pizza window at Enrico's, he waited till she was giving her order, and then did that twisting-jump that had gotten him loose from so many adult grips. He dodged behind her and slipped down the alley by Enrico's. She shouted but he could already hear the resignation in her voice. She must've known she couldn't catch him once he'd gotten such a start on her. He angled down the narrow passage between two buildings— piled with trash, rotting blankets, and old metal buckets to jump over—and around another turn of the familiar way, gasping when he got to the street, a block from Enrico's. He was surprised to hear pursuit—but turned to see Garvey coming.

Garvey grinned, leaping over a pile of old paintbrushes as he came. Huffing, he skidded to a stop beside Inchy on the sidewalk, both of them looking up and down the street for Officer Cat. "Why you make me run through that trash?" Garvey asked, not really expecting an answer. "Get shit all over my damn clothes. Look at this, scrape up my shoes. Shit, man."

"Yours tell you where she was taking us?" Meaning Garvey's Invisible.

"I was hiding behind the Tank, I heard her talk about it. I don't need Slink to tell me everydamnthing like you and that dragon. Come on, let's find Niall."

Getting past the librarians required a certain strategy—one they had practiced. It was an old library, but it had a modern security gate and a librarian sitting at the checkout desk where she could keep an eye on who went in and out.

Sometimes Inchy came in to get out of the weather and look at picture books. He couldn't read, much. Mina would take off her glasses and read to him now and then.

Inchy was grubby and smelled sour, and he knew it. They had a policy of keeping the homeless out, and he was pretty obvious.

Sometimes he waited till the librarian's back was turned, and vaulted the low railing by the gate, then ducked under a reading table and ran between the stacks. Today, though, they were in a hurry, so they did another bait and switch, with Garvey—who never got stopped—asking the librarian why they didn't have more books on black culture, and her protesting they had a great many of them, and him shaking his head in pretended outrage, waving his arms, to keep her attention on him, so that Inchy could vault the railing without her seeing.

After a minute Garvey said, "Hey—tell you what, white lady, I will check out what you got myself, and then we'll see."

He strutted into the library, heading for the Black history stacks, where he met Inchy as prearranged. They were between a high stack filled with magazines and slender books, and a silver-painted radiator under an old, high, smoked-glass window. The ceilings were high, in here, with dusty glass fixtures, way up there, that were almost spider shaped. "Where you think Niall'd be, Inch?"

"I don't know. Pearly feels distant. Ask yours."

He looked around; they were alone in the stacks. He took out his kerchief and bunched it up in his palm, whispering, "Slink . . . ?"

This time the little red-stained dollshape emerged, translucent and shivering, almost immediately. "What's the matter, Slink?" Garvey asked. "You're shakin'."

"The *fear* . . . like a scent in the air . . . I see books on the ancient gods, there . . . that way . . ." He pointed with a tiny indistinct hand, then surprised them by jumping to the floor and pointing again, urgently.

"Ancient gods," Garvey muttered. "Niall likes to read about mythology and stuff. Greek gods . . ."

They followed Slink, who was running down the aisle like a runaway puppet, ahead of them, pausing now and then to turn and gesture. *Follow, follow . . .*

A middle-aged lady with hair like a dyed-blond helmet turned her quietly angry eyes toward them as they ran past. She couldn't see Slink, but she snorted out a single derisive laugh, shaking her head and muttering something about grungey little urchins running in here, and she seemed happier, Inchy thought, to have something specific to be angry about besides the thing that frightened her that she never let come into the front of her mind—

He knew that view of the lady came to him from Pearly somehow—

Garvey and Inchy left her behind, jogging around a corner after Slink who was leaping and weaving down increasingly dim aisles, between high shelves of musty books; the aisles seemed to get narrower, edging closer and closer, and Inchy felt like they were starting to lean in, toward him; like the books were all going to tumble furiously down like the pictures Mina had shown him of the playing cards coming at Alice in Wonderland, when she'd read the book to him—

(Was Mina safe?)

—and then Slink turned another corner, went down another aisle, turned another corner, they were zigzagging through the library, past a startled black man and a tall man with a beard, and it seemed to Inchy that Slink must be confused, lost, because they were going back the way they'd come, until he realized that they were following some kind of trail in the air itself, a trace left by someone or something that had gone here before . . .

And then Slink skidded to a stop and spun around, like a figure skater in slow motion, and then fell on his miniature behind and stared dazedly at the ceiling, as if trying to understand the spidery light fixtures.

They stopped running, breathing hard. Looking around.

"We're here," Garvey said, gasping, "but I don't see Niall."

The aisle looked normal to Inchy, now, not too dark or narrow or leaning. Just library shelves of books, some of them old and leatherbound and tattered, some of them glossy backed. He saw a picture of a naked flying guy holding up the snake-headed lady, on the spine of one of the books, one of the myth books, for sure. But Niall wasn't there.

Garvey was staring at Slink. A slender woman with butterfly type glasses and leopard pattern pedal pushers, her hair in a retro beehive, was coming down the aisle, smiling at them; one of those hip girls that hang out in front of nightclubs. She said, "You guys lost?"

"Nuh," Inchy said. "Resting. Looking."

"Okey dokers." She walked on . . . right over Slink, almost stepping on him, not seeing him. He ignored her. She glanced back at Garvey who was staring, as far as she knew, at the empty carpet.

Then Garvey looked up at a top shelf nearby. "He's looking up there. I thought he was looking at the ceiling but . . ."

There was a set of books, on the top shelf, that stuck out a little so you could see the edge of the pages under the spine; and some of them were a wet-red color, that looked new, and some were white. They found a stool with little steps on it in the next aisle, and brought it over, and Inchy stood on it to look. There was a little space between a set of gold-covered numbered books and the wooden shelf-wall. In the space between books and wall, in the shadows behind the books, he could see a small, dirty hand clutching a curling, yellowed paperback book. And he saw there was blood seeping into the books.

He felt like he was going to fall backward off the stool, and had to clutch the back of the books to hold on; they were big books and stayed in place. He reached into the niche and took the book from the little, curled hand, having to pull sharply; the fingers curled up like a dying flower as Niall's charm came free.

As he climbed down off the stool, he felt a series of sensations in his chest. First there was a kind of electrical numbness, then a deep coldness, and then an aching hole. Just a hole that hurt.

Garvey was staring at the old paperback in Inchy's hand.

The retro girl was coming back toward them. She seemed to work here. "You guys sure you're . . . What's the matter?"

Garvey pointed. "We were looking for our friend. Someone left him up there."

"What?" She laughed. "He's in the *Golden Bough*?"

"Behind those books."

"You got a hamster or something in here . . . ?"

She climbed up on the stool, and said, "Oh my god."

Inchy and Garvey ran, while she was up there looking; Inchy stuffing the homebase for Niall's Invisible in his shirt.

As they left the library, he thought he saw the pouchy-faced man with the icy blue eyes; the man was walking around the corner of the building, on his way home from work. Looking at Inchy and Garvey; gone from sight.

Inchy clutched the paperback to his chest, under his shirt, as the wind soughed past him and Garvey, and through them too, it seemed to him. "Garvey . . . I feel like . . . like there's a window in my forehead that's just . . . left open and the wind is blowing right inside my head . . ."

"Yeah well, if it tried to blow through my head it couldn't get in 'cause there's a damn brain in there. Shit, it ain't no cold wind." But he sounded hoarse, scared.

"I got Leafjacket but . . . I don't know if he's in there anymore . . ."

"Maybe Pearly can tell you. I got to go home."

Inchy looked at him. Home? "You mean the old car? Why?"

"I just got to think."

"I don't know—I don't think we should be apart. I think we should get all the kids and . . ." He stopped on the corner, dizzy. He felt hot, and then cold, as a ripple of weakness went through him. Was he feverish? His arm ached, where the nail had punched into him.

"I meet you later, man, maybe at the McDumpster. You get 'em together. I got to think. I just . . . I got to think. I got to be alone . . ."

Inchy watched Garvey walk away, and wanted to chase after him. But he felt too sick to do it now. He felt sick about Niall and just sick. One blended into the other.

"Inchy?"

Mina's face hovered in lamplight, just around the corner of the library, her body in shadow. So shy with her bony fingers creeping around the cold gray edge of the building. He looked up at the massive building, thinking it looked like a tomb. He could hear sirens coming to claim Niall. He hurried toward Mina, grateful for her appearance, and took hold of her thin elbow through the ragged sweater.

"Inchy, you're hurting me!"

"We gotta get out of here, Mina. Come on."

"I—I came to find Niall."

His teeth started chattering. "N-Niall . . ."

"Did you tell him? What the Invisibles said, did you tell him?"

"Niall's dead," he spat out. "Garvey and me, we found him in there in the books. He's dead, Mina, killed." He had to bite his tongue; he didn't want to tell her more than that. He could have; he desperately wanted to unburden himself, but it would have been cruel to her. She had loved Niall, Inchy knew, loved him in something like the way Inchy himself loved her. Niall never really noticed Mina, unless they were talking about books, but Inchy had seen the way she looked at him and sometimes let her glasses slide down a fraction of an inch so she could peer at him clearly, shyly, when he wasn't looking.

She didn't ask any questions, he was grateful for that. She just started shaking and sniffing, and he tried to hold her up but suddenly she was down on her knees on the sidewalk, just wailing. He moved her over a little bit, out of the way, back onto the stoop of a massage place. A Korean woman looked out at him, fat and sweaty, fanning herself with a magazine; it felt so cold out here, but warm humid air pushed its way through the iron grating that held the woman. She narrowed her eyes and fanned the kids away with her mouth hardening. "You go!" she said. "You bad for business!"

Mina cried harder. Inchy had to get his hands under her arms and haul her to her feet. There was a park around the corner, a little place that used to be a vacant lot until they put in hedges and grass and benches; but the grass had been pissed on until it was burned yellow, and the hedges were so choked with trash they seemed to have browned scraps of paper for leaves, and the benches were long gone, just uncomfortable metal struts remaining. It was basically a vacant lot again. But he found a dirt knoll and brushed it sort of clean and sat there next to her, taking some comfort when she finally pushed him away from holding and hugging her, because it meant she was finding her strength again. She held her knees up to her face, arms wrapped around her shins, and rocked and moaned until finally she sighed and raised her eyes to him. He saw that she'd taken her glasses off. He thought maybe she was going to call Glimmish. Instead she just stared at him clear-eyed and said, "What now, Inchy? Who's next? Who's hunting us?"

"It's not that," he said. "There's . . . there's so many people out here . . . people getting hurt and killed and just plain lost . . . every day it seems there's someone else missing. Don't you feel that way, Mina?"

"I don't feel any way," she said. "I just know someone took Clyde and now . . . now Niall. And it feels like it's coming for us. And I want to know why."

He nodded, hanging his own head.

And found himself staring at Leafjacket.

The old book seemed to stir, the pages parting like a parched mouth trying to speak.

"Look, Mina!"

She looked at the crumbling paperback, then quickly scanned the street around them. There were people here and there, business on the corner nearby, men arguing up the block, some women leaning in to chatter at the driver of an idling car, which pulled away just as a black and white cruised through, but no one was watching the two kids. She ducked her shoulders and huddled in closer to Inchy, as if they were making a barrier around Leafjacket.

Inchy wondered if he should try to pry the pages open with his fingers, but there was no need. For the first time in his memory, Leafjacket opened. The pages crackled and ripples began to spread through the gray smeared ink, greenish brown stains puddling on the ancient paper like rain or tears. Forming letters . . . words. He could hear the book whispering, but it was too weak to speak. Inchy tried to mouth out the letters, but he only knew a few of them:

"I-N- . . . N . . . I-S-I- . . . D?"

"B," said Mina. "In-vis-i . . . Invisible."

"That's it?"

"That's all," she said. "Look."

Leafjacket cracked open all the way along its spine, sighing away bits of brittle dust. For a moment the letters hung across two smeared pages, then they faded out like the headline of a newspaper taped up in a shop window for years and years. Inchy caught the halves of the book before they could fall apart completely. He dug in his pocket and found a rubber band, snapped it around the remains of Niall's homebase, and shoved the whole wad down into his jacket with the remains of Koil and the warm pearls of his own Invisible.

"Garvey said we should get the others," he said.

"Garvey? Where'd he go?"

"His old car."

"Inchy, that's not a good idea. We shouldn't be apart tonight, we should . . . we should all stick together. It's the only way to get through this, I think."

"Maybe you should tell him that. Could be he'd listen to you."

Garvey would get into strangers' cars if he thought they would drive him a few blocks. "Saves me some wear on these shoes," he'd say when Inchy told him he was crazy. He didn't believe Garvey would take any chances at a time like this, but you never knew. He was suddenly stricken with fear and concern for his friend. Garvey on his own, always acting so fearless, and sometimes so genuinely trusting—sort of an idiot about it, really.

"We should go," he said.

"Yeah."

He was so grateful for Mina's company. They walked close together, stumbling on the uneven sidewalk and bumping up against one another. She was walking more steadily now; she hadn't put her glasses back on yet and he wasn't sure if he should say something about it. Without him even asking she said, "I want to see again. It's making me crazy, seeing everything all bent and foggy. Glimmish will understand."

"Okay," Inchy said. "Sure. Glimmish is probably glad. Makes her job easier."

"You think?"

They came to a stop past the wall of a brick building where the sidewalk just . . . ended. The Pit. For as long as Inchy could remember, there'd been a gaping hole here, all that remained of what had been a hotel or a skyscraper or some building they'd knocked down years ago. The Pit was all that remained of a basement two stories deep. You could see girders and beams down there, where floors used to be. Someone had come along and scooped out the center of the building and left this hollow place to be carpeted with broken glass and weeds and charred wood and cans and trash barrels. Piles of whitish foam and mold and shredded upholstery that one could no longer call furniture. And in the middle of all that, a car. It had crashed into the Pit one night, ending up crumpled like a can someone had stepped on. The glass was smashed from every window; it was rusted and crushed and dangerous to touch. But inside it, Garvey found shelter. It wouldn't keep a grown man dry, but it was barely enough for the boy.

They stood at the edge of the pit and yelled down: "Garvey! Gaaaarvey!"

A siren whooped and startled Inchy into leaping down to the floor below. He held up a hand to Mina, who knelt at the brink and then leapt down with him. They made their way over to the foundation wall of the adjacent building, where some bent prongs of rebar formed steps down into the Pit. At the bottom, they picked their way across the broken glass.

Back in the permanent shadows, Garvey's neighbors laughed and coughed and someone kicked bottle shards toward them.

"Garvey?" Inchy said, stooping toward the car.

"He ain't here," called a hoarse voice. A flame flared up; he saw a hooded figure with milky eyes. Old Mule. He was okay.

"You . . . you seen him tonight?" Inchy asked.

"Not since this morning," the raspy voice replied. "You're welcome to wait, though."

"Sure," said another voice, one they didn't know. "You come on in, and bring that sweet thing of yours."

More laughter. Mina scuffed away in the glass. Inchy had to stop himself from rushing in there, making them stop. Didn't they know what was out here in the night? Maybe they did. Maybe it was one of them.

"You watch out!" he called. "You don't know who you're talking to!"

"Woo-hoo!" called the voices. "Hoo-hoo!"

"Hey!" Old Mule, chastising them. "You watch your mouth around them kids."

"Mule," someone laughed. And then Inchy heard more glass breaking. Someone choked. The laughter got louder. Inchy moved back because he could see them surging forward out of the shadows. Old Mule made a wet broken noise and fell over into the light, his head slamming down on the broken glass.

"Run!" Inchy whispered. "Get out, Mina!"

She was already running, working her way onto the first of the rebar steps. Inchy found himself frozen in place, his fingers working furiously at the pearls in his pocket, squeezing them and clicking them together, *please let Mina get away, please let Mina be okay . . .*

Swirling mist. Pearlywhite cut the air, bridging the gap. The laughing ones hadn't even cleared the shadows before the pearly gray dragon was among them. Inchy knew they would see nothing but a blur, if that. But for Inchy it was clear enough. Pearly seized the darkness and tightened it, made a web and caught the lurkers in it, snarling it over their heads and throwing them backward. He heard them shriek. They didn't have a clue what was happening. He saw the smoky whiteness of his Invisible turn sharp and savage and tear into them like a mass of gnashing knives. Now they were screaming. He didn't care what Pearlywhite did to them . . . they deserved it, for scaring Mina.

"Inchy!" She called him from street level. He spun away, finding the rebar rungs, mounting quickly to the sidewalk. He turned to peer back down into the darkness. Pearlywhite was already drifting back toward him, wrapping around his neck, slithering down his arm. Not a sound came from the Pit.

"Was . . . were they the ones?" Mina said.

Pearly looked at her. Tendrils of fog curled around the smoke-dragon's broad lips like the catfish whiskers of a Chinese dragon, the fangs no longer visible. A gentle smile hid the dragon's fangs. Its opalescent eyes were heavy-lidded, reassuring.

"No," Pearlywhite whispered. "Not them. They're no danger to any of us. Not now."

"Where . . . but where'd Garvey go?" Inchy said. "He was supposed to come down here."

Pearlywhite reared back, nostrils flaring as it sniffed the air. "I don't smell either of them," said Pearlywhite. "Slink or his boy. Garvey's not here."

"Is that bad?" Mina asked.

Pearly made an urgent sound. Mina understood, and pulled the thick spectacles from somewhere in her pockets. At Pearly's cry, the Invisible unwound from her homebase, glittering up from the warped depths of the lenses. She polished the glasses on her cuff as Glimmish danced in the air. Pearly and Glimmish spoke for a moment, without either human understanding their meaning, and then both grew very still. Glimmish twisted around, said something abrupt to Mina, then swirled like a small storm of sparks and shot off into the night.

"He's going to look," she told Inchy. "He can see farther than Pearlywhite."

"Okay. Good. Should we . . . should we find the others?"

"They come," said Pearly. And at that moment Inchy heard footsteps rushing up the sidewalk, scuffing and slapping steps of bare feet and rotten sneakers bound with duct tape. And here came the pale, excited faces of the others—Vick and Cassandra and the twins. Vick stopped at the edge of the pit, out of breath, and barked out a hoarse cry into the dark maw below: "Garvey! Inch!"

"Psst!" Inchy waved them toward the shadows, where he and Mina hid. Rosalie notice them first, tugged Junebug's arm, and then the two of them kicked the back of Vick's heels until he turned. He came stomping toward them, his face so pink from running it looked as if it would burst. Cassandra stood looking back, until the twins grabbed her sleeves and pulled her along.

"We saw . . . oh, man," Vick said suddenly. "Inchy? It's you?"

"Of course," Inchy said. "Who'd you think?"

"We thought . . . we . . ." Vick didn't seem to know how to say it. Rosalie finished for him: "We thought he got you."

"Who?"

"The big man," said Junebug. "The one who's been doing it."

"—we think—" said Rosalie.

"We figured it out because we saw the same guy this morning, hanging around Naiad Lane, and just little a while ago we saw him again with a kid . . . a little kid about as tall as you—"

"—same color hair—" said Rosalie.

"We thought it was you," said Cassandra, and swallowed a lump in her throat. Tears sat on the edge of her eyelids.

"Big man," Inchy repeated. "Was . . . was he in a blue suit?"

Remembering the man at the alley this morning, the man he had seen this evening, walking away from the library. Two places of death, and the man in both of them.

"Yes!" said Rosalie and Junebug, their words blurring together. "Blue!"

"You saw him with another kid?"

"Well, it wasn't you, obviously," Vick said. "But we had to be sure."

"But it was a boy," Cassandra said. "He was walking him down the subway steps—forcing him along. Oh . . . we should have followed. We should have followed but we were scared!"

"*You* were scared," Vick said. "I just didn't want to be stupid."

"Oh, Vick, we should have gone down there! He wouldn't have done anything with all of us watching! And our Invisibles to help us!"

"Vick's right," Inchy said. "The Invisibles aren't enough."

He held out Leafjacket and let them all bear witness to the tattered bloodstained book. There were no questions . . . just shocked silence. "Garvey and I found him in the library. And I saw that man in blue there, too. I think you're right about him."

"Here's what we have to do," Mina said. "First we find Garvey, then together we go after the man."

Her eyes were so bright and clear now. Inchy found himself looking to her for the plan, for real answers. She was so much smarter than he ever felt, but usually she just hid that, pretended she wasn't . . . but she was using it now. He felt proud of her.

"Us?" said Cassandra with audible dread.

"Niall and Clyde are dead," she said. "That's too many already. If this man's hunting us, then only we can stop him."

"Alone?"

"We're not alone. We've got Invisibles. And that makes it our job, because somehow he can kill *them*. How do you make a cop believe that, huh? No, it's up to us."

"What do you think, Inch?" said Vick, staring hard at Inchy. But Inchy looked over at Mina. "I think she's right," he said. "We should listen to her."

Mina looked from face to face, then took out her glasses and gazed into the murky lenses.

"Glimmish?" she called.

The lenses exploded in her hands. Shining dust shattered from the plastic frames. Mina shrieked and dropped them. She stumbled back against the wall and stared at the broken spectacles and wailed: "What's happening?"

At that moment, the Invisibles came unbidden. Pearlywhite sharpened and solidified, bright in the night air. The twins' twinned Invisible climbed from their lockets and clasped itself into a single form. Catseye rose spinning and singing from Vick's pocket, its lighthouse gaze swerving over all of them, casting its rays over the streets and the grimy walls. Cassandra's little deity came out and stood on her shoulder and whispered in her ear and Cassandra's eyes grew even wider and more terrified.

"Children," said Pearlywhite. "There is danger greater than you know. It hunts us all tonight."

"Oh, God," said Cassandra. "Where's Garvey?"

"Glimmish was looking for him," Mina said.

The pain in her face was worse than anything she'd shown on hearing of Niall's death. Inchy could only imagine what it would mean to lose an Invisible after losing everything else in this world. But surely, while Mina still lived, there was some chance of restoring her friend.

Unless, as Pearly said, the lives of the children were of no consequence.

He had assumed the death of the kids had caused the death of the Invisibles. But if it was the other way around? What if the kids were only in danger because something hunted the Invisibles?

The world spun; the fever suddenly gripped him, and he found his teeth chattering so hard that his jaws clenched tight. No one else seemed cold . . . why wasn't anyone else shivering tonight? Chills swept him, and he couldn't separate them from fear. Something was paralyzing him. He fought to shake it off, to take action, but he was having trouble even breathing.

"Inchy, man, come on!" Vick was saying, and Mina was pulling at his hand but he couldn't respond . . . he couldn't come with her. They were all yelling at him to run and he wasn't sure why. He tried to swim up out of the fever dream, but by the time he broke free . . .

They were gone.

They were gone, and Officer Cat was standing over him, holding his arm with one hand, feeling his forehead with the other. "Inchy? Don't run from me, boy. You come with me now and no fooling. This is serious. You come with me for a little while, and if you still don't want my help getting you off the street, well, that's your decision. You need to get in the car right now. I'm taking you to the hospital."

He looked once more to see if there was any trace of the others, to see if they were perhaps peering out at him from the shadows, or up from the Pit, but no—they were gone. Something was very wrong with him, but that was just the tip of it all. The wrongness went deeper than that. It went all the way down.

"Come on." She guided him toward the car. He thought she was going to put him in back, in the cage with no door handles, but she helped him gently onto the front seat, next to her. He sat there listening to her radio going, looking at the shotgun set up in its mount by the steering wheel. And when the lights started streaming across the windows he couldn't tell if they were moving or if it was the fever again.

"You have a seriously high fever, Inchy. There's a virus going around. Leave it untreated a couple days and it could kill you. God only knows what inoculations you ever got. Your mother wouldn't want this for you, Inchy. She'd want someone looking after you, don't you think? Especially now. When none of you should be out there, not with all this evil going on."

"Perhaps that would be best," Pearlywhite murmured, in Inchy's ear. "A doctor."

"No, Pearly—I can't," Inchy said. "I have to help find the man. We have to stop him. Save you and the others. If I go with her, to . . . wherever . . . they might take your homebase away."

There, he'd said it—what he'd never said aloud before. The biggest reason he didn't want to leave the streets: he could lose the pearls and that'd mean losing Pearly.

"What'd you say, hon?" Officer Cat asked.

Inchy didn't reply. She shook her head, thinking he was delirious.

Then she made another noise, deep in her chest, and it filled him with foreboding. He felt Pearlywhite suddenly rearing back, winding up into thick tense coils of smoke that brushed the back of his neck and caused his jaw to clench. The cruiser slowed. Looking up, Inchy saw the lights above the 97th Street subway station, the plaza around the entrance. He peered up over the edge of the window, saw a cluster of cop cars thrashing their lights against the night, beyond a wall of bodies—the crowd that always clotted around the lights as if summoned to an impromptu carnival. Officer Cat rolled down the window to talk to a cop who stood by a taut stretch of yellow police tape. Inchy unbuckled his seat belt and got his knees up on the seat to crane past Officer Cat. The other cop pointed, and the gesture seemed to cause the crowd to part. Suddenly Inchy could see what everyone was looking at.

Three other cops and a woman in an ambulance attendant's uniform were standing over a limp, awkwardly skewed shape that was somehow ground into the pavement. Inchy recognized the suit jacket instantly, although it was hard to make sense of the shape that filled it. The only thing that made any sense was the hand, with upturned fingers, and the golden gleam of a ring with no jewel at its center, which therefore failed to catch the light. Garvey's ring, Garvey's suit . . . Garvey.

Officer Cat got out of the car. "Stay there, Inchy." She said that, but then she made no effort to stop him when he slid after her and slipped out through her door before it slammed. He felt like an Invisible himself at that moment, a wisp of smoke, merged with Pearlywhite. He walked beside her through the crowd, no more noticeable than her shadow.

"Oh my God," she was saying. "Not . . . not another?"

Inchy tried not to look at what was left of Garvey, but there was movement on his friend's body. Life . . . some stirring of life. His heart leapt. Garvey!

A crumpled face of blood-soaked fabric looked at him with hollow mouth, hollow pleading eyes. Slink raised itself slowly from the bloodied jacket, inching down to the ground. For a moment he thought it was coming to him and he knelt to snag it, hoping the detectives wouldn't notice—because there was no way they would let him have it. But instead, Slink seemed to gather itself for a last burst of movement. It pulled itself taut and poked a wadded limb toward the mouth of the subway station, back in the shadows where the lights had been shattered out. It was pointing at . . . at what?

Far back in the shadows, the pouchy face drifted away. The ice-chip eyes glinted and started to fade, but not before he saw the hunger in them.

"There he is!" Inchy burst out, grabbing Officer Cat's wrist.

"Inchy? What are you doing here? Get back to the car! Get back now, I'm telling you!"

"Don't you see him? He's getting away! Oh, he's getting away! That's the man! He's been in all the other places. We seen him all over!"

"Inchy, you're sick, you've got to get back . . . and you shouldn't be seeing this."

"Just look, Cat!"

She glanced back at the subway station, but it was too late . . . the man had been only the dimmest trace if you knew where to look for him, if you'd already seen him before. She thought he was raving from fever. The fever raged in him, true, but her blindness and his frustration were making it worse. His face felt unnaturally smooth and dry, hard and hot. Like burning bones. As if the skull had caught on fire inside him and burned its way out through his skin.

"Listen to her, Inchy," Pearlywhite said quietly. He didn't know what to make of that. Pearly sounded genuinely scared. It was the raw form of what he'd heard in Pearly's voice that morning, when going after Clyde's homebase. What he'd taken for a threatening tone was Pearly being afraid, facing something that could actually end Pearly-white's existence. He hadn't known there was such a thing, but Pearly had known. The Invisibles weren't what he'd thought them to be. So much had changed in one day.

She looked back at him, and he knew she'd seen nothing.

"There's no entrance there, Inchy," she explained patiently. "This whole side's been closed off for repairs. Gate's closed. Now—"

Her pistol was staring him in the face. Inchy saw his hand going toward it, a slip of pale smoke, invisible.

"—I want you to get back in the car—"

"... *No* ..." Pearly whispered.

"—and stay there while I get some things straightened—"

"... *Not alone* ..."

And he flicked up the snap with his thumb, dug in and grabbed the butt, had it out of the holster, still invisible, moving like a breath of hot wind, unstoppable. Or so he felt himself to be, though Officer Cat was screaming at him and grabbing at his arm, already aware that she had lost him. He could feel Pearlywhite frowning down on him. In a way that was the hardest part: doing something against Pearly's wishes. But he was committed now. He was running, stooping to snag Slink as he went, stuffing the bloodied rag down into his pocket. The other cops lunged at him but Inchy was white mist, unstoppable. He flew down the subway entrance, past the point where he'd seen the fat man standing, feeling both strangely energized and as if he might spin into oblivion at any moment.

Behind him, Officer Cat shouted, "Hold your fire, damn it, hold your fire!"

Then Inchy was leaping five stairs at a time down the trashy hole of the subway entrance. The floor-to-ceiling gate was closed and pad-locked, just as she'd said—but it was bent back at one corner. There was an opening just big enough for a kid to squeeze through. As Inchy wriggled through, the bars scraped over the inflamed wound in his arm, making him wince. He realized it was somehow connected with his sickness. Something had gotten into him through that little nail hole; it was eating away at him. Another invisible thing.

Pearly tightened around his neck. "Inchy, you must not do this. Go back! This place you are taking us . . . I cannot promise our return."

Inchy made no reply.

The shouting of cops fell farther and farther behind. It would take them a while to find a key to that padlock. Of course, they could go across the street and down the block to the other station entrance, and considering he had a gun they were not going to just let him go. But right now he had freedom, and he would use it. Feet banging out echoes, he ran through the moldy concrete darkness to the subway platform—and there he saw the man. The killer in blue, herding a boy ahead of him, down on the track. The boy might have looked a little bit like him, he supposed. He was about the same age with curly brown hair, but he wore dark blue jeans that looked like they hadn't been worn or washed many times; he also wore expensive high-top sneakers and a blue silk football jacket that was too big for him. Something bulky shifted in the jacket but Inchy couldn't tell what it was. The pouchy-faced man glanced back at the sound of Inchy's steps, and shot him a look that was first furious and then sneering, then he chivvied the boy up the ladder onto the other platform.

Lungs heaving broken glass, Inchy climbed down, jumped over the tracks and the lethal third rail, running to the ladder. Pausing there, Inchy shouted: "Boy—kid! Jump off the platform! I'll shoot him if he follows you! I got a gun! Mister—I'm . . . I'm gonna shoot!"

Pearly appeared, then, between him and the ladder—glimmering ghostly in the murk. "Inchy, let them go. You can give descriptions to the police now. You are a child and weak with fever, and *that one* is too strong. I can't let you go after them."

Inchy hesitated. There was something in Pearlywhite's eyes—was it tears? No, but it was an endless sorrow. As if Pearly had read his heart, already knew his answer. Maybe Pearly was right.

But then Inchy saw Garvey lying crushed into the asphalt, smeared there with incredible force as if dropped from a height and then hammered down. He saw Niall's hand tumbling out above the blood-soaked edges of the books he treasured. He saw Clyde's poor grubby bare defenseless foot. And he thought of Mina. Vick and Cassandra and the twins, sure, and the other kids in the city, so many of them. But especially Mina.

"No," he said. "It has to stop. It's up to us . . . you, too, Inchy. You, too."

He took the pearls from his pocket and held them out in the palm of his hand. Pearlywhite whirled in the air and drained away into the pearls. Inchy heard him whisper, as he went: "We might lose each other . . . we might lose . . ."

When Inchy got to the top of the ladder, a train was raging out of the dusty tunnel. The wind of it flung waxed-paper trash as it came, and then it squealed to a stop. A few people idled on the active side of the station, several moved toward the train, but there were still no cops.

Far down the dimly lit platform, the man pushed the boy ahead of him, onto the train.

Inchy hesitated once more. He was suddenly sickeningly tired and thirsty, his mouth paper dry. But the train made a chirping sound that meant the doors were about to close.

Inchy hid the cold metal bulk of the gun in his coat and dodged into the last car just as the doors closed. There was a chunky black lady, a transit cop, sitting across from him. He waited for her to grab him, but she only glanced at him, frowning.

It looked to Inchy like she was going home after a long day on duty. She had her belt radio turned off and zero interest in turning it on. She hadn't heard about the kid who'd swiped a cop's gun and run away. Still, he imagined they'd be searching the stations up ahead, if they had time to organize. He hoped the man wasn't going too far. He had few enough advantages in this chase.

He started to go through the door to the next car, to find the man and the boy up front, but a hard grip on his arm stopped him. "Boy, you stay right in here. We don't want you kids running around between cars now. Jus' sit your ass down and wait for your stop." He nodded. But instead of letting him go, she cocked her head and peered at him. "You okay, boy? You look sick."

"I'm okay. Goin' home."

"That right? Well tell your mama to give you a bath."

A stab of painful sadness went through him at that. "Yes, ma'am. I will." She let go and he went to sit down. To wait.

The train rattled and grumbled through an endless chain of stops. At each, a few people got on or off—but never the big man with his captive boy.

That didn't happen until the end of the line.

He let them get ahead of him, because he felt so vulnerable here—so exposed. No one else had gotten off, and the station was bright enough that he couldn't follow them too soon. Poplar trees poked their swaying feathery heads up beyond the fence at the end of the raised, open-air platform. From up here Inchy could see a parking lot, and across from that houses. Endless miles of houses on long regular streets spreading off into darkness toward a line of hills. Low roofs with warm lights glowing out from under them. None of the hulking buildings he was used to. None of the city noises. It was quiet. He stood feeling the cool wind on his cheek, wishing it would take the edge off his fever. Instead, it only made him shiver, and instantly he felt sicker.

Down below, coming out from under the edge of the platform, he saw the man urging the boy ahead of him toward the parking lot. It suddenly occurred to him that they were probably going to get into a car and drive away, and then he'd have lost them for good. In a panic, he hurried down the escalator, leaping steps so fast he felt he was flying. The station was deserted down here, too. Seeing no station agent, he leapt the turnstile and rushed out to the street.

The man and his boy were just passing under the last row of streetlights at the edge of the lot, moving on foot toward the houses. They weren't driving after all. Inchy breathed a sigh of relief, and followed.

It was a pretty house in a street of pretty houses; a two-story white house trimmed with open green shutters. Curtains, soft-looking as cobwebs in the tall windows. Someone hadn't mowed the thatchy lawn in a while, and one of the tires of the station wagon that sat in the driveway was flat. There was a light shining out from around back—the kitchen, Inchy thought, as he walked past the glossy bulk of the station wagon.

His head throbbed, and he felt sort of dreamlike; the gun was heavy against his rib cage. He wanted to see if the car was unlocked, and if it was he wanted to lie down on those wide soft seats. But he kept going, through the open wooden gate into the backyard. Crickets sawed away. A nightbird chattered and fell silent.

There was a fountain in the back, built into a terraced garden; the upper spillway was dry, the pool brackish. Inchy heard an electrical humming from the little black-plastic pump, half hidden in the grass. A pipe in the base of the fountain made a sucking noise as it sipped at the shallow, stagnant puddle where the light from a kitchen window surged and rippled.

Inchy turned his attention to the house. The back door stood ajar, atop a flight of red-painted concrete steps. Another flight of flagstone steps led down to where a second light issued from a white wooden door. Through a pane in the basement door he could see, distorted by the beveled glass, the boy from the subway, crossing a dull gold carpet. He couldn't see anyone else.

"Maybe the man's upstairs," he whispered. "Why doesn't the boy run? Pearly?"

He waited but Pearly neither emerged nor answered.

He started down the steps to the basement—and then dizziness whirled up in him and he had to stop to steady himself on the stairwell wall. Pearly wouldn't abandon him now—wouldn't leave him alone, to this. Maybe Pearly was too scared to come out. He thought of the times Pearlywhite had helped him, had given him the courage he needed to go on.

He wished he could do the same for Pearly now. But the only one he could do it for was himself.

He took a deep breath and reached for the doorknob. It turned in his fingers. Unlocked!

He pushed the door open quietly, searching for the boy, afraid of seeing the man. A fire burned in a black-metal fireplace, but the logs it danced upon were fake, cement. A pool table sat somewhat slanted on the gold carpet; all the balls had gathered in one corner, or fallen into pockets. At the far end of the room was a little cocktail bar; bottles tried to gleam in a glass case under it, but a thin layer of dust seemed to choke them. To the left of the bar, stairs led up to the kitchen.

He took a step into the room, and suddenly heard a gasp.

Inchy stiffened as the boy rose up from behind the padded bar, mouth and eyes wide. His head jerked sideways, toward the stairs, obviously listening and looking for the man. Inchy listened too, but he heard nothing.

"Kid!" Inchy hissed. "Come on! He left the door unlocked!"

The boy had tired brown eyes; he looked as skinny as Inchy, despite having grown up out here where people didn't have just one refrigerator, they had two. Inchy waited for the kid to respond, waited with his head throbbing, wanting to get out of here and take the kid to the cops and lie down somewhere safe. But the boy just looked at him. Too scared to move, maybe.

Inchy decided to help him. He came all the way into the room and edged past the fireplace, past the pool table, circling the bar.

His foot bumped something and he looked down, saw a small wooden baseball bat, the kind you give to preschoolers. He stepped over it and crossed to the boy.

"He left that back door open! Let's go!"

"No," the boy said. "I can't."

"I know all about him," Inchy said. "We can get out of here. I can hide you somewhere he'll never find you, and we'll tell the cops and . . ."

"If I try to leave," the boy said raspily, sounding like he had a bad cold, "he'll come out and get me."

Inchy could see that the boy's nose was running, his eyes red; he'd been crying.

"It's ok, uh—uh—what's your name?" Inchy said.

"Errol."

"It's okay, Errol. I know about him. I know what he's been doing."

"No . . . no you don't. You only think you know, but you were stupid to follow us. Now he'll get you. I saw you in the city. By the alley this morning, and at the library, and then at the train station. I thought maybe you would get away, but then you had to go and follow me, so I know he was still using me. And it worked. Other kids, he made me talk to them till they followed. Telling them I had food and stuff. But you . . . he must have known you wouldn't fall for that. You, he had to lead on a chase. Used me again."

"So stop letting him. Get out of his house."

"It's not his house. It's mine. And . . . and hers."

Errol turned and for some reason looked at the bar refrigerator. It was long and white, like a big white coffin, and suddenly Inchy felt

Pearlywhite's claws sharpening on his shoulders, underneath his clothes, tightening around his rib cage, right where the gun rode. He thought about reaching for the gun, just as the boy was reaching for the chrome handle of the fridge.

Errol pulled on the handle, hard, and cold mist streamed out of the open case; cold white light streamed out of it. It wasn't a refrigerator, it was a freezer. Full of frozen meat pies and plastic-wrapped steaks and chicken parts all crammed into every last bit of space that wasn't taken up by the two hard-frozen bodies of grown-ups. The stiff wrinkles in their clothes looked like snowy valleys; ice bearded their faces, pressed so close together; bearded the woman's face as well as the man's. One of her eyes was red-crusted shut, her blue lips parted; the frost on her lashes looked like some kind of exotic white makeup. She'd been a smallish, foxy-faced woman, with curly brown hair, closely resembling the boy. Her face was pressed into the man's face. The freezer had turned his pouchy cheeks and jowls into hard, bluish ice. But Inchy knew him at once.

"It's—it's—you killed him!" Inchy looked at Errol in awe, wondering how it was possible—how anything could have frozen so quickly, even in a freezer this size.

"Because he hurt her. Like that, you see?" Errol's voice went flat as his eyes roved the frozen wasteland of her features. "He—he gave me the bat when I was little, and then he used it to hurt me when, when he said I was bad, which was all the time. And then he used it on her." Errol's eyes welled up with tears. "I heard them, I heard it happen, but I . . . I didn't see anything until I came in and saw him next to her, on his knees, drinking from one of his bottles and laughing and sort of crying too. The . . . the bat was there, on the floor, and he didn't hear me pick it up. He didn't hear a thing until I hit him in the head. He didn't see me, but he knew it was me. He had to know. That's why he stayed. He tried to get up but he slipped and I hit him again and he fell and I hit him again and . . . it didn't matter. He still wouldn't go away."

"Inchy . . ." Pearly's voice. Pearly was constricting around his chest, squeezing him so hard he could hear his heart beating louder than Errol's voice. "Inchy get out of here *now*."

Errol's eyes widened. "What . . . who said that?"

"Move away from him, Errol," came a deep, mocking voice from behind Inchy.

Inchy spun, heart leaping, and saw the man standing there holding the little baseball bat. The man who . . . what was he, the brother of the man in the freezer? A twin?

Inchy pulled out the gun, catching it on his coat-zipper—tore it loose as the man lunged at him, shoving Errol aside. Raised the gun and squeezed the trigger.

Pulling the trigger was harder than he'd thought. He had to use both hands as the man towered over him, raising the little baseball bat to bring it down on Inchy's skull.

The gun went off, dead center into the man's chest.

The man stopped—

—As the bullet splashed into his chest.

Inchy fired again—

—The second bullet making the man's substance splash and swirl so that for a moment Inchy could see right through the hole where the bullet had gone, could see the light from the kitchen and the gas flames flickering on the wall. Then the hole closed, like heavy fog, and re-formed as before.

Inchy staggered back. "You're . . ."

"Invisible," whispered Pearlywhite, slithering up along his back, clawing up to the top of Inchy's skull. And the man caught sight of Pearlywhite, his head literally splitting in a grin obscenely wide. He paused, chuckling, and raised one finger, beckoning. Not only to Inchy, but to Pearly. His pouchy features starting to squirm and tremble and flow into distinct, writhing pockets. The icy eyes began to slip below a surface of bubbling, molten flesh, but the man didn't need eyes to see. He saw with his whole horrible essence, beyond physical form.

Hopelessly, Inchy threw the gun at the man, but of course it passed harmlessly through him.

At that same instant, with a snarl that traveled down Inchy's spine, Pearlywhite tore itself free, leaving stinging gouges in his scalp, and launched itself at the . . . the Invisible who was starting to lose the form of a man. The blue suit of the other Invisible flickered and reformed into some kind of horn, an armored skin. Pearlywhite was a blur of teeth and claws, as Inchy had seen him earlier at the Pit, but this time Pearly could find no purchase on the scaly coat. The smoke-dragon grew dense and knifelike, striking and plunging repeatedly, but the "man" was nothing like a man now—even his laugh became less and less human as it cackled on and on and on.

Inchy saw Errol sunk to the floor, watching the struggle in terror, his hands clamped over his ears. Pearly was weakening, he saw that now; the poor thing had used up nearly all its strength. As if, somehow, the man-thing was drawing Pearly's power out of it. Every time Pearlywhite flashed into a new form, the enemy Invisible seemed to thrust out some part of itself—a face tendril, an amorphous finger—and wrap it deep in Pearly's misty core and rip out a bit of the stringy stuff that suddenly didn't look so insubstantial. And every time it ripped a bit of Pearly loose, it thrust the filthy finger deep into the writhing pouchy face and sucked at it with a juicy sound that echoed the dry slurp of the evaporated fountain.

Inchy crawled back toward the fire because he had to get away, and there was nothing he could do for Pearlywhite—he knew that with complete certainty. Pearlywhite was giving his essence to save Inchy. The smokedragon whirled for a moment and cast a desperate look back at Inchy, a pleading look, as if warning him to flee while he had a chance. Alone, they had no hope of beating the thing. It fed on Invisibles, sucked them dry, turned itself into this fat, powerful monstrosity. Look how many it already had consumed.

Thinking of the others it had taken, Inchy felt a stirring in his pockets.

"Let . . . us . . ."

The man-thing heard the whisper, just as Inchy did. It slipped its triumphant stranglehold on Pearlywhite and started toward Inchy. But Pearly hissed and slithered, tightening like a bit of moonwhite noose, binding with translucent sinews, throwing the monster back toward the bar where every bottle shattered as they hit it. And Inchy dug his hands deep into his pockets and removed the coiled ball of string, the bloodied paperback, the kerchief freshly steeped in gore.

The man struggled up, tearing Pearly free, shredding Pearlywhite to its last bit of matter—but thankfully not consuming the stuff. Some of it floated free on the air. The monster's arms widened to surround Inchy, but he had already hurled the homebases of his murdered friends. He could see them uncoiling, awakening in the flickering air, rising above the man whose face was no longer a face or anything much at all except a void, a hunger, an absolute emptiness. The man's arms clamped reflexively around Inchy, and his breath was just . . . gone. It was not like the physical touch of another human being—it was like gravity pulling when he jumped from a fast swing, or a heavy wind all compressed into a man-shape. Inchy's life was almost squeezed out in that instant.

Then the man released him. Inchy collapsed on his back, paralyzed and stricken, gasping up at the scene above him. The man stood there, thrashing at the forms of the other Invisibles, snatching at the weakened bits of them. Koil and Slink and Leafjacket and a storm of white froth that seemed to be all that remained of Pearlywhite. They were so weak, so insubstantial, that the man couldn't get a purchase on them. He swatted and they swarmed; he tried to snag them but came up empty and a black rage poured from the vacuum of his mouth.

Inchy saw Errol, then. Errol standing behind the man, with the bat raised as if to try once more to brain the thing. Utterly futile. Errol pulled back and the man-thing, Errol's enraged and insane Invisible, turned and took a swipe at the boy but the other Invisibles closed in around the thing's mouth, choking it with themselves.

Inchy felt pearls in his fingers, sensed Pearlywhite whispering something to him, and he managed to choke out to Errol, "Burn it!"

The man-thing struck at Errol, struck him hard in the head, clapped his two massive hands together so hard on either side of the boy's head that his life was extinguished. All the rage he hadn't been able to bring to bear on the elusive Invisibles, spent in a final blow that made of Errol's skull a thing misshapen.

The bat flew. Went spinning. Struck cement with a hard clink, and a moment later Inchy smelled burning wood.

The man let out a roar and tried to rush to the fire. His foot struck Inchy's leg, but the blow felt soft and unreal. The man toppled flat across him, but the weight was almost nothing. The other Invisibles followed him to the ground, harrying and tearing at him, diving into his eyesockets, tearing at the folded flesh. He shredded them with his bare hands, clawing them as a man would wave away cigarette smoke, but they just reformed. He opened his gulf of a mouth to howl and they stuffed themselves inside and allowed nothing out. The Invisibles caught the edges of the man's face and pulled him inward, drawing his extremities down into the hungry maw. The thing was consuming itself, and all of them as well. Inchy prayed that as a result of what the Invisibles had done, they would find another way out, once they had destroyed this one. They deserved something more than the void into which they threw themselves.

The man's fleshy fingers, arms, and thrashing blue limbs all stretched and drew into the center of the blackness, caught by the relentless pull of something graver than gravity, which he had experienced for less than an instant and would never forget. There was no escaping it now, not even for the man itself. The collapse when it came, came quickly. A sudden indrawing, a quickening, and then an explosion that made Inchy wonder how he could ever have called his friends and guardians "Invis-ibles." *This* was invisibility. It was an absence of sight—of everything.

They were gone. All of them.

He raised his head weakly. "Pearly?"

White mist still hung in the air, but he couldn't tell if it was Pearlywhite or smoke from the burning bat. He looked at Errol. He was dead, very for-sure dead. Inchy turned away—and almost fell over. The fevered weakness was pulling him down like a drain.

Inchy knew, now, that he needed help—help that Pearly couldn't give him. He needed real help, and he needed to help himself.

The last thing he did, summoning all his strength, was to drag himself behind the bar, where a telephone sat. He picked it up. And although he couldn't remember it later, he must have called a number he had never called before.

Officer Cat was sitting beside him, in a chair, and he was in a bed. A bed with crisp white linen. That was the first thing he noticed: He was lying down in a white bed in a white room, and Officer Cat was sitting beside him. The second thing he noticed was that she wasn't wearing a uniform. She was wearing some white slacks and a soft yellow blouse. He felt weak, but the throbbing was gone. There was a tube going into his arm, he saw then, from a bottle hanging from a metal stand on the side opposite Officer Cat.

She smiled at him. "They said you'd probably feel better this morning. Looks like it's true. They've had you on IV antibiotics for two days. You had a bad infection, on top of everything else."

"Two days?"

"Seemed like longer, to me," Mina said.

She came from a doorway behind him, a half-eaten candy bar in her hand. She was cleaned up, and she had a new blue shift on, and— no glasses.

He looked at her and she shook her head. Glimmish was gone. Pearly!

He sat up, fumbling in the bedclothes. "You looking for those pearls?" Officer Cat asked. "They're in that drawer by the bed."

There was a little white table next to the bed with a vase of daffodils on it. He opened it and found the pearls, clutched them to him.

"The others?" he asked Mina.

She shrugged. He turned to Officer Cat. "There was a book, and . . . and Garvey's handkerchief, and a ball of string. Where they found me . . . ?"

"I haven't been there, Inchy. But I imagine it's all in Evidence now. What do you need to trouble yourself with that stuff for? I know the history. It all belonged to your friends. But those are morbid memories, Inchy. Blood-stained and all . . . even if you could have them back, why would you want them? Some things you're better off putting away. Believe me."

Beyond her, Mina was nodding slowly, and he knew it was the truth.

"Of course, no one's saying you should throw away those pearls, Inchy. I know what they mean to you."

A beeper sounded from Officer Cat's purse. She opened the purse, looked at the beeper, and said, "Be right back, have to call in." She got up, patted his arm, and went out into the hall.

Mina seemed to know he was thirsty. She poured him a glass of water from a plastic pitcher at the bedside. He drank deeply as she sat on the edge of his bed; she waited. Then he told her what had happened.

"So the man won't be back?" she asked.

"I don't think so. But neither will Errol." He pressed the pearls to his cheek and whispered, "Pearly? Pearlywhite?"

There was no answer. He had known somehow that there wouldn't be. He could feel some sort of difference in the pearls. They didn't seem lighter: they just seemed *less*.

"Glimmish is gone, too," Mina said, looking at her feet. New tennis shoes on them. "I don't know if it's because my brother's glasses broke, or if it's because I . . . I told Cat yes."

"Yes what?"

"She filled out some forms and talked to some office people— asked if we could live with her. They said yes and I said yes. Now it's your turn."

"Me?" His head spun. "I don't know. Pearly . . ."

But Pearly wasn't here to advise him anymore. He had to guide himself now. He remembered how it had felt to know he could do that, could make the hard decisions without looking to someone or something else. He thought, This is the way it's supposed to be—or anyway, the way it's going to be from now on. Pearlywhite had taken him most of the way, past his mother's death, down the hard streets. But the last few steps, well, he'd had to go those alone. And they had brought him to a place where he might not have to be alone any longer.

He closed his hand around the string of pearls and lay there feeling how the warmth in them, now, was simply the warmth his own flesh gave them. Before he realized what was happening, Mina was holding him, and holding his hand around the pearls. He was crying and it was okay, she understood what he had lost. What they had lost.

And when he told her one last thing he had to do, she understood that too.

Three days later, he walked away from Mina and Officer Cat, leaving them standing on the gravel road while he stepped through the wet grass toward a line of graves. He was wearing new clothes, new shoes, and he was surprised at how annoyed he felt when he saw mud splattering the nice new shine. "Damn, these are new shoes!" he thought, then he let out a surprised laugh. It was Garvey's voice, almost. Garvey living on in him.

The rain had been falling steadily all morning, and it didn't let up for a minute as he knelt by the plastic marker. Someday he would replace it with something nice—real stone, something lovely and permanent. But for now, he was already soaked through the shoulders, and he didn't want to ruin the suit Cat had bought for him. She had already told him not to worry about that, but anyway, it didn't take long. Just long enough to push the pearls, and, in a way, Pearly too, down into the soft earth over Mama's grave, and say goodbye to both of them.

Love

Suzzy Roche

THAT AFTERNOON Jean ran into Adele, who works at the Silver Tray. She's the one who snickered when Jean told her about the concert in the first place. Adele's son plays a tuba in the St. Louis orchestra and apparently she has the opinion that if it isn't classical, it isn't music. Well, maybe someone finally told Adele that Jean's daughter was on *The Tonight Show* once, because she was whistling a different tune now.

"Are there any tickets left?" asked Adele.

"You'll have to check at the high school" was all that Jean would say. After all, why should she facilitate the tickets? Sure, now she wants to go. Now that there was an article in *The Woodside*. "Get your own damn tickets," thought Jean.

At the crack of dawn Jean had picked up several copies of *The Woodside* and cut out the article from each one. There was a big picture of her daughter Mary, taken at least ten years earlier, with a ring through her nose and her eyes heavily lined. The caption read, "Mary Brennan from Sliced Ham comes to Woodside High for a solo concert." Anyone could see that she was a pretty girl under all the makeup. The article went on to describe the breakup of the group after the death of the bass player, who unfortunately fell out of a hotel window. It didn't say in the article, but Jean knew drugs were involved.

There were lots of things that hadn't been said in the paper. The breakdowns, the four months at the rehab hospital, the abortion, and the lingering heartache. Mary's and Jean's. No one wrote about the brutality at home under the heavy hand of Bub, husband and father, now in Three Forks Home, paralyzed from a stroke. Mary and Jean knew the story well. But it was over now. Jean had started life in a new town and it was no one's business.

Mary's success in Sliced Ham came and went in the space of about five years and was a bewildering surprise to Jean. One minute Mary was a teenager strumming sweet songs on a folk guitar in her room with the door locked. Then all hell broke loose. Within a month of her eighteenth birthday she started mouthing off to Bub, and the fighting escalated until she left home one Saturday with a carful of boys. Jean didn't hear from her until three years later, when she received a letter from England with a clipping from a paper about Mary's band.

Jean was relieved. Mary's disappearance had shattered her life. But when Mary started writing regularly and it became clear that the band was considered a success, Jean was reunited with the idea that God was watching over the world, and she even felt a little puffed up by her daughter's popularity.

Apparently Sliced Ham had a fringe hit with a song called "Feet and Knuckles," which hurled them into the outer edges of the mainstream. The neighbor's children seemed to know the band and when she'd run into acquaintances at Shop Rite they'd often refer to some piece of news about Mary they'd read somewhere. The band was on TV, of course, that time on the *Carson* show, they were popular on college radio stations, and there were write ups in magazines. Not the kind of magazines that anyone would actually read, but people were impressed. Though no one said a word, they all knew very well about the troubles at home, and somehow Mary's success put a different slant on things.

Jean was suspicious of the hoopla, however, and had never even listened to the music. She had the collection of CDs, but they remained unopened, tucked away in the closet alongside the newspaper clippings and the letters that Mary wrote. The pictures on the CD covers were disturbing and they had unhappy titles like *You're a Pig* and *I Can't Stop Eating*. And though Mary kept in close touch during those brief years of success she never came home.

Mother and daughter kept connected through the mail. Mary told Jean everything. The struggle with drugs and drink, the reckless romances, the sold-out shows and the sleeping pills. Jean always wrote back to Home of the Stars, a management agency in New York City, with words of encouragement, and sometimes she'd include an inspirational prayer card from Sunday's service. She never referred to the horrors at home, Bub's violent eruptions or the slow loneliness that lurked around the house. Sometimes Jean just sat on the edge of her bed and wept without making any noise.

Then, when Bub had the stroke six years ago, Jean moved to a town a hundred miles upstate to be closer to the nursing home. Her life began to blossom. She became quite active in the church, did volunteer work at the hospital and knew people in town. She could stroll down Meadow Avenue waving and smiling. And if the question "How's your daughter?" came up, Jean would say, "Fine! Just fine!"

But in truth, Jean had actually laid eyes on Mary only a few times since the day she left home. There was that afternoon in the rehab, when Mary was a blubbering mess, cursing at the aides. And before that, they had an encounter at a Holiday Inn lounge outside Albany where Mary chain-smoked and drank rum and cokes at four-thirty in the afternoon.

So when Bill DeSockie, head of the English department at the high school, called Jean and said he had heard that Mary was doing solo appearances and would she consider coming to Woodside, Jean got nervous. True, the wild and crazy days were over. Mary had finally straightened up and settled in a small town in Northern California. Sliced Ham was now passé and though some people were aware of who Mary was, not many seemed to remember or care. But Jean wasn't sure what to expect. And besides, she was enjoying a peaceful anonymity since she moved to Woodside, a life of her own. But Bill DeSockie's enthusiasm was endearing to Jean, he was a real fan and referred to Mary as an important poet. So she called Mary and, to her surprise, Mary was quick to agree to come to Woodside High for $850. She sounded very upbeat and said, "Mom, I'd love to see you and that'll pay for my ticket."

In the weeks leading up to the concert, people in town seemed to become aware of Jean in a new way. They would stop her on the sidewalk to say they were coming to the show and she found herself enjoying the attention and starting to feel like a bit of a celebrity herself.

Jean looked lovely that night in a powder blue sweater with a dolphin pin and floor-length navy skirt. All her friends were there, members of the choir, her best friend, Betty, and several neighbors from down the street that she hardly knew. Even the priest came. A table had been set up for CDs and and Jean volunteered to sell them.

To her chagrin, there was an opening act whose merchandise table had many more items. For example, T-shirts and a mailing list, as well as pens and buttons with the name of the duo. They were called the Tennessee Twinsters and there was a glossy photo of them, all smiles under one giant cowboy hat. Jean thought it was a cute picture and felt a secret embarrassment about Mary's appearance.

Mary had shown up at the house two hours before the concert in a beat-up leather jacket; she was thin as a toothbrush, with strands of gray beginning to spiral up out of her thick black hair, which hung like two curtains over her face. But she was so loving and affectionate, she brought wildflowers from a field and handed them to Jean with the dirt trailing into the kitchen. She kissed Jean four or five times on each cheek and held her tightly with genuine feeling. Jean was overcome and felt years of lost joy rising up.

At a quarter to eight Jean stood in the lobby of the theater, greeting members of the community and noticing strangers, too.

There were a few unfamiliar groups that arrived together, clad in dark, dirty denim, with different shades of dyed hair, orange and pink, streaked through greasy blond and brown matted clumps. Not the usual Woodside clientele.

It was going well. The Tennessee Twinsters gave a rousing show, which ended with a hand-clapping sing-along. The audience poured out of the tiny theater during the intermission, laughing and stepping up to buy CDs. Jean enjoyed the show too; it turned out that they were in fact twins and they had delighted the audience with funny anecdotes about their childhood in Tennessee.

When Mary's concert was about to begin, Jean slipped into the theater and stood by the door just under an exit sign that shed a soft glow upon her, as if a spotlight had been focused just for her. Mary came out onto the stage to eager applause with a smattering of whistles and screeching yelps from her diehard fans. She was dressed in what looked to Jean like an unwashed nightgown and an old pair of soldier's boots. She didn't say a word. She strapped on an electric guitar and strummed down hard. A loud ugly scraping noise filled the theater and then she stopped and said, "This song is called 'The Back of My Ass.' " Jean's heart thumped and she froze. She had no idea what the song was about, the words flowed inexplicably into each other and it sounded like slurred gibberish. Mary had a sweet, disturbing childish voice, but the guitar screeched like a garbage truck as if to underline an obscure, elusive meaning that rolled and floated over the audience like a bad smell.

The songs kept coming. There was "Tom's Dick and Harry," a horrifying rant that appeared to be about a gay man's murder. "Lay Down Upon My Smarmy Liver" was a bitter dirge obviously alluding to her alcohol and drug use. In between each song she let the awkward tension lay in quiet agony. Applause was polite except for the occasional whistle from a dying fan. Jean stood stoically, watching her daughter's slender body sway to and fro . . . to an inner rhythm, impossible to detect. Mary's eyes were scrunched shut; her face seemed about to break from sorrow. The melodies were mournful and though the words made little sense, they somehow threatened to tell the ugly story that Jean had been so careful to keep to herself all these years.

Before the last song, Mary looked up for the first time and said, "I'd like to thank my mother for sticking with me through the tough times."

Jean heard the words but made no move. She felt eyes upon her, but kept her gaze fixed on her daughter, her jaw tensed, and rage boiled up into her chest. Hatred cooled her cheeks. She longed for privacy, no spotlight, no attention. Somehow, of all the words she heard that night, these were the hardest to handle, and among the few she understood.

As the audience filed out into the foyer, Jean busied herself, rearranging the CDs on her table and eyeing the the crowd, which was gathering around the Tennessee Twinsters. They had come out to shake hands and sign autographs. Betty, with awkward exuberance, rushed over to Jean, her arms extended.

"Mary's quite a poet!" she exclaimed and then whispered, "Honey, I'll call you in the morning."

Then Father Michael approached cautiously with a Twinster CD in his hand and said, "What a lovely voice. Like a bird, Jean, like a little bird."

Jean noticed Adele at the Twinsters' table getting an autograph and the words *my son, tuba,* and *the St. Louis orchestra* rose like crescendos above the crowd. Meanwhile, a bearded fan with a small glass bone in his nose came up to Jean and grabbed her hand. "Your daughter is AWE-SOME, man," he said solemnly, and bought a CD with fifteen crumpled dollars that Jean was afraid to touch. It was the only one sold.

The high school was empty and Jean waited on the sidewalk, leaning up against a parking meter. Bill Desockie had helped her pack the CDs, and before he said good night he shook his head and commented that he didn't think the audience understood Mary.

"I guess times have changed. We made some money, though," he snickered. Jean didn't know what to say. She sneezed into a napkin, blew her nose, and watched him drive away.

Mary finally came out, lugging her guitar. She walked up to her mother. The two stood together in silence for a long minute. The moon was bright as a white tulip and cast a brilliant glow on the crab-apple trees that lined the small town street. Mary was holding a Twinsters CD. She smiled, but Jean could see that she'd been crying.

"Did you like the show, Ma?"

"Yes, Mary, I did."

They went back to the house and cut into a lemon cake that Jean had specially ordered from the Silver Tray. Pink lettering on white frosting spelled the words *Welcome Home.*

Crazy Carl's Thing

JOHNNY STRIKE

7:45 A.M. My first intake at the methadone clinic; "Raven" was a twenty-five-year-old stripper. She spilled some coffee on my desk, giggled, and made a halfhearted attempt to wipe it up with her sleeve. Her right eye was swollen and I thought she'd been slugged.

"No," she said, "I tried to hit a vein in my neck. But I was drunk."

Raven wiped her runny nose with the other sleeve. "I thought maybe I'd hit an artery because I went into a seizure. This morning my eye was all swollen and shit."

"Are you working?" I asked. She said yes, no, that some money was owed and then added huffily, "I can work whenever I want."

For something to do besides the mundane paperwork I decided to ask these incoming clients what the most exciting thing was they'd ever done.

I asked Raven and she said, "Oh I dunno."

8:30 A.M. Thirty-three-year-old homeless man who stank: something like compost and rotting rubber sandals. I directed my fan at him.

"What's the most exciting thing you've ever done?" I asked trying not to breathe through my nose.

"When I went to Tucson with my dad," he said. "I'd just turned fourteen. My life's been pretty boring."

After he left, I sprayed the chair with Medi-aire, a "biological odor eliminator."

Bryan stuck his head into my office and said he'd do Dark City Man's intake. I took a look in the waiting room: long black coat, black hat something like a bowler, shaved head, pale as chalk, definitely reminiscent of the aliens in the film.

My office was saturated with the soapy smelling Medi-aire.

Bryan sniffed. "Had a ripe one, eh?"

9:17 A.M. Fifty-year-old man called "Jacko."

Most exciting thing?

"That had to have been the time I parachuted from a plane at twenty-five hundred feet. I was a bartender then. My boss was always getting us together for some damn fool thing."

Forty-five-year-old homeless man who looked twenty years older. This premature aging was due a lot to the lifestyle: poor diet, lack of medical attention, and so forth.

Most exciting?

"Probably when I was in the navy. I was on a submarine crew in Hawaii. One time we surfaced and a whole group of dolphins appeared and started leaping over the sub. That was pretty exciting."

9:53 A.M. Thirty-six-year-old man who in spite of his Wild West mustache looked his age, maybe even younger. Nickname: "Slim."

Exciting?

"What, like fucking a supermodel or something?"

"Okay," I said. "Did you?"

"No. I went with a few dancers though. But that was a long time ago."

During the intake I could see that Slim was still thinking it over.

"What, like winning the lotto or something?"

12:15 P.M. Sixty-eight-year-old ex-con. Ex-biker. Moniker: "Hog."

Most exciting?

"Oh I guess when I went to Germany. I went to this huge castle out there in the Black Forest. I had to walk for miles to get to it; but it was worth it. There was a moat, catapults, even some wild boar."

Fifty-two-year-old man who bore an uncanny resemblance to Shakespeare.

Exciting?

"Two sexual encounters," said William.

"There was one fine lady who made love to me. She got on top and rubbed her breasts right in my face. The other, a nymphet, began the lovemaking by sucking on my toes. I'll never forget either of them."

Fifty-one-year-old computer programmer, "Nick," screwed up his face and gave the question some thought.

He laughed and said, "Oh, maybe the first time I tried heroin."

Later Nick came back to my office to say, "No, I believe it was the time I did some acrobatic flying with my brother. But that was twenty-some years ago."

1:03 P.M. Twenty-three-year-old homeless man who told me he camped by a phone booth and used that number for his own. I told him about a family in Morocco who lived in a wrecked car and used the license plate as their mailing address.

Most exciting?

"I fired off a fifty-caliber BMG machine gun out in the desert once."

1:23 P.M. Seventy-three-year-old, ex-seaman. A ghostly character right out of Conrad; his arms were smeared black with crude tattoos.

"It had to have been the time I swam in the Marianas Trench," he said. "Its the deepest area of sea in the world."

2:10 P.M. Forty-four-year-old parolee. His dark, reptilian eyes scanned the room in a series of quick moves.

"People call me Slick," he said. "Cuz I'm always hitting licks."

Most exciting?

"Some people feel it was their crimes," I said to prompt him and his eyes danced.

"Yeah," Slick agreed. "I've done lots of stuff, robberies, I shot a guy in the ass once." He snickered.

"I love guns but I can't have 'em anymore. Once I was shanghaied by this nut who was gonna kill me, his old lady, and then probably himself. He had me driving her car. He was in the back with a shotgun. In the rearview mirror I seen that he'd dropped his cigarette. I slammed the brakes and me and the bitch jumped him."

"He begged me not to kill him." Slick snorted. "Then the cunt comes back to my place for his fuckin' jacket. I had my gun and told him to get the fuck out. Then I shot him in the ass." Slick's smile contrasted weirdly with a vacant stare.

2:15 P.M. My last intake of the day was a timid man with short black hair wearing red-tinted black frame glasses. He was thirty-two and received an SSI check that was almost as much as I was making for working full-time. When I asked "Carl" the "most exciting thing question" he asked if he could close the office door that was just barely open.

After shutting the door he sat back down and in a hushed voice, said, "I can't tell you. I'd have to show you. It's something I've recently acquired."

Although we were forbidden to fraternize with clients I agreed to meet him at a café a few blocks away. When I arrived Carl quickly steered me away, anxious to show me his "most exciting thing."

"Its not far," he said for the second time, on the fourth block of the walk. Finally we stopped and he gestured to a weathered, apartment building that brought a short, melancholy shiver over me. Around the back we traveled a path through a mostly dirt yard. At the end was a concrete shed. When we got to the door Carl turned and said, "I'll have to charge you two dollars."

"What?"

I had come this far so I peeled off two George Washingtons. He opened the serious-looking padlock and then the door itself. He turned to me again.

"Please wait for just one moment. I'll be right back."

Could Carl be dangerous? There was something downright creepy going on.

When he returned I insisted that I follow him in. Carl led the way with a small flashlight even though the room could be made out from a dim light on the other side. Another even dimmer light shone from inside an old-style tent.

"Well, you've paid your money," he said. "You're entitled to your look."

He directed his flashlight's beam at the opening of the tent.

With one eye on Carl and one on the tent I approached the entrance, squatting down to completely pull back the flap. A stuffed two-headed calf greeted me. One head looked right, the other left, and the eyes were dark and sad and strange. The floor was covered with straw and there was even a bucket of water. Carl was staring at the floor. I took one last look at the freak of nature.

Outside, Carl smiled beatifically. "He's from God you know," he said softly. "And he still has the power of God even though he died."

"Sure, Carl," I said and thanked him and went on my way.

The James Dean Diaries
A WORK OF FICTION

PAMELA DES BARRES

INTRODUCTION

I'M A big yard sale person. Too often I get up at the wee crack of dawn
just to make sure I'm the first shopper poking around in other people's
tragic fifty-cent toss-aways, things that once held all kinds of signifi-
cance and meaning. I have found some pretty awesome items over the
years, but it's the hunt that thrills me. You never know what you're
going to trip over. Especially when sweet old ladies take their final
powders, leaving behind their beloved collections of dusty doo-dads.

I collect various things myself, from thirties silhouettes (extremely
delicate reverse paintings on glass—usually of romantic couples or
cavorting fairies) to serene Jesus portraits. (No crucifixes. I don't like
to see Him forever dangling in agony with that beseeching upward
gaze. And no exposed, drippy hearts wrapped in thorns, thank you.)
I have also amassed several heavily made up porcelain deco lady wall
heads and close to forty reel-to-reel tape recorders. When I was a kid,
my handsome, Clark Gable daddy bought me a reel-to-reel in the
shape of a '52 Buick, and I've been wild about them ever since. Not
too long ago, I was featured on the cable TV show *Collectibles* as a reel-
to-reel Super Collector. I guess there aren't too many of us. My
favorite has always been the red naugahyde with loads of chrome. At
least, until last Saturday.

I live in Southern California. Sherman Oaks. A very warm chunk of the San Fernando Valley. Earthquake country. I was raised just west of here in Reseda, where we had a lot of baking, hundred-degree summers. I know the Valley like the lines around my eyes. Most of my treasure hunting takes place in the upper-crust hills west of Ventura Boulevard. Sherman Oaks, Encino. Woodland Hills. Original owners of the postwar pads pass on and leave behind closets full of old memories to be hawked for pennies in the front yard. The bereaved usually can't wait to be rid of the stuff. I could tell you all kinds of tales about the extraordinary estate sales I've plundered, but this story isn't about me or my silhouette jones. It has nothing to do with me, really . . . except for the fact that I happened to be at the right place at the right time. And that's putting it real (to reel) mildly.

When I pulled up to the heavily shaded ranch house on Sutton Drive last Saturday morning, my heart started palpitating. The drapes must have been drawn for years. The grass was a foot high; the ivy was unkempt and overgrown; delinquent foliage spilled onto the side-walk. The once-swank auto in the driveway had four entirely flat tires and was over forty years old. I think it was some kind of Chrysler—I could tell by the sweeping would-be Caddy fins. (My daddy always drove Cadillacs and continuously pointed out the inferior fins of lesser vehicles.)

The sale was taking place inside the house (which is always a bonus), and as I hightailed it to the front door, an old sweetheart in a rakish beret stepped out to welcome me.

"Good morning, dear. Benny couldn't be with us today," she trilled, "but if he could have, he would have sent you an invitation, so come on in and take a piece of precious Benny home with you!"

Stepping inside, I saw that I had the place to myself. I scanned the fusty, musty living room and hoped I had brought enough cash with me. Every square inch was crammed—from floor to ceiling—with all manner of stuff. A slim trail had been created to get from room to room, and as I adjusted to the muted lighting I realized with breathless glee that the walls were completely covered with old movie stills and posters. The furniture was classic tattered movie set. Hollywood memorablia a-go-go times ten. Slam the door! Nobody else gets in! I was smack dab in one of those pinch-me-I'm-dreaming moments.

"Is everything for sale?" I squeaked at the beret lady.

"Yes, indeedy!" she replied. "Benny would have wanted it that way!"

I heard cars pulling up outside, so I gathered up as much Hollywood glory as my arms could hold and started asking prices.

"Oh, two dollars for Gary Cooper, a dollar for Robert Taylor"— my Mom's favorite—"oh, and little Jimmy Dean, he's three. A special friend of Benny's." She winked conspiratorily as the house started cramming up with gawkers.

Peering around to see if there were any more James Dean items, I snatched a bolt of old fabric decked with the images of Laurel and Hardy, a manuscript of *The Thirty-Nine Steps*, a decanter emblazoned with the Warner Brothers logo—and then the place was entirely overrun. Squeezing out the door with my loot, I overheard the aged dame telling somebody that the late Benny had been a very important movie makeup artist in his day. "The Hollywood elite just adored him," she sighed. Then I noticed the for sale sign on the old Chrysler in the driveway.

A pencil-slim, John Waters-looking fellow had opened the trunk, and inside (among many other gew-gaws) gleamed a magnificent old turquoise reel-to-reel and a whole bunch of tape boxes. I just about lost my breath.

"Are you interested in the tape recorder?" I peeped nonchalantly to the mustachioed ogler.

"What?" He squinted back at me. "I'm not even sure this old clunker is worth the time it takes to think about it." He absently kicked at one of the deflated tires as I dashed back to the old doll and offered her five dollars for the trunk's treasure trove. She winked at me again and took the money.

The reel-to-reel sat next to me on the front seat of my T-Bird like Sleeping Beauty. It was a humdinger—a Webcor, one make I *did not* have in my collection. I almost stopped at another parade of promising leftover yardifacts, but my anticipation got the best of me. I couldn't wait to plug the thing in and press play. On occasion I had found a few reels with the recorders, but never a pile like this! Mostly what I had discovered on previous tapes was big band music, Dean Martin Volaré-ing, or Frankie and Tony in their prime, swaying it up. or somebody stiff-reading thee and thou poetry like they knew what it meant. I still have my own old reels of me and giggly girlfriends plotting the demise of Paul McCartney's mid-sixties freckle-faced fiancé, Jane Asher, so I'm always hoping to come across somebody else's personal, long-lost mortifying memoirs.

Listening to the old tapes is always a titillating experience, sort of like buying a very peculiar lottery ticket. But when I got home and cleaned off the old Ekotape, wound the first reel around the spool, and pushed the play button, I could not believe what I was hearing. What? Wait just a bloody minute! Stop the presses. Order in the fucking court. Could it be? That voice! That wicked laugh! My heart was slamming out of my chest as I listened jawdropped to the rest of the reel, slowly realizing I had just struck gold in Sherman Oaks.

Oil, that is. Texas tea. Just like in *Giant*, when the black geyser hits Little Riata and covers Jett Rink from head to toe with the same glorious goop while he laughs the very same wicked laugh. "I'm a rich un," he spits spitefully at the hapless Rock while devouring Liz with his eyes. "I'm a rich boy." I would know that voice anywhere.

The same voice, tape after tape. After the initial mind-blinding shock, I decided to put the tapes in order. It took quite a while to get them in some kind of sequence, and I'm still not sure they're exactly right. From what I've gathered, James Dean began recording his life story—keeping a spoken journal, really—on February 8, 1954 (twenty-third birthday). He must have carted the heavy damn thing everywhere—once even back to his hometown of Fairmount, Indiana. Not only did he record his own thoughts and ideas, but he taped conversations with all kinds of people, mostly without them knowing anything about it: friends, lovers, family members, photographers, girlfriends, boyfriends, artists, agents, movie-makers. He vented, raged, wept, and sang. He laughed his ass off. He practiced his lines, gave interviews, banged his bongos, quoted Plato, Shakespeare, and a Hoosier called Riley, and played a lot of Bartók and Sinatra on his fancy new hi-fi—really loud. He quarreled, philosophized, ached, argued, and made love—all with his tape recorder on.

The final recording was made the night before his death on September 30, 1955. What follows are selections from the tapes— not the entire incredible story, not even a fraction of it, but enough to give you an idea of how I felt that Saturday, when a dead icon sprang vividly to life with the flick of a switch. His familiar, unforgettable, unmistakable voice reveals the complex young man behind the legend, and I have had the distinct honor of getting his words down on paper—like an old-fashioned secretary taking diction from a ghost.

.1.

(FEB. 13, 1955)

JD: Grandma, I played a character in the movie *East of Eden*, his name is Cal. And it's so funny, because Cal was your father's name, too, right? What was he like? Did he have any interest in the arts or anything?

Grandma Emma Dean: He was an auctioneer, one of the best there ever was.

Grandpa Charlie Dean: He was one of the best auctioneers I ever did hear. And I heard hundreds of 'em.

JD: Well, what's it take to be a good auctioneer?

Charlie: You gotta be a good judge of stock. You gotta be a good judge of human nature. You gotta have a talent for it.

JD: How do you do it? C'mon, Grandpa, show me how it's done!

Charlie: (laughter) Hey, I have three dollars, will you go four? Will you make it four? I got a three, now four, would ya go a five? Who'll make it five? I gotta five, lets get it up there, do I hear six? Now I gotta six . . . (lots of laughter) I'll tell you what kills auctioneers. You take a man who talks to the public every day, he'll eventually get too much confidence in himself. He fools himself by thinkin' he's gettin' by with it, and as soon as the people find out, they quit him. And that's what kills all of 'em off.

JD: That's what kills an actor, too.

.11.
(FEB. 13, 1955)

IN MY old room, exactly the way I left it. Tuck's here with me, on his back beggin' for some scratchin'. (big sigh) Just put on my old comfort clothes so Dennis can hone in on my farm-boy history with his Hasselblad. I saw my old acting teacher, Mrs. Nall, this morning, and she was tryin' to tell me I have to accept my lot because acting is what *I* chose to do in the first place. What about my private life? Hey, what about my private *parts*? It's *all* up for grabs! (laughs) I love everybody here in Fairmount, but they can't fathom what it costs, and I can't help but bitch about it sometimes. It's almost as if the decision to act was made for me, and I'm payin' the big-bucks price. It's like my soul's being raided, having to explain myself to all these fuckers with their X-ray glasses. They need to know what I had for dinner last night and what it looks like comin' out this morning. Maybe I'll learn how to play chess with the fatboys, and maybe I won't. I sure as shit can't fake it, and it's not something I can plan. Plans are for people with a whole lot of time on their hands. I told Mrs. Nall today I have to get there fast! OK, Dennis, you ready? I'm comin' down! Soooeeee!

.III.

(FEB. 14, 1955)

ALL'S QUIET around here. I been lookin' through my old Riley book—
here's a fine selection from that sly old bramble of a man:

> *Little Orphant Annie says, when the blaze is blue,*
> *An' the lamp-wick sputters, and the wind goes woo-oo!*
> *An' you hear the crickets quit, an' the moon is gray*
> *An' the lightnin'-bugs in dew is all squenched away,—*
> *You better mind yer parunts, and yer teachurs fond an' dear,*
> *An' churish them 'at loves you, an' dry the orphant's tear,*
> *An' he'p the pore and needy ones 'at clusters all about*
> *Er the Gobble-uns'll get you*
>
>   *Ef you*
>
>   *Don't*
>
>   *Watch*
>
>   *Out!*

I grew up with ol' Hoosier Riley; he's the one who made me aware of
the gobble-uns in the first place, and I'll always be grateful to him. I
made sure to say my prayers and eat my peas just to be on the safe side.
But I suppose I've strayed a bit left of the safe side lately. Can't help
it. Listen to his dedication at the beginning of the Orphant Annie
poem: "To all the little children—The happy ones; and sad ones; the
sober and the silent ones; the boisterous and glad ones; the good
ones—yes, the good ones, too; and all the lovely bad ones." All the
lovely bad ones. That always gave me some confused, nameless kind of
little-kid relief. It still does somehow. The Gobble-uns are real,
though. I've run into 'em plenty of times. (chuckles) So watch out.

.IV.

(FEB. 14, 1955)

HAPPY VALENTINE'S DAY. We took pictures all day around the farm, then stopped by Wilbur Hunt's in town. Wilbur runs a kind of general store in Fairmount. He's also the town mortician, and in the back he's got a swell selection of caskets. He grinned like crazy when he saw me. "Mind if we shoot some stuff in here?" I asked Wilbur. He's a wonderful guy. "Help yourself," he said, so we went in the back. There were all these satin-lined deathbeds, and I climbed into one of them and said to Dennis, "Start shooting." He thought I was kidding, but I always wanted to see how I'd look in a casket. And after seeing Mama in the cushy thing, I always wanted to know what it *feels* like. Besides, you should have seen the expression on Dennis's face! Wish I'd had the camera! At first he refused to take any pictures, said I only got into the casket because I was afraid of death, that my way of dealing with death was to make fun of it, laugh straight in the face of the demon. But he's wrong. I'm not afraid of death. Hell, I respect it. That's right, it's just about the only thing left in this world to respect. It's the one inevitable, undeniable truth. Everything else can be questioned, but death is truth. In it lies the only nobility for man, and beyond it the only hope. (pause)

When my Mama died, I traveled with her casket across the country in a train and kept runnin' back to the luggage compartment to make sure she hadn't left me all over again. I can see this little kid just like I'm watching the whole thing from way up above; he's rushin' back and forth through those rattling train cars, panicky and disoriented, just about out of his head with a new kind of grief, the real kind, the kind that'll never be over for the rest of his life. And, oh God, I wish I could reach down and help that terrified little kid. But the gobble-uns already got him, but good.

.V.

(FEB. 15, 1955)

As USUAL, everybody's snoozin' except me. Me an' Tuck. He's been trailin' me around—knows I'm leavin'. Don't you, boy? (lights a cigarette) I've been scribbling here with a candle for company, and I came up with a poem about Back Creek, where me and my pals used to paddle around in the old swimming hole. Went out there in the damn February cold today, and it felt like maybe the last time. For better or worse. Here goes:

> *I took a little drink from an ample stream*
> *I fear thereby result in fertile jest to her source*
> *Her current swift, direct, and crystal*
> *There is a want to be there and drink long*
> *Nature's plea, ovum, stem and pistil*
> *But there is more to streams*
> *Than the water to gorge on*
> *Plunge your face in a brook*
> *To wash the desire away*
> *A fool to drink*
> *To drink and not to taste.*

James Byron fucking Riley. Right? (laughter) You damn well have got to taste what you drink, or what's the use?

Dennis and I are leaving tomorrow. We've got to shoot some stuff in New York before heading back to Hollywood and *Rebel Without a Cause.* (long drag) Better pack this thing up. Carting it around is a pain, but it's good for posterity. (laughter) I'll miss the folks, and my cousin Markie. And I'm gonna miss good ol' Tuck. I'd take him with me, but I don't think he could handle all the bullshit. Could you, Tuck ol' boy?

.VI.
(FEB. 20, 1955)

BACK ON 68th Street. February 20, the great year of 1955. This city yanks me right out of the crap. So many smells! You pass so many different faces on the street, there's no time to ask yourself a bunch of impossible bullshit questions. Too much to look at and take in. Dennis and I have been taking pictures all over the city. I pulled on some tights this afternoon and did some barre exercises with Eartha. Miss Kitt to you. (laughter) Looks like Nick Ray is coming to swim around in my psyche for a few days. Just a peek'll probably send him running back to the palm trees. But I want to pick *his* brain. He's directed eight pictures. I got me a movie camera, a Bolex 16mm, and I've been fucking around with Billy Gunn and Marty Landau. Just for kicks. I think I'd make a good director. A director has to be a perfectionist, a man of wide knowledge. That's me! (laughter) But you know, there are too few fucking hours in the day for me to even begin to learn what I need to know. Still, I just can't stop. I wouldn't even sleep if I didn't have to, and sometimes I don't. Gonna give it a try right now though. Gonna give it a little try. (yawns) I haven't been able to get through to Barbara. Guess it's true that she's met somebody else. I don't get it. With the great James *Dean* back in town? Shit.

.VII.
(FEB. 21, 1955)

I played chess with the fatboys today: well, one fat cat in particular; Howard Thompson at the *New York Times*. Something inside me makes me do such dumb shit. I know on the outside it looks like I'm full of loathing and disdain for the whole scene, but it's not like that, really. Honestly, it's like I can't fucking help it! I *make* myself late for the interview, knowing damn well that Mom Deacy is going to be sitting there pissed as hell, and it's not fair to her. But there I am, wandering through Times Square like clocks were never invented. Late on purpose. So Mr. Reporter is sitting there, leveling me with condescension, and I stretch out on the floor, looking the other way, and say "Shoot." So we're off and running. First off he asks me if I read *East of Eden*, and I tell him no—the way I work, I'd much rather justify myself with the adaption rather than the source. Told him that I didn't think I'd have too much trouble with Cal's characterization once we started because I understood the part. I knew, too, that if I had any problems over the boy's background, I could straighten it out with Kazan. Shit, maybe I was too damn lazy to read the book. I'm only in the last third of it, anyway. And despite his belief to the contrary, I had Kazan in my hip pocket. He was hidin' out in the teeth of my comb. I didn't tell Thompson that, though. I made some stuff up about how I studied law at UCLA, and how I busted a couple of kids' noses and got kicked out of the fraternity.

When he asked how I became an actor, I actually got sincere for a couple minutes. I told him acting is the most logical way for people's neuroses to manifest themselves, that an actor's course is set even before he's out of the cradle. Sounds good, right? Must be true. Should've told him I'm interested in the craft, not the crap. So then I went on about the "cadence" and "pace" of New York (laughter) and how "fertile" it is. That's the word I used, "fertile." I told him that behind all that brick and mortar in Hollywood, there are human beings just as sensitive to fertility. Just look under the nearest rock. (dark laughter) And that the problem for this cat—myself—is not to get lost. That last statement might be the one thing I'm sure about.

.VIII.

(MAR. 8, 1955)

(BARTÓK'S *Miraculous Mandarin* is playing) Barbara's on her way over. I think tonight'll be the live version of my "Dear Jimmy" letter. I've got a pretty little surprise for her, though. Might make her change her mind. (long drink, loud swallow) Me an' my bottle and good ol' Bela Bartók creating the perfect mood. Not to mention some reefer here. (loud inhale) C'mon, Barbara honey, I's a'waitin'. (long pause, Bartók plays. Knock at the door) Holy smokes, there she is, Bela, finally got here. Better hide this thing. There we go. Well, now, there, then . . . Hi, sweet honey, come on in. Come right on in. (door closing)

Barbara: Jimmy, you're flying. Are you OK? What are you drinking? Whatever it is, you've had enough, I'm sure.

JD: You want some? Here, honey, just take a little swig out of the bottle. Oops, seems to be all gone. Sorry, so sorry. Let me see if I have something else for you . . .

Barbara: No, Jimmy, come on, I don't want anything. I came here because I want us to have some sort of understanding about all this . . . What in the world?

JD: This is all for you, honey. Every bit of it.

Barbara: Jimmy, what are you trying to do? There must be a thousand dollars in that suitcase!

JD: I owe it to you anyway. Take it, it's all for you. You deserve it.

Barbara: Jimmy, you seemed to be able to accept the situation last night at dinner. You even seemed to get along with Eddie. You insisted on meeting him. What's happened? What's going on in your head? I told you in no uncertain terms that I'm getting married next month. Oh God. Oh my God. Stop, Jimmy. Just stop it.

JD: Here! Take it!

Barbara: This is so unneccesary, Jimmy, so damn sad. Please, I don't want any of this money. You're breaking my heart. Stop it. Put the suitcase away, Jimmy! Put it back in the closet, please!

JD: (weeping) Must I *always* be miserable? I try so hard to make people reject me, even you! Why do I *do* that? I'm so sad most of the time, and awful lonely, honey. Awful fucking lonely.

Barbara: Jimmy, you have this open wound that's never gonna heal.

It's the size of the Grand Canyon, and who could patch that up? I don't have the strength. It's over, Jimmy, and you know it. I have to go. I have to get out of here. Eddie is waiting for me.

JD: Go on, then. Go to the wonderful fine gentleman Eddie with all the proper fine manners. But you'll be sorry.

Barbara: Good-bye, Jimmy. I'm sorry, I really am.

JD: Go! Just go! But don't forget this!

Barbara: Stop it! I don't want the money!

JD: And just remember—you *better* remember—when I die, it'll be your fault! All your fucking fault! (Sound of slamming door. Long, deep sobs.) She's gone. Got all that? Got all that for posterity? (Hysterical laughing and sobbing.)

.IX.

(MAR. 16, 1955)

IT'S MARCH 17, way late. Went to Hollywood Boulevard tonight and watched people come out of the theater talking about me. Hollywood fucking Boulevard. It was like being privy to my own birth—or funeral maybe! (laughs) I parked on Caheuenga, me and Frank. He's in *Rebel* with me has his own car-club. We stood around, my hat low down, hidin' out in plain view, and lo and behold, seems like I moved some of these people. Lo and fucking behold. I even spotted a few wet-eyed girls. Seems like James Dean made 'em weep here in Hollywood, Cal-i-for-ni-ay. (long cigarette drag)

They gave me a lot of guff last time I was out here. Now everybody's payin' a whole lot of attention to me—but I'm still the same guy. I haven't even changed my pants! I suppose I was too small. All of a sudden I've grown a few inches. When *Rebel* is done I gotta get back to New York. I sure as fuck don't need Hollywood. Maybe they don't need me either, but I've got the advantage. I've got something they want, and they're going to have to pay to get it.

The New York *Eden* premiere was last week, but I just couldn't make that scene. Jane was pissed, but I told her I just couldn't handle it, just *could not* make it. So on to the next—(cigarette drag, rustling pages). Hey, how about this description? "Jim—The angry victim and the result. At seventeen he is filled with confusion about his role in life. Because of his 'nowhere' father, he does not know how to be a man. Because of his wounding mother, he anticipates destruction in all women. And yet he wants to find a girl who will be willing to recieve his tenderness." Awww, shucks.

There's so much crap being written about me. Maybe publicity *is* important, but I just can't get with it. I've been told by a lot of guys the way it works. The newspapers give you a big buildup. Something happens, they tear you down. Who needs it? What counts to the artist is performance, not publicity. Guys who don't know me, already they've typed me as an oddball. And you can't trust critics as far as you can bounce 'em—but maybe Zinnser is right about this one. In the *New York Tribune* he said even though you sensed the badness in me, you liked me anyway. Or was he talking about Cal? (laughs) I even read where ol' Steinbeck said it was the best picture he'd ever seen. Hmmmmm, I wonder how many movie theaters he's got up there in Salinasville? It's all a bunch of shit anyway. Yeah, my name's up there in the marquee lights, but it's not my be-all and end-all. (phone rings) Well then there now, should I answer that? Let's flip us a dime.

.X.

(MAR. 22, 1955)

BOUGHT ME a horse, a Palomino. I'm calling him "Cisco." Cisco the Kid, the new member of the family. He's the brother I never had (laughter), and he can't give me any guff! He gives me confidence, makes my hands strong. I love ridin' him.

I'm thinking of getting rid of my motorsickle cause of all the guff from the studio. It's funny: I've always wanted a bike just like the one I've got now, and they don't want me to ride it. Screw 'em. I'll keep it for spite. *And* I'm gonna get me a Speedster. When I'm flyin', I've got no fear at all. Doubts—and even *reasons* to doubt—drop out of my mind like bricks in a hay bale. Riding Cisco up in Santa Barbara is a temporary emancipation from the pesky facts, but he's not fit with a 1500 cc motor. (laughter) I've got my eye on a certain white Porsche Speedster. Just as soon as I sign the Warner Brothers fat contract, she's my new baby. (Lights up a cigarette, long drag.) I'm headin' out to Ella Logan's in Brentwood. Brando is supposed to be there. I guess I'm supposed to be jazzed. He's already accused me of wearing his last year's wardrobe and using his last year's talents. Who does he think he is? The greatest living actor or something? (sighs) I wish I didn't give a shit. I have my own personal rebellions, and I damn well don't need to rely on his to screw things up.

.XI.

(JUNE 1, 1955)

(LONG BLAST of bongo drum pounding.) I'm drunk, so what of it? Leaving the party, Brando came up to me and told me to give up my motorsickle. "It doesn't go," he said. It doesn't fucking go! What does he know? "I found out," he said to me, "an actor with half a face is no actor at all." I was riding a sickle way before he ever did. My first one is still out in the barn back home. I've had it so long it's like an old friend. Awwww, shit. Ella's worried I'll total out, so she must've asked him to tell me off. I don't know why I go to these showboat parties. Either I fade into the wallpaper or start some kind of ruckus. So here I am alone in this four-walled trash can. I can't sleep again. I never seem to get more than two or three hours in a row. And there's only so much room in this fancy-assed little dive to pace back and forth. But hey, do you realize that if you sleep eight hours a day, you have slept twenty-five years by the time you're seventy-five? There's not much difference being asleep and being dead, so you might as well say you've been dead for twenty-five years! Thoughts are sweet, then wicked, then perverse, then penitent, then sweet. The moon is not blue. It hangs there in the sky no more. In antiphonal azure swing, souls drone their unfinished melody. When did we live and when did we not? In my drunken stupor I said a gem! (long pause) I suppose Pier is sitting in front of a roaring fire in Beverly Hills, swooning over that putz she married for no good reason. Awww, shit! She's having a baby, and it isn't mine. What would I do with a baby anyway? I'm just gonna do what I have to do and shake it all off. At least I'm a goddamned star out here in Hollywood. Maybe that'll ward off the gobble-uns.

.XII.
(AUG. 4, 1955)

I HAVE a hunch there are some things in life that we just can't avoid. They happen *to* us, probably because we are built that way—we simply attract our own fate . . . make our own destiny. I've been reading about the Aztecs, and I think I'm like them in some ways. With their sense of doom, they tried to get the most out of life while life was good. And I go along with them on that philosophy. I don't mean the "eat drink and be merry for tomorrow we die" idea, but something a lot deeper and more valuable. I want to live as intensely as I can—I can't seem to be able to help that anyway—be as useful and helpful to others as possible—but live for myself as well. I want to feel things and experiences right down to their roots—even when it hurts. Maybe by not avoiding painful emotions, I'll be able to feel all the good stuff in life while life is good. And accept the difficult shit when it's downright unavoidable. I'm feeling pretty damn chipper this afternoon. Maybe because I'm about to go pick up my Speedster.

.XIII.

(SEPT. 29, 1955)

I WANT that line from Alan Seeger's diary on my tombstone—"One crowded hour of glorious life is worth an age without a name." In fact, I sent Jack Warner a telegram asking him to make *sure* that it got carved deeply into my tombstone. He responded by revoking my driving privileges on the lot. Jimmy Dean is such a naughty boy. (dark laughter) Seems my new Speedster shook 'em up a little. Too damn bad. Everybody's too damn serious around here. They're in the business of celluloid, don't they know that? Stuff that'll disintegrate not too long after they do. (Lights up cigarette.) Maybe even before. So what am I doing here? Driving a real fast car—but not on the lot— and pretending to be other people. Folks with life-altering problems that get all worked out in the allotted hundred minutes. Ha! Wish I could say that's all there is to it. Sometimes that *is* all there is to it, but way down I know exactly what I'm doing and why I'm doing it— just can't put how it feels into words. Guess that's why I'm doing it. To see what it feels like. (laughter) Didn't Shakespeare say that men and women are merely players? OK, who are we playing for then? There's gotta be an audience, a witness of some kind. Who's to say that all this shit— frying an egg over easy, making yourself come, begging Jesus for some kind of mercy, growing old, wrinkled up, and all bent over—Goddammit, who's to say that it isn't all taking place in God's private screening room? (pause—inhale, coughing, pages turning) Anyway, I'm reading this cool book, *Actors on Acting.* It's confirming my suspicions. My new bible. Almost two and a half thousand fucking years ago, Plato said that the true artist, when he is in the throes of his art, *is not in his right mind.* (laughter) I can confirm that one! What a relief. Listen to this—"When a man has acquired a knowledge of a whole art, the inquiry into good and bad is one and the same!" It's hard to even get my head around that one, but I *feel* the truth of the statement down in my guts. He calls the poet "a light and winged and holy thing . . . out of his senses . . . the mind no longer in him." I reach that state—I'm sure I do. I'm just *gone*, man, you know? In this passage he asks the actor when reciting a "striking passage"—"Are you not carried out of yourself, and does not your soul in an ecstasy seem to be among the persons or the places of which you are speaking . . . ?" And the actor answers, "I must frankly confess that at the tale of pity my eyes are filled with tears, and when I speak of horrors, my hair stands on end and my heart throbs . . ." (huge sigh) I'm on to something here. This thing inside me is bigger than I can stand sometimes. And it aches to get out. It yammers and yammers at me until I'm almost impotent with a crazy mix-up of rage and sorrow and out-of-my-head fucking *rapture*. I don't want to be just a good actor. I don't even want to be just the best. I want to grow and grow so tall *nobody* can reach me. Not to prove anything, but just to go where you ought to go when you devote your whole life and *all* that you are to one thing. Being an actor is the loneliest thing in the world. You're all alone with your concentration and imagination, your heart throbbing and your hair standing on end. And that's all you have. Being a good actor isn't easy. Being a *man* is even harder. I want to be both before I'm done. (long inhale) Shit, is *that* all? God, I guess I'm really fucked up. I hope I can sleep.

END OF TAPE.

THE JAMES DEAN DIARIES—EPILOGUE

AFTER I digested these stunning revelations, listening again and again to this living, breathing young man speak his peace (and angst), I finally took Southwest up on their no-frills direct flight to Indianapolis. I had long wanted to visit Jimmy's grave (he will now always be Jimmy to me) and in fact, had carried a grainy magazine shot of his headstone around in my plastic wallet all through junior high, gazing at it often with bleeding teenage sorrow. Those goofy, gangly boys at Northridge could never measure up to the dead, holy perfection of James Byron Dean—1931–1955.

But I learned from listening to these tapes that there isn't much difference between this determined, long-gone Midwestern lad, and anybody who's had a burning desire to splatter his or her heart all over the screen, page, canvas, or stage. He still inspires and instills that desire to this day. When Nicolas Cage accepted his Oscar, he thanked James Dean. Have you watched *Rebel* or *East of Eden* lately? I slid my *Rebel* DVD into the player last night, took a deep breath, and was once again transfixed by his hungry, fearless truth humming through the air.

After the four-hour flight, I rented a car and drove through miles and miles of endless Indiana cornfields, taking Exit 55 to Fairmont, "The Place Where Cool Was Born." It's as if time stands still here. I slowly cruise Main Street, recognizing the old brick buildings from studying copious photos featuring Fairmount's most famous son. Here's the hardware store where he posed in the casket. Here's the storefront where he proudly sat astride his first "motorsickle." I wander through the museum, where the very bike sits encased in glass, along with a pair of black leather boots and a set of worn bongos. His face beams at me from all sides, and I long to hear his laughter.

And here I finally am, at the graveside, in front of the simple, familiar headstone, paying my respects to a man whose thoughts were sweet, then wicked, then perverse, then penitent, then sweet again. The moon is not blue. It hangs in the sky no more. But James Dean's rebel soul is a light and winged and holy thing, forever saying gems in God's private screening room.

Letter to the Drummer, April 8, 1998

JOHN ENTWISTLE

Dear George "King of the Skins" Thumpit,

The reason you were fired from the tour (during rehearsal) was that in my mind you were ill prepared and badly equipped. In my opinion a biscuit tin and a dustbin lid does not constitute a kit worthy of stadium performance. The fact that your previous letter was on audio cassette makes me suspect either that you do not own a pen or (and this is more likely) you cannot READ. This perhaps is why you were early on the second day of rehearsals. In future you should remember ENTRANCE is four letters longer than EXIT. You can count can't you? Oh no I remember you CAN'T. When I asked you to count us in you counted the BAND MEMBERS and even then you got it wrong. You forgot yourself (which I intend to do from now on).

Your ambulance-chasing lawyer has tried reversing the charges to me one time too many. Tell him any more and he's going to catch up with the ambulance. By the way, my drum roadie has managed to buy you another stick. You might as well have it as my next drummer will probably possess two or hopefully more. I feel cheated by your resumé as when we checked it out we found most of the stars you worked with were deceased (two of them before you were born). In fact the three surviving employers of your talents have restraining orders out on you.

So—George "King of the Skins" Thumpit—I'm gonna open the door—shove this letter/cassette into your hand—PLAY IT LOUD—AND GET THE FUCK OFF MY LAWN.

Yours Threateningly,
Phil Depressed

The Plate

from HORSE'S NECK

PETE TOWNSHEND

SEPTEMBER 3RD

I was a detective; brave and fearless. Like Sherlock I had my idiot partner. We called him Fan and he was black. I always listened carefully to whatever he said, then disregarded it. Why, at that point in my career, should I have even bothered with such buffoonery? I suppose I felt some pleasure in being snide. It all seems so long ago, like a previous life. I will explain everything soon, as best I can.

"Tell us again. Exactly what happened, for the Inspector." Fan talked to the girl indifferently as though he were dealing cards.

"Miss Lazenby," I said. She was a fairly plump girl of about twenty-three with blond hair. Her face was weary, and small dark crescents capped her green eyes, which were hypnotizing and slightly reptilian. Her look was spellbinding and gave her heart away: she was sad, and she was sick. Behind those dilated pupils there was a mystery flashing that intrigued me. There was a call from her body that had me opening and closing my hands involuntarily. She did not appear beautiful at first—her chin was too petulant, her lips too thin and her hard eyes too widely spaced—but if you had a soul with a nose, you were sunk. I looked at my blotchy palm and the itching scar that ran from thumb to little finger. I turned the middle-aged hand over, and scratched instead the few hairs on the rivulet-veined skin.

"I'm sorry to have to take you through this again, but I assure you it will be helpful—most helpful. Of course we could continue without further questioning, but it's important that I, the senior detective here, should hear your story." Fan was smirking visibly as I spoke and I felt like hurling something at him.

"I told your friend here the poem." She started to talk suddenly and I leaned forward, obscenely obsequious. Already my mind was feeling the beginning of blood-lust.

"She didn't mention a poem, sir." Fan looked at the girl, pokerfaced. She suddenly began to recite like an absent-minded schoolchild.

> On a painted plate
> My body lies, like an ornate pattern
> On an ornate pattern;
> A willow-story corpse in state.
> My body lies on a painted plate.

The girl stopped, a fold of her blond hair falling over one eye as she tried to light her cigarette. The noble Fan stretched over with a lighter. The flame was set so high she had to struggle to avoid being branded.

"Watch it!" I snapped.

He ignored me and stabbed another question at the girl: "What does this peculiar poem mean and where did you hear it?"

"He used to say it over and over."

"Who?"

"Robin, the boy who used to come to see me here, to bring my drugs. I'm not a heavy addict or anything, it was just the odd delivery of smoke or coke for parties. He was my boyfriend."

"Your pimp, you mean," Fan sneered.

God, I hated him. I couldn't bear to think that he might be right.

"I'm glad you're being so frank, miss," I said. "I'm sure it will help. Now, tell me again what you saw this morning."

The girl's mascara-smirched eyes cut into me and didn't soften for a second, but I could tell she was in bad shape. I was determined to help her get to the truth.

She began: "It was him. Robin. He was out there in the garden. He came back. I'd seen him in my imagination a thousand times. When the landlord came in and looked out he saw him too."

At this point she did crack and I had to rely on Fan to give me her complete story.

SEPTEMBER 5TH

Fan wanted me to forget the whole thing. Raston, the only other black detective in M Division, was brought in to interrogate the girl again. It was suggested I do nothing more. At first I capitulated, but listening to the girl's story again I only became more deeply convinced it was true.

Now I am here in the ceiling, locked deeply in love, holed up like a poisoned rat scuttering between floorboards as I die, shuffling the loose cork installation chips lining the beams, whiskered nose covered in dust. I am steeped in fury, determined to make my mark, to win the day and the lady in distress. My back aches. My eye is glued to a hole in the ceiling of her room.

I still watch her. Two weeks ago I lost my job. I am no longer a commissioned detective. The landlord doesn't know this. I began my intimate surveillance soon after I was dismissed. I enter the building from the adjacent house, which her landlord also owns, into the roof via the attic door. Through a series of small holes I watch her. Now I am so desperately in love that I want to call out, or turn to snow and melt through the plaster into her hair.

Once, after watching her undress, pull aside her robe and ply the dusty hair between her legs with slow, pushing and pulsing finger-dances until she breathed and collapsed, I could restrain myself no longer. I wriggled from my secret place quite noisily, squeezed down through the attic door, down the staircase into the street, through the high-hedged garden full of weeds and flowers, and up to the adjacent house, knocking on the door, pushing the bell bearing her name.

She appeared on the balcony above me. "What the hell do you want?" she shouted.

"I need to talk to you." I lied. "I have learned something."

I scratched my palm and looked at my scuffed shoes and chalky clothing. The landlord had come to the door, and stood looking at me as I looked up at the balcony where she had been. I studied it as a sacred spot, appreciating the cracked and eroded stone, crumbling and green in places. (It was Raston who got me dismissed. He and Fan had done some very cursory investigation, but they never really believed the girl's story. I did. I believed it as though I had lived it, and neglected every other case I was ordered to follow up, until it all got out of hand. The only consolation was that Raston himself quit when a full investigation was threatened. I wanted the truth, for me—and the girl.)

She arrived downstairs, her robe drawn around her. Her face glowed and she seemed more beautiful than I had ever seen her. I thought I smelled a fleeting scent of female sex. Perhaps it was my imagination, but it sent me into a dizzy, spiraling sparrow-hawk glide from which I thought I couldn't recover.

She immediately tore into me: "What the bloody hell do you want? Why don't you bastards ever leave me alone? I'm sorry I even told you about all this."

Her eyes were crisp slits, and her hands were shaking. With a boyish memory I climbed the boughs of a wind-blown tree far too high; exhilarating, dangerous, no way up or down. She had to let me in. I think tears may have filled my eyes, or the earnestness I tried to communicate may have penetrated—I'm not sure. We went to her room. I knew it so well. I knew exactly where to sit.

OCTOBER 2ND

Lying here now, in the roof, looking through the little hole next to the place where the rose of the lamp hangs through the ceiling, I can see where I sat. I don't know why I am even thinking of telling this story. I can't tell now whether the things I said to her were lies or truth, whether what I write here is what I remember of what happened, or pieces of fact and fiction.

Why have I humiliated myself? Why have I degraded the love I feel for her?

After the first interrogation I grabbed Fan and walked into the street, which was full of flying paper and filthy children. I had felt confused but resolved never to go home again. After a few hours' work at the station I went to the Common and smelled the trees and listened to the rush-hour traffic in the middle distance. I kissed every living thing. From afar I watched faces; each one seemed attractive and belonging in some way, old and young.

All I saw in my mind was that fold of hair, that shaking hand, her eyes as cold as a snake's, and from each a strange tear frozen against her smudged mask of make-up. Probably a dozen times I have watched her wake up in shafts of sunlight, sheet to one side, her breasts floating with the tiniest movement of breath, her hand always touching her sex in sleep. How I cursed the winter when the morning light came too late, when I strained to see her in the darkness. I hardly ate or slept, I didn't dare, I might have missed a second of some new movement, some special action from my precious tragedienne.

Once I saw a man in her room. I had become so excited I didn't know whether to die there and then. I hated him so desperately. He had been black. (No, it wasn't Fan or Raston.) She was a diffident lover. She'd lain on the sofa, legs spread, awaiting him and he'd thrust into her with little real attention to himself or her. He took at least an hour and a half to come. My own center, veined and blood-flooded, felt the length of two palms. In their dismal hour and a half I came three times. The black man had thrown money to her before he left.

I sat down on the same sofa.

"Well?" she demanded. "What have you found out?"

So close to her, filled with the smell of her in the room she had lived in for months, I wanted to be sucked into her womb then and there. Her legs were tightly crossed, her robe pulled over her like steely armor. She seemed to be ready to resist anything I told her.

"Please listen to what I have to say. I'm sorry to bother you with this, it might not mean a thing, but I need to know." My slashed palm and once broken fingers itched and ached.

"I was following up a very tenuous lead—one of the names of Robin's friends you mentioned—I was watching a club in the factory area behind the railway, Yard Street. It's well known as an area where pushers operate. On several nights the same thing happened. A large old car would pull up in the street, and the driver would get out, without being furtive, and go into the club. He was about five-eight, with bleached hair, but normally dressed. About ten minutes later the boot of the car would open, and out would struggle about three or four kids—not always the same kids as far as I could see—they were differently dressed each time. They were always brightly turned out, with extreme make-up. On one occasion they looked like punks of the old order, belts and chains, their faces pale, but very carefully painted . . ."

The girl was getting interested. She shifted, leaned forward.

"On another occasion people emerged from the boot of the car dressed in rags like tramps, but again their faces were made up so delicately that each one was beautiful, and hard to identify. Once they were wearing flowing gowns and suits, then military coats, sashed and emblazoned, but worn with shoes like children's woolen slippers. Then the hair would be long and flowing on the males, shaved to the scalp on the girls. Then the girls might have hair like wire attached to their scalps, their men Aryan or like ancient Yehudis, with earlocks and scruffy gaberdine suits . . ."

Was I lying? I was at least keeping her attention.

". . . but always this incredible make-up, so carefully applied, as though by some fantastic theatrical expert. The whole affair is totally confusing."

The girl was up and pacing. Her hips swung beneath the robe, her hair, pulled into a rough ponytail behind her head, tossed as she pulled on her cigarette.

I broke the short silence: "Did you know my friend Raston quit the force over this case?"

The girl whirled on me, almost sneering. "Why should I know? Why should I care?"

"No, no—I didn't mean because of you or anything. He quit because he felt I was going too far, he was worried by my actions, he said I was becoming obsessed. I wouldn't let him work on anything else. He put in a protest and I threatened to have him sacked for indiscipline. He quit."

"Am I beholden to you then? Jesus Christ! Someone once lectured me about the danger of nuclear war. She spouted on about how little warning we will get. What I need is a bloody two-minute warning from the likes of her, and you, and the rest—bloody hell, here I am with an aching habit, no one will deal with me anymore, you had the bloody house under observation for so long. All my friends think I'm barmy . . ."

"I believe you." I was playing my only real card.

She stopped walking, her arms dropped to her sides. She fell into the sofa like a discarded child-doll. Tears flooded over her face even though her expression remained that of a cynical, frozen mannequin.

I went on: "I want to protect you—I'm worried about these people. I'm sure they park their car just over the road. It's there for an hour or more sometimes—yet I know there are probably, at least three, sometimes four, people dressed like fops squashed into the boot! There must be some connection!"

She stared at me blankly.

I hurried on: "I want you to let me watch from this room for a few nights. You can sleep in the back room. I will keep out of your way."

"No!" She put her hand under her robe and scratched her breast. "Yes—yes, all right."

The girl had told Fan that she had seen her boyfriend, Robin, murdered in the garden outside her home in a strange ritual killing. She had said that three men had dragged this man Robin into the garden where she had heard his cries. The men were dressed at the very height of the latest fashion of the time, a romantic look, long gowns over flowing trousers, almost like Arabs, hair Hitler-youth, faces made up white with a single line from ear to nose on the left side of the face. They had stabbed him repeatedly, then left. The part of her story that made Fan question her sanity was her claim that the attackers had then squeezed into the boot of a car and were driven away. They took the man's body with them.

She had said nothing to anyone until early morning. On the day we met, she had looked from her balcony and seen Robin's pale, decaying body laid out on an absurdly large china plate in the middle of the garden. By the time she had found her sense of balance, bringing the landlord up with her screams, the vision—or reality—had vanished. The poem Robin had often repeated to her had suddenly manifested itself. At first the landlord corroborated this second part of her story. I think he changed his mind when he realized how absurd it sounded.

OCTOBER 9TH

Of course, everything I've written is in fact true. I was a detective and I have now lost my job. All that has happened since is that I am convinced that I am losing my mind over this, my infatuation with the Lazenby girl, but there is nothing I can do. She depends on me a little now. That is precious to me. At least I no longer sleep in the garret.

OCTOBER 13TH

She hates me. I love her. I am back in the roof again. I annoyed her. The landlord let me have the room below the attic area I use to observe her and I can now see the street. I'm still very confused about the young people getting out of the car boot in Yard Street. I can see it so clearly I feel sure it must have happened. Yes, of course it happened; it just seems too incredible to be true. But it does add substance to her story. My relating that single event to her was what persuaded her to allow me into her flat for those few weeks. To confront her on the stairs was all I dreamed of. To say hello. The sun is shining.

In my new room in the house next door I made some coffee. As I poured the water over the grounds in the filter it all overflowed, black and gritty. I took a cloth and started to wipe it away. The coffee clung to the rag, and on each successive sweep dry grounds fell over the area I had wiped. I became infuriated and hurled the rag and the muck to one side. As I gazed at the mess on the scratched wooden table, inspiration hit me.

I rang some agencies and told them I was planning to make a short surrealist film. Once I had sketched out my idea they rang off, promising to call back. They never did. I tried some villains, contacts from the past. Again, once I told them my plan, they slunk away across the billiard halls laughing behind their hands. Nothing gives a villain as much pleasure as a fallen copper. They all thought I was doing drugs or something, but I had simply been inspired. I just needed a few people to help.

For a few evenings I visited Yard Street again. I was doing a recce.

I stood in the shadows and watched the kids arriving. I hoped to see the car-boot crew. The whole idea was, of course, peculiar but still I waited. It didn't occur to me that the girl's story might have changed as a result of what I had said I'd seen. She was an addict on the slope, after all. I remember a friend of mine on the Force telling me that when an addict, of his own volition, elected to go to a clinic for a cure, his friends called the act "going to the police." The expression made me feel warm inside when I repeated it to myself.

People arrived and left. The clothes some of them had the courage to wear at night were astounding. Sometimes, amid the young and vital explosion of colorful dress, there might loiter an older man in dress clothes or a woman in an evening gown. Somehow they would be absorbed without looking out of place. That was something notable about these kids—their outfits were so various that they absorbed anyone and everything. After a couple of nights I gave up.

OCTOBER 30TH

I am back in the attic. She never goes out. Sometimes she watches the television late at night with the sound turned off. The sofa is ragged, one arm falling away, the stuffing pulled out in a heap on the floor. A tribal rug, appearing to be moth-eaten and burned with cigarette holes, hangs on one wall. Her robe is perpetually hanging open, her naked body so familiar to me now that I can open and shut my eyes and see, and feel, every inch of her. I've watched her pick at her nails and her nose for hours on end, so insistently that a sudden flood of blood has rushed over her hand and she has leapt up in horror, thrusting a tissue to her nostrils. I've watched her pull up her leg at an angle and rub her toes, squeeze them together, the toenails uneven, or too wide. She has then cut delicately at them with tiny scissors. With her legs spread widely apart I have seen her clitoris, the lips of her vulva.

I fall asleep watching her. I dream of strolling by the side of a dark canal and meeting a man walking a dog. As they pass, I turn and look after them, the dog's behind is her exquisite cunt, moist and rouged. In sleep the sudden scent of lavender, invaded by a pervasion of sex, floods through my sleep-starved brain. Starting awake I hear a car horn in the street. I go down and look out of the window. There is a car outside and the horn sounds again. Looking through one of the peepholes back in the attic, I see she has heard. Still awake she is sitting cross-legged on the craggy sofa, gazing at the silent TV screen, but she doesn't move.

Now when I watch her she seems to have a golden aura. Perhaps it's because I'm letting myself get so deeply tired. Or maybe it's just the phenomenon that occurs whenever you stare too long at something. I remember as a child that I loved to scare myself after the vibrancy of a hot bath by gazing into my own eyes, my hair swept back, my face reflected in the mirror. I would stare and stare until my face started to become recognizable as the face of an animal. I remember the distortions vividly: my nose bent and blotchy; my eyes like bloody gashes; the eyeballs, never still, like oscillating slugs caught in an oily bath. The tiny hairs and blemishes on my face enlarged and mobile; my hands ugly when held up beside my face.

It would feel unendurable, but for some masochistic reason I endured it, almost recoiling in revulsion at the unfamiliar vision that I knew was my own face. Then, after about ten minutes, everything would clear and become peaceful. I would end my mirror-gazing, a ten-year-old boy looking at the face of his own father. One quick blink and everything returned to normal. It had just been an illusion.

It felt like a unique power. I could carry myself safely through an appalling hallucination and then pull myself rapidly and confidently back to secure reality. My whole life had become such a dangerous game.

The furtiveness of my position is a peculiar delight to me. I like the deceit, and the feeling of true subterfuge. I never feel claustrophobic as long as she is in the room below, as long as my eyes are on her. The peephole I arranged over her bed is in a far corner of the attic, well under the eaves. When looking there I can sometimes hardly breathe, but as long as I can see her in the dim yellow light from the streetlamps, I feel as though I'm on an ocean. There is nothing she can do that makes her look unpleasant to me. When I gaze at her at length, keeping my eyes open without blinking, just as I did as a boy gazing at my reflection, she seems to become ever more pure and transparent. Her skin glows and her eyes wish through their half-closed lids, perhaps recalling memories of wafting trees. Her hair, always falling and moving, seems to become liquid.

The pain of my love for her is beyond all words. It is the most unbearably delicious sensation, but agonizing and despicable. My chest feels pitted as though by the boot heel of a Cossack; my face burn-scarred by the iron of an inquisitor. There is no torture I have not endured, none I would refuse to undergo, in order to remain close to her. If a miraculous potion was forced to my lips that made me forget her forever, that flooded me instead with a conventional ecstasy, that made me feel as though I sat at the feet of God Himself, surrounded by hosts of angels, bathed in celestial music, if I was released from pain, then ironically I would scream forever. I would know intuitively that I had lost something more precious than an eternity of bliss: the exquisite pain of separation from some unknown object of my desire, more attractive than the gravity of the center of the universe itself.

I stood outside the door of her house for the first time in over a week. I rang her bell just as the landlord came up the path behind me carrying a bag of groceries.

"If you're calling for the Lazenby girl, you can give her these."

He didn't even pass them to me. He placed them beside me and walked in leaving the door open for me. She had, as usual, not responded to the bell. I craned my neck up at her balcony. She didn't appear. I rang once more and waited. The balcony doors were open and the tatty lace curtains blew slowly back and forth. I picked up the bag and went up the stairs. Outside her door I waited and listened. I could hear nothing. From under it, daylight from the open window shone over my feet. I felt I wanted to bend down and bathe my hands in the sacred light, gather it up and fill my pockets with it, drench myself in it. Finally I knocked. She opened the door. I spoke: "I've lost my job you know." I don't know why I said this: I couldn't even remember whether I had already told her.

"Come in," she said, taking the groceries from my arms. As she turned and walked to the little kitchen in the back of the room, I realized this was the first time I had seen her wearing anything other than the robe. She was in a blue dress. I have never seen a blue like it: it glowed, carrying an energy like the blue of the summer sky.

"Thank you for bringing up the groceries. Did he leave them downstairs?" She turned to face me as she took things out of the bag. Her eyes were carefully made up. She was wearing make-up on her skin too; deep, slightly sparkling blusher accentuated her cheekbones and temples. Her lips shone and glittered, her teeth sparkled moistly.

"Yes. Does he help you?" I gestured at the groceries. I sat on the sofa and put both hands on it, sensuously feeling the surface of the cushions.

"I never go out. He gets them for me. Always. I can't go out. Why did you lose your job?"

She knew why. I felt so close to her, so familiar to her, that I almost exploded at her with the license of a familiar lover. I wanted to enjoy a tiff, to explore dangerous territory, then collapse into forgiving embraces. I caught her dispassionate, inquiring look and came to.

"I lost it because of you. Because of the case, I mean."

The stiffening I had expected from her never came. She calmly carried on putting tins into a high cupboard and I looked at her back. Her shoulders. Her spine. The soft material of the blue dress was simply there. I was feeling ever more daring. I mouthed her name: "Rhea."

As I spoke, the sudden rush of impatience and irritation I had anticipated arrived in her. She laid down a food packet on the ledge below the shelves and looked at her hands. She leaned forward on both arms, her shoulders hunched up slightly. When she finally spoke I could hear that she was crying. Her question began low, rising in pitch and intensity almost to a doodlebug scream. "Why, why— please tell me why you won't leave me alone?"

At the end of the question she slammed the doors of the cupboard, but they flew open again and one of them hit her on the face. When she turned to me, black streaks of mascara ran down her rouged face, blood trickled from her left cheekbone, a gash about half an inch long gaped below her eye.

"Fuck it. Why do you keep coming here? What the fuck do you want?" She took a step toward me and I was scared. I had never been as scared of a woman before.

"It's your story, I just can't get it out of my mind. You know I believe it, just as you told it. I was blathering. Wiping at one side of my neck I felt an icy warmth. It felt like blood. I surreptitiously looked at my hand to check. It was sweat. She was the bloodied one. "Your face," I said, "it's cut quite badly you know."

She slumped into a chair by the sink and grabbed a small, dirty mirror that sat behind the water taps.

"Oh, screw it!" She dabbed at her face with the cuff of the blue dress. It seemed sacrilegious to me.

"Here—use my hanky." I pulled it out but it was filthy.

She didn't even look up from the mirror. "Listen, just piss off, will you? Go. I've got a visitor coming. Thanks for bringing up the groceries."

She glanced up for a second. I hesitated, then moved to the door. She spoke when I was halfway out. "Why did you move in next door? Are you spying on me?"

She looked up and I faced her. My arms, already by my sides, slumped as I answered, "Yes."

NOVEMBER 3RD

I've become a worm. Not a beetle, but a worm. Little point in spying anymore: the girl is in a mental hospital somewhere. Landlord told me, loving every minute of it.

NOVEMBER 17TH

Today I saw her come home. She was with her mother. I don't think she saw me. I feel elated. The landlord sneers as he sees me scurrying back into my flat. Maybe he knows. I must be careful. Now she knows I spy on her. I admitted it. What a bloody fool.

Her mother put her into bed this morning, left for the day, and is back now. I want her to go away.

NOVEMBER 24TH

For weeks now I have waited. The girl does not seem to be getting any better.

I couldn't wait any longer to find out how she was and stopped her mother in the street.

"How is Rhea? I'm a friend."

"She is very confused. She thinks she is crazy." Her mother stopped before walking down the path to the house. She looked at me carefully. "How do you know her?"

"I was a police officer assigned to her case." I tried to seem natural and assured.

"It is you people who are to blame."

"Why is that?" I asked defensively.

"Because you believed her absurd story at first, then didn't follow it up. You have made her believe she is crazy. What about the landlord? Didn't he corroborate her story?"

"At first—yes," I agreed, "but there was a lot of confusion. I left the Force. Then the case was taken over by another man who also left the Force. Finally it was dropped. In the end your daughter changed her story. We think she did it so it would fit a poem of her boyfriend's. I was trying to help her when she cracked up.

Her mother responded immediately. "It was you who was spying on her?"

"Of course I wasn't spying on her. She was delirious, upset." I wondered if I looked as red as I felt.

The woman seemed impatient with me then, and went inside.

NOVEMBER 26TH

I have decided that I will help the girl. I will definitely carry out my inspired plan to re-enact the story as she first told it to Fan six weeks ago. I have managed to get some out-of-work actors together. I have cut the back seat out of an old car and tomorrow I am going to shock her out of her depression. I want her, but I am still so much a copper I also want the truth. I feel sure she told me what she thought was the truth, or what was close to the truth. When she sees again what she thinks she imagined, she will remember everything, she will tell me all. Then I can help her.

That night I couldn't help but spy on her again. She lay sweating and naked on her bed, her breasts rolled, and her belly, a little heavier since her mother had been feeding her every day, lolled from side to side as she tossed and turned. Asleep she was more beautiful, I think, than any woman I have ever seen, and her skin became transparent and luminous. Her hair fell into strands over her face. She nearly always slept with her legs wide apart, her cunt covered in hair that spread a little way inside her thighs and generously over her lower belly. Whenever I watched her for very long, tears would fill my eyes. I had stopped masturbating while looking at her; it seemed wrong. She was too much a beloved icon to me, even when naked like this. When morning came I went to bed for a few hours' sleep. The actors would be around at midday.

Everything had been rehearsed. It was simple: they were to put on the various costumes I had provided. One of them, a younger man, was to do the make-up for the four others. The actor who was to play the corpse tried on his trick death-knife and monkeyed around on the floor pretending to die. The plate, which was to be fashioned from an old circular table top I had picked up at a junk shop, was to be delivered to the garden at four that afternoon. At 4:30 I knocked at her room door.

"Who is it?" Her mother's voice.

"It's me."

She opened the door and let me in. The girl was in bed, looking radiant. I bowed and scraped. "I hope you are feeling better, Miss Lazenby."

"What the fuck do you want?" she sneered.

"Rhea!" rebuked her mother. "How dare you? This young man is concerned about you. At least you can be polite." She turned to me. "I'm sorry. I know you are a friend and you understand what she's been through. Talk to her quietly for a minute. It will help her. I'll go and make some tea."

I went over to the bed and sat on the chair beside it. The girl looked at me sideways and started to laugh.

I was starting to feel worse. "Please don't laugh at me. I really want to know how you are," I stuttered.

She seemed hurt by this request. The smile turned to tears; suddenly she put her face into my lap and lay across my body shuddering with sobs. I held her beautiful head in my hands and thanked God for the moment. Then she said something I hardly heard or understood:

"Apart from losing the baby and finding out I had cancer, everything has fallen into place beautifully."

It was so pathetic, so moving, that I had to fight off my tears. She became silent, her face still in my lap. Her sighs were deep and distant. I didn't dare to ask what baby or what cancer she was talking about. I turned her face up to mine and touched the spot below her eye where she had bled.

"It's healed okay," she said. She looked straight at me. I leaned down and raised her face toward mine. Just as my lips touched hers the prearranged car horn sounded from the street outside. She ignored it and pulled my hesitant mouth back onto hers and kissed me deeply.

"I'm happy now, with you I'm happy—I know you love me. The doctors told me that it was having too many sexual partners that brought on the cancer. It was down there," she pushed at her belly, "and it was the junk that made me lose Robin's baby. I just went crazy, totally crazy, but I'm happy now."

The car horn sounded again, this time for a full ten seconds. My actors were ready to play. The plate was in the garden. Robin's "body" was spread out on it, a knife in the chest. As soon as she appeared at the window my troupe would drag the body away and all climb into the car through the boot. They would then drive away. The horn sounded again and Rhea got up to walk to the window. Just then her mother walked back into the room, cooing, "Everything's fine now. Tea for you two and everything's fine."

The Devil's Racetrack: Ray Trailer

LYDIA LUNCH

PRISONER #32578 is shitting himself to death in the next cell. Every twenty minutes another round of bowel-splitting explosions wrack his body. He coughs, cries out, pounds his head on the cinder-block walls and wails. The smell is awful. As thick as oatmeal. His impending death from dehydration signals small relief, as its horrendous aroma wafts down the hall, walloping the senses, mingling with the already heady fragrance of thousands of spent bladders pissing into eternity since the turn of the century. The smell of old men's fecal remains, their sour and rancid flesh rotting from the inside out reeks until it stains the interior of your own nasal cavity, forcing you to become one with the smell. A seething odorama contaminated by the decay of hundreds of lost men whose very souls have started to stink.

Pickled feet and dirty fingernails. Silent pleas have been scratched into every surface, deep grooves in the floors, walls, bunks, sinks, an homage to endless days ill spent, locked inside this human warehouse of disease and petty disasters. Where wasted lives count the days until release, relief, return or death.

Another notch on the wall to keep you sane . . . keep you insane . . .

On my back in my bunk. A waiting game. Poisoned stalactites hang heavy with a toxic runoff steeped in decades of disappointment. Years of nervous, bored sweat cling to the ceiling and walls. Threatening to drown me. Drip by drip. In the eyes, the nose, the mouth, the ears. Browning like nicotine stains forming a Rorschach Test in every corner.

Sticky to the touch, foul to behold its ceaseless descent. I pull my T-shirt over my head. At least the smell is my own. Smells like sorrow. Like spoiled meat. Like a beaten man, tricked on by his own gullibility. Tricked into believing . . . tricked into someone else's beliefs . . . I close my eyes and meditate. Fooling, with all of my will, myself, into summoning Her smell. I breathe slowly, deeply, inhaling my own aroma, a bittersweet stench whose undercurrents, with much torque of the imagination, are magically transformed into Hers. Into Her smell. Into what I remember of Her. I will never forget Her. The scent that emanates from the small of Her back. The smell of butter. Clove. Coffee. Cayenne. A spicy, pungent fragrance whose mysterious depths sting with intrigue. Rebellion. Deception. A perfume so steeped in magic, that a mere mortal's most strident resolve disintegrates, once intoxicated by the ether of its undertones. A perfumed poison whose fragrance scrambles the synapses. Turns men into obedient little puppies whose only wish is to please the Bitch Goddess. The witch whose wanton desires manifest themselves in a catalog of criminal behaviors whose essence in turn fuels Her need for domination. And it's her smell whose spell casts dominion.

I pull my T-shirt tight around my face, forming a noose, snug on my neck. A tourniquet which I twist just enough to cut off my breath. To thicken the pulse, causing dizziness. In a dream state of asphyxia is where I find Her. Lurking in the corner of my impending death. A bewitching pariah summoned only when everything else has been blotted out, chased away, erased, when nothing else remains but Her. And the mind is free to roam the inner recess of my imagination. The imagination She stained with Her scent. The images saturated with Her effervescence. The fantasies and recollections with which I shall remain forever trapped . . .

A Downtown alley in the back of a run-down Theater, once glorious, now in ruins . . . a sleazy European soft-porn skin flick milks what little life is left in the six or seven scummy patrons who scrounged up the two-dollar-and-fifty-cent admission fee. The cheesy soundtrack of Seventies synth is offset by overdubs whose grunts and groans simulate real passion. It bleeds through the brick. I'm leaning against the damp wall slippery with greasy rain. Her right hand is cocked around my throat. Her left unbuckles my jeans. She pulls me out, half hard, shiny with heat. I can smell myself. She begins squeezing. Tugging. Jerking. Whispering "I'll suck you until you cry like a little girl . . ." I pull Her into me, my lips touch Her neck, the pungent musk, my eventual downfall . . . She shoves my hands away, slaps my mouth, insists I do not move. Stay still. Don't speak. Don't breathe. I hold my breath.

She slides down my body, into a squat, legs spread wide, exposing Her pink. Tells me to not even dream of peeking. I'm not allowed to look. Insists I turn my head left, no right, to keep an eye on the entrance to the alley. To keep a lookout, make sure no porn patrons decide they need a piss, no cops come nosing around, no teenagers or gangbangers. No dogs or dopers. She puts me in her mouth. Her soft fat lips encircle the purple tip. Nip on it. Bite it. A little too hard. Enough to make me wince. Nestling teeth inside the foreskin. She coos on it, making sarcastic sucking sounds, loud enough to startle. Then swallows. The whole of my cock. Lips flush to pubis. I fear She will somehow disgorge the meat from my body. Suck it off. Spit it out. Step on it. She holds my cock in, undulating her throat. Squeezing. Forcing me to spasm, flinch, thrash. Come. Her mouth slowly subsides, leaving me limp. She slaps at my prick, insisting I put it away . . . get it out of Her face, that filthy thing, a discarded toy, no longer of interest. I scramble to stuff it back inside my pants. My belt buckle chimes against the brick wall. The jingle of silver and stone is transformed into wood against steel.

My daydream fades as Holtzer & O'Leary begin their afternoon shift. Rattling the cages with nightsticks. With bullshit and intimidation. Dirty jokes and catcalls. The stink of their aftershave. Body count begins. I don't know why they bother. No one has ever mastered a successful break. The last man that tried was riddled with fifty-two bullets. Back in '73, or so I've heard. I've only been inside for six months, twelve days, seven hours, and forty-one minutes. I'll be released in twenty-four-some-odd years. If I can make it. I can't believe I have for this long. Don't know how anyone does. Surprised the suicide rate isn't higher. More manslaughter isn't committed. Homicide's not on the rise. The smell alone makes you pray for Murder, for only in Death will there be the freedom of relief, that portal of escape from which release will breathe new air, an air devoid of ghosted scents whose putrification stains the brain stem.

Second only to the smells are the sounds. The moronic chattering, nonstop bantering, petty squabbles, chronic bickering, inflated bragging. The ceaseless tedium of being forced to endure countless conversations full of run-on sentences whose main objective is to overflow every second with a hideous din which murders silence . . . The cruelest of all punishments. The caterwauling of stupid men in love with the sound of their own voices . . . The endless boredom and monotonous routine occasionally eclipsed by the static sounds of shitty reruns that sputter from a broken-down black-and-white TV propped at the far end of the corridor, featuring only the finest in adult entertainment. *America's Most Wanted. The Price Is Right. Family Feud. Candid Camera. Cops.* No distraction great enough to ever allow you to forget where you are, what you did, what went wrong. How easily a stupid mistake, which could have been avoided, should never have happened, was not intended, and was not my fault, for which I am forever fucked, can ruin your life.

We never went to Her place. She never even mentioned it. Not in the three weeks that I knew Her. I don't even know if She had one. She couldn't stand to have sex in enclosed spaces. She said it made Her feel trapped, domesticated. Depressed. It was boring. Dull. Too damn rote. It always had to be outside, in plain sight, in public view.

The threat of being caught, possibly arrested for indecent exposure, turned Her on. Made Her rabid. She claimed it was one of Her many personal attacks against the ridiculous and outdated regulations fasted on society by government issue. Viewed public indecency, lewd behavior, and exhibitionism as a personal vendetta against the abolition of the individual. If we were truly free in a free society, pleasure would be rewarded, not punished . . .

I know. I know I should have known better . . .

A Korean late-night mini-mart. We went in for cigarettes, two cups of rank coffee, something sweet. Last aisle near the frozen food. Between the baby diapers and the dishwashing detergent. We were babbling like school kids, giggling like idiots. Spewing convoluted utopian rhetoric like college freshmans. She pulled me close. Stuck Her tongue in my mouth. Started sucking it. Instant arousal. And my hand between Her legs. Petting sweetly. "Pinch it." She insisted. Biting my lower lip, Her eyes trained on the mirror above us, the view it afforded the cashier. Making Her twitch. Wiggle. She unbuttoned my shirt, eyes glued to our reflection. Began sucking my nipples. Licking them, slurping loudly. Her slippery little tongue, a rattler, darting back and forth across my chest. Chewing, a hungry little orphan eating a gum drop.

The small things are what you miss most. The inconsequential. A warm breeze on the back of your neck. A fresh pack of cigarettes. The smell of wet leaves. Mud. Music. The Sunday paper. Silence. Try keeping your mouth shut when Holtzer, impeccable in his freshly starched uniform, lightning-bolt tattoos barely concealed under his black armband, poster boy for the Aryan Brotherhood, makes his afternoon rounds . . . interrupts my reverie . . . I could almost scream at the bastard to just back off, shut the fuck up, drop dead.

Big man. Bigger mouth. Feels it his duty to comment on every man in the ward. "Make up that bunk!" "You pussies look a little pallid today . . . what's the matter, meatloaf no good?" "Another beautiful day in paradise." "Greet the day, you lowlife shits!" Thinks it improves morale, his useless drivel. Please . . . Pretends to befriend all the white cons. I get his trip. Sieg Heil and all that bullshit. I try to keep to myself. Toe the line. Not talk. An almost Zen existence where days, weeks, and soon years will disappear in mediation, daydreams. Memories.

A light rain . . . quarter past midnight, bus stop. Downtown. All but deserted. Only the truly desperate out on a night like this. A wino or two in drenched cardboard, stooped down low in the corner of a far building . . . a crack whore waiting to roll an unsuspecting mark, the rustling of tin cans as they scamper up the sidewalk. I'm with Her again . . . She straddles me on the bench. Climbs over my lap.

Long black raincoat, short black dress. Not a word is spoken. She's devouring my face. Biting cheeks, forehead, ears, neck. I thrash my head from side to side, trying to avoid those pointy incisors. A manic dingo, ferocious, feral. She keeps up the attack. It's all I can stand. I stuff a musty leather glove in Her mouth, damp from rain, smelling of cigarettes and mildew. She clamps down, glowering. Not much time before Her next attack.

I grab Her hands behind Her back, holding Her small wrists in one meaty fist. Hard. I tweak them a little. Until I hear Her gasp. Quiver. I rip Her panties aside, now I want to hurt Her as She hurt me, my face still throbbing full of love bites from this petite piranha. She struggles against the force, pinned in place, but there's nowhere for Her to turn. The other musty glove grabs at Her pouty puss. Her musky smell mingles with the wet streets ringed with garbage. Inflames me beyond belief. I stuff my fingers inside, two at a time, poking viciously at Her tender pink.

Now She's the one who thrashes. Left and right, a slow gurgle of excitement slips past Her mushy gag. Both mouths now stuffed with the stink of moldy leather. I force another finger inside, and then another. All but my thumb. Which rests against Her swell, that niblet of pleasure. Mashed against the pressure. Causing Her to buck, a wild little bitch, sent into heat . . . Until I begin a steady pummel. Punching at that little hole, pounding, forcing a grand expansion, explosion, expulsion. She comes, spraying all over the glove, my coat and jeans, the bench.

An abstract portrait rendered in spunk.

She set me up. But I was stupid enough to take the fall. She slipped into my life like a low-grade fever. A bacterial infection that quickly poisons every reasonable cell in the body until you're defenseless against the virulent blows of her night sickness. My whole being tainted by Her toxic succulence, a psychic pollution so potent that the only recourse was acquiescence, as She leeched at my life force. Devouring small pieces of myself that fell away like dust, dry bones, dead skin, desert wind.

Now time keeps me. With slow dissolve every hour dribbles away, every second stretched to eternity, the minutes mere interludes with which I count my heartbeats. Leaking life from my caged existence like sand in an endless hourglass whose bottomless pit mocks without mercy . . . stealing from me the most precious commodity. The choice to decide just how I'll waste the day. Do not take this lightly. It is the finest of luxuries. Now my days are wasted for me. Locked up and lost in thoughts whose instant replay is my only salvation.

I calibrate time by plucking hairs. Off my arms, my legs, my pubis, and eyebrows. Glued to the four-by-eight-by-nine-foot walls with spittle. Prehistoric as a miniature cave painting. My private museum. Filled floor to ceiling with masterpieces I create in invisible ink, sketched by fingernail into the canvas of my flesh, projected through the filter of my brainpan unto the gallery walls whose seething funk I erase with my gluey iris and replace with much eye strain and a headache-inducing squint, with pristine white plasterboard filled with nonstop rotating film loop replicating Rubens, Bruegel, Bosch, Bellini, Bernini, Goya, Caravaggio.

The Masters whose subjects, not unlike myself, were forced by circumstance beyond their control into playing victim at the hands of cruel gods and vicious monsters whose only offering of salvation beyond this tortured existence was in the knowledge that a suffering that wounds beyond the shallow exterior of flesh and bone, penetrating through the multiple levels of epidermis into and beyond every fiber of your being, an agony from which no solitary moment without would ever again be complete, is offered up in loving submission to a greater being. A being with no equal. Whose godlike powers and omnipotent understanding no matter how cruelly projected, or simultaneously you are rejected from it, is reward unto itself. A being who, in my case, has disappeared completely from my life, appearing only in visions as apparition and savior.

Perfect World

from VIRTUAL UNREALITY

EXENE CERVENKA

THEY WERE perfect for each other. They kept a little jar of guitar picks and rose petals next to the bed.

When they weren't feeling exactly the same, they were feeling different; and that was interesting, too. Their songs were like flowers that bloomed sober and straight from the water in a whiskey bottle vase. The clock, the moon, the sun were all round, friendly faces that marked happiness; not time. Not the miles, not the minutes, not mortality. They were free and unopposed. There wasn't one thing she didn't like about him. He had never made a complaint against her habits. Already a month had passed, and still they loved each other.

She woke up this morning and the first thing her eyes landed on was one of his shoes. She felt funny. She didn't know why. She wondered, "Does it bother me, where it is? In the middle of the floor? Where's the other one?" and as she rose half-covered and touched it, he awoke and said, "You gonna hit me with that?" He smiled at her. She told him that it just bothered her for some reason. He said he was sorry, and he said, "I told you before I moved in that I was a slob." She set the shoe gently down on its sole.

He put his arms around her and kissed her face and neck; and as she introduced her tongue into his mouth, she knew that things weren't perfect anymore; and that his shoe was the beginning of the end. A few months later she watched him tie his laces and walk away with the moon under his arm. She cried all day to the rose petals. But they were dead, and the jar was dead, and the guitar picks were dead, and the air in her apartment was dead air, and her hair was dead, and the sun was brutally, unmercifully alive.

Perfect worlds roll like balls through people's lives. Today, through mine; tomorrow, through yours. How lucky we can be sometimes. But how lonely and desperately sad we can be when our perfect worlds roll away.

Where are you, little star? Did you see this bitter earth roll by, a ball you shouldn't play with? It belongs to me and I want it back! Just like a child, I don't want my happiness to end. Just like a child I'll get over it. And just like you, I'll find someone else to play with. I'll wait until a perfect world rolls to a stop at my feet; and when it does I'll get back on. And I'll know you when I see you, because you'll be barefoot.

Narcissus

ROBYN HITCHCOCK

IN THE blue light of dawn, the Chateau stood motionless at the end of the straight drive. The Chateau never went anywhere, after all: you went to it, not vice versa. Hence the drive, lined with poplar trees whose surviving leaves hung still in the autumn air. Mist hid the legs of the beasts in the fields that flanked this avenue. Jean-Yves heard one of them cough and he dismounted his bicycle, trying to keep his progress as muffled as possible . . .

• • •

Narcissus starts here . . .

"Good night! Good night!" Guy Kincaid, lead singer of the band Narcissus, waved from the center of the stage at the Marsupial Winter Gardens: "We love you all, with no exceptions."

Actually, that wasn't quite true; Guy thought he had seen both Myra Kwok and Harry Penrose in the audience. On the other hand, there had been no sign of Merry Kakouli. Guy bowed, his long form fairly supple in a dark green body stocking, and walked to the side of the stage, pausing in the wings to allow Easy Chapman, the drummer, to exit first. His olive eyes gazed up at Easy from beneath wet strands of hair that clung to his head like seaweed. Some people thought that Guy drank chlorophyll.

"After you."

"As it pleases your dude-ship," responded Easy, clicking his heels together and saluting. He had an ear-to-ear beard and a habit of addressing people as if their heads were nine inches to the left of where they really were, but he didn't miss much.

" 'Dahlia Thweet' was *right on*, man," said Easy over his shoulder as they clambered up to the corridor. He was referring to a new song of Guy's entitled "You and Me and Dahlia Thweet," a dialogue between two paintings at an art exhibition discussing a critic named Dahlia Thweet as she stood peering at them.

Guy grunted. He wasn't good at taking compliments, though he'd had enough practice. He was even worse at taking criticism, at which he'd had virtually no practice at all. If he seemed inconsolable at times, perhaps it was because everybody appeared to love him.

Seven gold-painted doorways lined the backstage corridor. The Marsupial Winter Gardens was an accomodating gig.

Guy peeled away from Easy and stepped through his own golden doorway into his dressing room.

The room had pink walls, a matte black ceiling with a solitary sticker affixed to it advertising an act called Thruckfash, and a long mirror surrounded by light bulbs that ran along the left-hand wall. Beneath the mirror was a dressing table, on which were a number of things. Guy switched on the mirror lights, switched off the dreary overhead bulb, and began to look at some of them.

There were some pink roses that echoed the walls, in a glass bulb of a vase that looked surgical. Guy hadn't noticed them being there before the show. There was a glass of red wine that made a pool of darkness below the head of one of the roses. A pink petal dangled lasciviously over this miniature lake.

Moose, the road manager, had thoughtfully poured out this after-show drink for him. Guy took an oafish swig, forgetting that he'd instructed Moose to put the rest of the bottle in the conference room, where he and his bandmates would reconvene to groove with their guests.

By anybody's standards, it had been a brilliant show. A packed house full of faces trained like sunflowers on Guy and his cohorts had brought them back to the stage three times. Three times! This city had always rooted for Narcissus, but never beyond the point of two encores. We must have played well, thought Guy.

But, he thought, you can never be totally sure, can you? The more they loved him, the more he asked himself, "Who, me?" Guy thought he had better check on who it was that all these people were really loving.

Wineglass in hand, Guy surveyed his frogman-like torso in the mirror. He looked like a scrawny super-villain; indeed, with his top hat and cane (discarded after the first song of the show, "My Friend Day One"), he was a passable descendant of The Shade in Flash Comics.

Guy toasted his reflection, which returned the favor. For a man in his late thirties who was strong on alcohol and soft on exercise, he was in reasonable condition. He now performed the entire show sober, did thirty sit-ups almost every morning, and eschewed bread while on tour. He also sweated half of himself away on stage every night. It was time to ease himself out of the sticky wet costume that was cooling on his skin.

He replaced the empty wineglass on the table. Next to the roses were two phone messages that Guy hadn't spotted before. In a mechanical, childlike hand, someone had written two names and two phone numbers. *Yes, of course*—Myra Kwok and Harry Penrose had both requested after-show passes and wanted Guy to call them! There was nothing, however, from Merry Kakouli.

Guy felt the cry of the bathroom. He unwrapped himself from his one-piece body stocking, discarding it over the chair in favor of the towel that Moose had left there for him, a big white hospital-type towel that he draped over his shoulder. His naked body accompanied him in the mirror to the lavatory. He sighed; his paunch was still there, a polyp of flab linking his meager chest to his inadequate penis.

Narcissus was a joke and always had been, really; that had been the concept when he and Easy Chapman (the other surviving long-term member) had launched the band from the ashes of The Vermeers ten years previously. A pantomime extension of Bowie's classic Ziggy

Stardust persona, Narcissus, like all good pantomime, worked on two levels: upstairs and downstairs. The kids downstairs—the Real People, as Easy called them—enjoyed the show, the chutzpah of the front man (who obviously didn't take himself too seriously), and the catchy songs.

The people upstairs, meanwhile—the savants in the balcony—dug the irony of the whole thing. Here was a man clearly uncomfortable with himself and his self-selected role in the world, who was making that point *precisely* by emphasizing the opposite. Narcissus was no whinger: "No Kvetchup on Mr. Kincaid," as the *New York Times* had put it. Guy maintained a facade in the great Glam tradition, blowing kisses to the house at the end of every show. But the folks upstairs and the Real People downstairs took those kisses back to very different homes, and remembered them very differently. That's what the folks upstairs thought, anyway.

Guy emerged from the bathroom and washed his hands in a small basin that stood before the long, lit-up mirror. Further along the table, the roses looked as if they were growing out of their own reflections. Guy noticed a cardboard label he hadn't seen before. He saw in the mirror that his penis was slightly tumescent. Turn yourself on, and you turn on the world, he thought. Yet he was still a long way from Port Sex in his consciousness. The morbid analysis of his own performance on stage, that nightly needed extinguishing with alcohol and other personal assistants, was already beginning, and although sex—or the idea of sex—often came as a welcome antidote to the way his mind attacked itself, by then he was usually past it.

He doused his libido with trousers, a T-shirt, and a jacket. All black. His paunch was hidden now. His dark brow and craggy features were enhanced by the somber gear. There he was again in the mirror, this time sitting down. But, thought Guy, I'm rather too brightly lit. He was still pink as a prawn from his exertions under the lights on stage. He rose from his seat, went to the door, dimmed the ring of lights a little and sat down in his chair again without ever taking his eyes off the mirror.

Reaching into his jacket pocket for a cigarette, Guy could truthfully say that he had never fancied himself. Not that he looked bad, he conceded to his reflection, with a flick of his dark green mane. But in the end, he didn't really care how he looked, except for professional purposes. That was what was so irritating about this paunch he was developing, he thought as he stood up to reach into his trouser pocket (having found nothing in the jacket). In this schtick all the eyes are on you. He found some matches in his trousers, but no cigarettes. His fingers returned to his jacket, probing the inside pockets. Although, of course—he proposed with his upstairs mind while the downstairs department continued to search for cigarettes—to think of Narcissus as a mere schtick was to belittle it . . .

No cigarettes in the inside pockets, interrupted the fingers. Shall we try the outside ones again?

Yes, OK, replied the downstairs mind.

It was just, continued the upstairs mind, that Great Pop should always be slightly ludicrous. Look at Elvis and the Beatles and their hairstyles: the world mocked them at first, then reached into its wallet.

No cigarettes—No cigarettes—No cigarettes! chanted his fingers and the downstairs mind together. It was obviously time to hit the conference room and get some supplies. He wanted a cigarette so badly, he could actually smell a freshly lit one now.

Then a new message flashed on in all areas of Guy's mind at once: *Read the label on the flowers.*

Guy obediently got up from his chair and twisted the vase of roses around until the label was in his hand. Inscribed upon it in green ink were the words: "Look in the wardrobe."

All at once Guy became aware that there was indeed a wardrobe behind him. Consisting of four double doors, it ran the whole length of the wall opposite the dressing mirror. He walked to the nearest pair of double doors and pulled them open. A wave of cigarette smoke broke over him, and from the midst of it stepped Merry Kakouli.

Guy's eyes became monster olives.

Merry was brandishing a cigarette holder, and her bobbed black hair suggested the flapper epoch, but the rest of her slim frame was encased in black leggings, skirt, and T-shirt. Black globular beads adorned her pale white throat.

"Gee, you always read the small print, don't you, Guy?" she cawed in a thick Boston accent. She cleared her throat, held the cigarette holder at arm's length behind her, and embraced him with her free arm. Her bangles clacked behind his head.

Merry was a woman in her late twenties, on the shorter side of tall. Guy had met her several times before in this city. He felt a little diversion in his bloodstream as they hugged, but tonight something wasn't there in Merry's embrace. Their lips came nowhere near each other, and their heads fitted neatly around each other's shoulders. However, she did hold on to Guy long enough to feel his interest. Then her voice hollered in his ear:

"Heidi!"

Merry disengaged her head and called into the wardrobe. "Heidi, sweetie, are you OK?"

There was no reply from the wardrobe.

"Wow, I hope I didn't suffocate her," she said and climbed back into the wardrobe. So Merry had brought a friend.

Guy spoke for the first time since entering the room. "You've been sitting in there smoking with somebody? How long have you been sitting in there smoking with somebody?"

"Oh, I don't know," came Merry's voice from the wardrobe. "I never time my smokes."

"Heidi! Hey, Guy—is this your regular closet? She's not even *in* here, for Chrissakes!"

Guy opened the remaining double doors, letting the residue of the smoke dissipate into the pink and black room. Merry stood in the shell of the wardrobe like a forgotten passenger in an abandoned railway carriage. She bent forward and pushed one side of her bob back behind her ear to keep it out of her eyes.

Guy kept looking at her. Then he noticed a deep recess behind her at right angles to the wardrobe itself. He clambered in beside her. "I think your friend—Heidi? Do I know her?—went that way. The Marsupial has some pretty *involved* closets."

Guy took Merry's hand and led her into the recess. Her fingers felt light-boned, like a bird's would probably feel if it had fingers, he thought. But he had to let go almost immediately to turn right into a further recess. The light from Guy's room was feeble here, but a red oblong outline ahead of them indicated that they stood behind another doorway. Guy was picking up heat from Merry like an infrared scanner. He reached for her hand again, but she had already placed it on his shoulder.

They stood amid coat hangers.

From beyond the red outline came the sound of human activity, like a radio play in someone else's room. There was a murmur and then a sigh. After a pause came a creak and a whisper. There followed the discreet rhythm of something that the listeners could guess at, but not identify. Then there was a sneeze, followed by the sound of a woman and a man laughing.

"Should we knock?" Guy whispered to Merry.

"Get outta here!" she whispered back, then raised her voice. "Heidi? You in there, girl?" The noises stopped abruptly. "Heidi!"

"Just a minute! Hang on just one minute, please," came a man's voice. It was Lord Anchovy, the keyboard player in Narcissus.

"You rat, you bailed on me," cried Merry, who leaned her full weight on Guy and pushed them both through the crimson portal into Lord Anchovy's dressing room.

In a room that mirrored Guy's—but with red walls, a red overhead lightbulb, and a pair of low-slung lamps that crouched on the dressing-table—Lord Anchovy was rummaging in a rubbish bin stuck under the table while a young woman leaned back against the same table and smoothed down the front of her skirt. She wore a beret, a discreet black halo. Her hair looked red, and she had dark lipstick and disappointing teeth.

Lord Anchovy kept swishing his hands through what sounded to Guy like liquid rubbish until he realized that it must be ice.

"I can't believe this," mumbled Lord A., without so much as glancing up: "There's no Anchor Steam."

He stood up. His blond curls seemed glued around his cadaverous face. The ring through his ear gave him the look of an aristocratic pirate. To Guy's chagrin, he noticed that Lord Anchovy still had no trace of a paunch under his tight black and white striped sweatshirt.

Merry had meanwhile spotted a cooler behind a small armchair and extracted from it a chilled bottle of Anchor Steam beer. She unscrewed the top and presented it to Lord A. "Here you go."

"Oh, er . . . right . . . cheers. Hey, Guy! Er, this is . . . um . . ." Lord A. indicated Heidi sheepishly.

Merry completed the introductions. "That's Heidi Melrose, and I'm Merry Kakouli."

"And it's a pleasure to meet you both. Lord Anchovy, at your service," he clicked his heels together and saluted. It was a Narcissus thing. Heidi tittered. Lord A. rolled his eyes toward Heidi, and Guy shrugged his eyebrows.

"OK, you guys," said Merry. "It's party time—take us to your party!"

• • •

Jean-Yves reached the door at the side of the Chateau. As soon as he pressed its peeling brown boards it yielded, and he slipped behind it like a beetle. He wheeled his bicycle into a dark outhouse, hung with moldering saddles like so many carcasses. He bobbed his head up and down to avoid bumping into them. At the end of this room light was strained in through the cobwebbed panels of glass that formed the roof of a small atrium. In there, Jean-Yves propped his bicycle up against the milk churns.

• • •

"That's the whole point, man—there was nothing before Charles Shaar Murray."

Karl Blight, the guitarist with Narcissus, was discussing rock journalism with some people as they huddled around the wine at one end of the conference room. The males, in the form of Karl and two members of the support band, were leaning against a table laden with beer and fruit. Facing them were the females: Eileen Fanshawe (rock writer for the *Sun Times*), her friend Carla Provolone, who had a big orange sweater and two capped front teeth, and Myra Kwok. Karl Blight continued.

"That bit, where you know, he gets locked out of Keith's dressing room, I mean, it's the alpha and the omega of music writing . . ."

The others stared at him blankly.

"I mean, it's like you're actually *there* with them, y'know."

"Where are you, Karl, man?" inquired Dickie Bollo, second guitarist for the opening act, Frame by Frame. He was a little in awe of Karl Blight, who was hunched intensely over a roll-up cigarette, smoothing his greasy black hair off his stubbly face and puffing hard.

"Up Keith's nose wi' a flashlight," interrupted J. J. McIntosh, the bus driver for Narcissus, who had appeared from nowhere and was now reversing back there clutching a carton of grapefruit juice. "Looking for all the other poor cunts!"

"Yeah, right—huh-huh-huh-huh-huh-hah-ha-ha-ha!" The dead-eyed laughter of Myra Kwok came forth. Bad language, said Myra's autocue: time to laugh.

"There was Lester Bangs," said Byron Hunter, the leather-trousered front man for Frame by Frame, exhaling menthol smoke. Byron Hunter had a certain presence. Not enough to threaten Guy

Kincaid and capsize the tour, but enough to keep Frame by Frame in the picture. Guy didn't mind Byron; like the ever-circling moon, the support star always presented the main man with the same face. Byron was good at keeping still, and he wasn't afraid of silences in the conversation. His tangled brown locks were beginning to thin on top,and this endeared him to Guy no end.

" 'Rest Bangles,' " said Carla Provolone, who had been silent up till now. She was looking at Myra Kwok when she spoke.

"Excuse me?" said Myra, distracted from looking over people's shoulders in search of other, more important, people.

"It's an anagram of 'Lester Bangs,' " explained Carla, happy with her first one off the production line.

"An . . . anagram? Is that, like, some kind of antidote?" Myra was irked at having to engage with somebody who wasn't Anybody Special, and she spoke snootily to Carla.

" 'Bengal Trees', " sighed Carla happily, looking like someone who had bitten into a quite acceptable profiterole, and who, furthermore, had several bites left.

" 'Angers Belts'?" offered Eileen Fanshawe, twinkling behind her glasses. "Lester was a little chubby in later life."

"Uh, 'Breast Angels'?" said Dickie Bollo, gamely. Eileen pursed her lips like a blackberry for a moment, then shook her spectacles at the guitarist.

"No, dear," she said. "There's only one 'a' in 'Lester Bangs' "— Dickie looked puzzled, but he nodded—"and I hate to break it to you, but 'Breast Angels' has two in it."

"One for each booby," said Myra as the elevator finally stopped at her floor. She periscoped the room again, watching as people came drifting in through the pouch of a giant replica kangaroo that served as the entrance to what had formerly been the ballroom of the Australian High Commission—now Marsupial Winter Gardens.

She was about to go refill her empty glass when she spotted her target: "Ohmigod! Guy!"

Guy had ambled into Hospitality (or Hostility, as the band called it) engaged in conversation with Merry Kakouli. He had deliberately held back his pace, allowing Lord Anchovy and Heidi Melrose to enter the room first and flypaper some of the backstage ghouls.

Nevertheless, as soon as he stepped through the pouch, people were upon him as if he was sweet and they were hungry. Why else would he be in show business?

"Guy—hey, dude!"

"Hey—it's the man!"

"Great show, man—I LOVE THE NEW STUFF!"

"It's Mister Narcissus!"

"Guy—we're over here!"

"Guy-uy-uy! Ola, big boy!"

Guy and his companions had made it as far as the wine. Guy helped himself to a pint glass, which he almost filled with Chateau Penfold. Then he bummed a cigarette off Merry, but not before being gallant enough to get her a glass of rum.

"The Coke is—can you see it, over there? If you like, I'll get—"

But Merry waved his mouth shut and excavated herself from the swarm. Guy drank half a pint of wine in thirty seconds—"That's more like it," thought his downstairs mind—as he held court. He saw, but didn't consciously register, that Lord Anchovy and Karl Blight were centers of their own respective circles elsewhere in the room. And, at the back of it all, holding a glass of ale as if he were in a pub full of strangers in Sussex, stood his old school friend Harry Penrose with his Abe Lincoln beard and his briar pipe.

Guy didn't see Myra Kwok, because she was standing right next to him. Myra was a legacy of Narcissus' previous keyboard player, Leslie Fade, who had been faded out several tours ago in favor of Lord Anchovy. She was handsome, wore red dresses and black leather boots, often with ebony bangles rattling on her lean wrists. She had crimson lipstick around her heart-shaped mouth, and she had no sense of humor. Perhaps because of her agitated décor, Guy's eyes never came to rest on her; they always slid away to someone else— just as Myra herself was usually looking for someone more important to be with.

Guy had never liked her, and she had never appeared to notice. Perhaps he also resented the fact that somebody technically attractive could be so boring; although, as he himself would be the first to acknowledge, a bore is only somebody who talks when you don't feel like listening. Leslie Fade's disappearance from the group had made no difference to Myra; every time Narcissus hit town, she was in there like an antibody, come guest list or high water. She came into her own at that stage of the aftershow, when nobody was listening but everybody was agreeing. Then it was time for flattery, sex, or oblivion.

"Guy, when are you guys coming back?" asked Lois da Figuera, the genial music director of KUMC radio.

"We haven't gone yet," replied Guy, not for the first time in his life. This got a big laugh. As the laughter retracted, fragments of sound— more laughter, sighs, cackles, hisses, burps, gulps, and yawns—ricocheted around the room beneath the gaze of the kangaroo. The aftershow was the true encore. The wine and the spare adrenaline from onstage combined into one of Guy's favorite cocktails.

"Did you see yourself on MTV the other night?" Lois was asking.

"What's MTV?"

Guy looked puzzled for a second, and then relaxed his face so that everyone could laugh. Even Myra Kwok; that is to say, she made the laughing shape with her mouth. Although, looking at her, she could just as well have been in agony.

Guy was feeling good, but he realized he had a need that was not being met. The glass in his hand had been mysteriously replenished, but his other hand lacked something. He looked over to Merry, who was standing in conversation with Byron Hunter.

"Merry?" he called. "Can I bum another snout off you?"

Merry fumbled for another cigarette in her bag. Beside her, Byron Hunter pushed his fingers down into his leather trousers, making a show of looking for a cigarette for the Headliner.

"Hey, Guy! Take it!" Myra Kwok prodded him in the ribs and handed him a freshly lit cigarette. "I got a whole pack."

• • •

From the scullery that led off the atrium came a saw-like snoring. Jean-Yves peered in and saw a man in a suit that was dusty with flour, curled up in a fetal position on the sacking. A cabbage leaf covered his ear, as if to protect it from the flour. One of the man's hands was clasping the handle of a big black hold-all. Jean-Yves now edged himself into the scullery, and his foot clinked against a bottle, but this did not disturb the sleeping man.

• • •

Guy was in his dressing room toilet. He was rocking back and forth gently, as if the dressing room was heading out onto the high seas: but it was only Guy who was chugging. He found the zipper at the front of his trousers and successfully located his penis. This he aimed with terrific accuracy at the toilet bowl. He waited, stable and contemplative. A sudden lurch caught him—the dressing room must have moved abruptly to starboard—and he had to support himself against the wall with his spare hand. Time went by, and Guy noticed that nothing was leaving his bladder. Of course: he had already just pissed a moment ago! The lavatory chain was still swinging. No wonder he was in the toilet! It would be best to leave now before he repeated the process.

For the wings of a dove, he sang in his mind as he washed his hands. Then, sensing an intruder, he looked up into the mirror above the sink.

Reflected there was Harry Penrose, still cradling a glass of ale. He wore a dark blue blazer and a turquoise necktie. His bald, squishy head looked as if it had been boned by headhunters and then filled with sand until it approximated its original shape. His full lips would have looked beautiful on a woman, but not with Harry's straw moustache draped over them, let alone the bristling beard below. Yet his deep-set blue eyes were windows onto a perceptive soul.

Although only a year older than Guy, he looked like a man from the previous generation. Twenty years back, Guy and Harry had played guitars together at school, like the Everly Brothers. It was Harry who had shown Guy the way chords worked with each other, linked by ascending and descending bass lines. Guy's early songs were a lucky dip of chords randomly slung together to accompany poems taken from his school notebooks. Harry gave these misshapen prototypes a proper spine and sent them walking away upright, and although Narcissus had never recorded any of the old Penrose-Kincaid numbers, ("Crab Radio" sometimes appeared in the encores.) Guy felt a debt to Harry. But Harry was no longer the same person.

"Ah, there you are, old boy! Thought you could give me the slip, eh?"

Guy kept on washing his hands. Marshmallow-skinned in the makeup lights, he croaked back at the reflection of his old friend. "To be honest I don't think I could even give you that at this time of night."

"Jolly good! As long as I'm not intruding . . ."

Guy shrugged fatuously in the mirror. His head was full of riffs, but he owed his old friend at least one half of his upstairs mind.

"Well, then," Harry continued over his ale glass. "I think it's time we had a chat about Christ."

Guy had seen this coming. He couldn't very well bar his old colleague from the show, but his pleasure at finding Harry relocated to this big foreign city had turned to dismay when he discovered that Harry had brought Jesus with him.

Compassion, thought Guy. We are all branches of the same tree. And if the tree were upside down, the branches would become roots. He sniffed, still feeling a little euphoric numbness at the back of his throat. Give Harry a couple of minutes, Guy, one of his minds told the other. You owe him time, even if you cannot give him love. He continued washing his hands and spoke gently to Harry's reflection. "Oh, yeah?"

"You know what He's done for me, Guy? It's absolutely knocked me for six the way the market's turned around since I've been out here."

Harry swilled his ale in the bottom of the glass and looked candidly at Guy back-to-front in the mirror. Guy had finished washing his hands but hadn't managed to leave the sink yet. Harry continued: "And then He found Laura for me."

"That's . . . that's very efficient of him," Guy concurred, taking care that his words didn't stick together in a lump.

"And I came along tonight—"

"I'm sorry." Guy swayed in the mirror. "I forgot to put your name on the door."

"Oh no, you didn't—my name was right there at the top of the list."

Guy sent Moose a silent thank-you. Good old Moose!

"—So anyway, I saw the concert, and I thought, Wonderful to see old Guy doing so well."

"Thanks." Guy was leaning with both hands on the sink and had forgotten that he was talking to Harry's reflection, not the true Harry.

"But, all through the show I could feel a sort of . . . despair, I suppose is the word I'm looking for. Don't get me wrong, old chap . . ." Harry cleared his throat and looked down into his glass again as if it might prompt him. "I mean, it was a faultless performance, and you've come on, you've obviously come so far as a songwriter, compared to our early efforts. But I looked at you, and the adoring crowd—and by the way, they really love you out here, Guy—and I thought: it's like a priest and his flock. But the priest isn't happy. Your mouth says one thing, and your eyes say another. You know—Guy, I don't know if anyone's pointed this out to you—but there's a hunger in you that will *never* be satisfied, not without Christ—just as there was in me. I mean, I still have the occasional beer now and then . . ." Harry glanced down to verify this, and the beer seemed to nod back in affirmation. "But it's not like it used to be. Laura and I prayed together, and our prayers, Guy, our prayers were answered. Now, you may say, 'Harry, old chap, I need that hunger—it's the fuel I need to earn my daily bread.' But take it from me, Guy: all the adulation in the world will not appease that howling mouth of yours . . . even though you're singing very beautifully these days, I must say."

Guy whispered the ghost of a thank-you at his friend's reflection.

"Because, you see, there *is* a higher power, Guy. Hunger can only consume itself, like any appetite. But there is something greater than ourselves, and we can only reach that something through Jesus."

Guy had been riveted, but now he was irritated. Harry had been right about him, in a way. The evening had left his ego hungrier than ever, wailing on the floor in its filthy diapers, and he was now indeed tipping anything he could into himself to appease it. Out of the corner of his eye, Guy spotted a bottle of red wine that someone thoughtfully—Guy himself?—had brought for the hotel after-aftershow.

Harry had been right, giving a diagnosis that only someone with his perspective, from outside the carnival, could bring. But then he had to go and bring Jesus into it and drag the whole thing down to a kindergarten level! He talked of Jesus in such a matter-of-fact way, too—as if He were somebody that Harry ran into most afternoons at the country club. As if Jesus did, in fact, exist out here on the West Coast.

Harry had blown it; his two minutes were up. But he was still talking. "So, what d'you say, old chap? I've got a Bible in my pocket; we could kneel down and see if Jesus is in—Oh!"

Harry looked troubled. "I say! Don't move, Guy—there's a demon on your shoulder! Ugly brute, too, by the looks of him. At least, I think it's a him. I wonder how long it's been there. They sometimes take a while to manifest, you know—sort of like a photo developing. Don't move—no, don't turn around . . ."

In the mirror there was no sign of anything on his shoulder, but Guy watched in disbelief as Harry did indeed pull a Bible out of his pocket and advance toward him on tiptoe, with the book held open at head height.

"This'll fix you, you brute!"

Harry snapped the pages of the Bible together right next to Guy's ear. When Guy turned around, the room was empty.

"Harry?"

But the room stayed empty. There was a pint glass with a shallow drop of amber in the bottom standing next to the pink roses. Most of the petals had fallen from the stems, surrounding the vase like the fruits of a sudden autumn.

"Harry?"

Guy looked through the carcass of the wardrobe, then stepped outside into the aquamarine corridor. He looked into the womb-red dressing room next door, where Myra Kwok had made his nose an offer it couldn't refuse. The other lucky noses had belonged to Lord Anchovy, Heidi Melrose, and Shane Haemorrage, lead guitarist of Frame by Frame. In fact, it was Shane who had supplied the stuff.

Lord A.'s dressing room was now empty of people, though littered with undrunk wineglasses. Guy managed to drain a glass of something pale (Chardonnay?) in one gulp and found a cigarette to put in his mouth. It was time to sober up with some alcohol. He made the journey back through the wardrobe to his own dressing room.

He half-expected Harry to be sitting in his chair, waiting for him, greeting his face in the mirror. But, no. Harry had disappeared so quickly that Guy began to assume he'd imagined him. Already the encounter was drifting into the swamp where memory and imagination mate with each other to produce gorgeous offspring. The room was so still. The motes of electricity seemed frozen as they blazed from the bulbs around the mirror.

Guy looked at the roses. The last of the petals had fallen, leaving the label with the green writing on it. The writing had been changed.

"Look in the wardrobe" had been crossed out and replaced, in the same handwriting, by "Look out the window."

Guy walked to the window. It was open, the lower casement pulled up to reveal a fire escape. Guy stuck his head outside and inhaled the city air. Anyone could have gotten in or out of his room all evening. Not that Guy cared much at this point. Maybe this was how Harry and his demon had made their sudden exit. Guy smiled at a vision of Harry running away to an empty lot where he could open his Bible and let the fiend fly away into the darkness like a moth that had been trapped between the pages.

The fire escape led down three flights to a back alley. It wasn't too dark. Then Guy noticed that the tour bus was gone! The long maroon vehicle with the Navajo painted on the side, in whose pink womb Guy and the others protected themselves from America, was not parked outside. Beneath his aftershow breastplate, his heart skipped a beat. Hadn't they parked there before the show? Moose usually winkled him out when it was time to leave, or at least made sure that he was fixed up with a ride. All Guy could see now were dumpsters. Was everybody back at the hotel already? In the time it had taken him to go to the bathroom and wash his hands?

An orange sports car drove into the alley, headlights raking the dumpsters. The car stopped, and Merry Kakouli climbed out. She waved up at Guy's head as it poked out of the window like something waiting to be guillotined. She called up to him.

"So, where did you go and hide yourself, Huh? Everybody's gone. They've just locked up front. I've been calling out like you were a lost goat, mister!"

Guy's heart replaced that missing beat. Merry hadn't abandoned him! What a great woman she was! Maybe he should move here and cultivate a proper relationship for a change.

He plucked all his damp stage clothes from wherever they lay and stuffed them into his bag. He decided to risk putting the bottle of red wine in there, too. The bottle had been opened, but the cork had been firmly replaced, and all the wine was still in the bottle. He walked to the window and swung one of his legs out over the fire escape.

"No, you jerk!" called Merry from the alley. "You'll break your neck on that thing. They bribe the fire department—no one's checked it for years. Take the stairs! I'll let you out . . ."

Guy heeded her advice, lurching, bag in hand, out of his pink and black dressing room. He stumbled happily down the corridor and the steps up which he had walked—was it tonight or on their last trip with Easy Chapman? Then he began to clamber down a spiral staircase. His heart beat fast, and his breath was labored, as if he were walking up the stairs and not down them. The palms of his hands developed small oases of clamminess. His footsteps clattered in the deserted theater. Many lights were still on.

He descended, backward, a steep wooden staircase. He had no memory of coming up this way. He had the presence of mind—barely—not to drop the bag with the bottle onto the concrete floor below. When he reached the bottom, he found himself in a khaki corridor that curved away to the left and right. He stood there with his bag, tight-chested, and brushed his dark green mane behind his ears.

"Hey?" he called out. His voice echoed from both ends of the corridor.

"It's right here." Merry's voice came to him from the same angles.

"Merry?"

She shouted back something that he couldn't make out. Setting off to his left, Guy soon passed the elevator that had originally taken everybody up to the stage level. He carried on walking around the corridor and was soon back where he started, at the foot of the steps. So where were the exit doors? He had just walked a complete circle!

Again, Merry shouted something that Guy couldn't catch. This time he decided to set off to the right. He was breathing heavily through his nose, high on himself with a side order of paranoia. He placed his bag on the floor, as a marker. It looked black and portentous against the drab khaki background.

His upstairs mind was still handing round the cocktails and patting itself on the back. But occasionally an acrid stench would waft up from below, where in the galley of the downstairs mind a black, resinous worm had boiled over out of a saucepan of self-doubt (which itself had been filled up by the overflow pipe of self-confidence upstairs). This worm was expanding, growing extra limbs with cankerous mouths full of pointed, rotten teeth, and in those mouths writhed supple tongues the same color as Guy's hair. The worm became a brooding hydra that squirmed around itself, bumped against the low, mean ceiling, and disturbed the soignée gathering above it. The hideous creature downstairs never quite ruptured the floorboards of the party upstairs, but it was always a bad sign.

"Merry! Merry? I can't find the bloody door!"

Guy still saw no sign of an exit. He noticed, on his right, the elevator. This time it was open. No matter: keep the hydra out of the upstairs brain. What a brilliant version tonight of "I Can't Cry" . . . or did they actually play that one? Or—wait a minute! Guy stopped walking. He had reached the wooden steps again, but his bag was gone.

"Hey, you . . ." Merry's voice came from out in the alley. "Mr. Rock Star Man—I've got it."

Guy turned around. Directly opposite the wooden staircase was a pair of metal doors, open to the alley outside. On both of them was stenciled in fluorescent pink:

PUSH TO EXIT

This made no sense. Guy could have sworn that neither the stencils nor the doors themselves were there when he descended the wooden steps, as much as he could have sworn that, half an hour ago, Harry Penrose had been preaching in the dressing room. Oh well, we live and . . . forget, said Guy to himself.

His breathing had calmed down, but his palms were still clammy.

He wiped them on the side of his jacket and headed for the stenciled doors. The black worm in his downstairs mind popped a new limb suddenly, so Guy amplified his thoughts of Merry. She was going to take him home. That was worth three encores.

The doors had drifted shut again. He stalked up to them and thrust them open wide.

There she was, leaning back against the car with her elbows on the roof. Her head was tilted slightly, and one of her knees was raised toward Guy. Snub-nosed and wide-eyed, she grinned at him. Her eyes crinkled at the corners. The car engine was switched off, the head-lights doused. Merry was largely in silhouette because of a lamp that shone down directly behind her, but Guy could sense her expression.

She nodded toward the one foot that she had on the ground. "Your bag, sirrr." She drawled out the words in a French accent. "It's been er-waiteeng for eeyou justa like ma good self."

She lapsed into her normal voice: "Lucky for you your friend's got cars."

Guy was now standing two feet away. Merry's knee was pointing right at him. He could smell the antique hippy musk that she wore, flowing off her in the night air. She uncoiled herself from her car and slid up toward him.

"You turkey," she murmured as for the first time that evening their mouths opened up to each other in a kiss. Their arms engulfed each other, too, and they became a dark rustling mass beside the orange car. But in a much more positive way than the black larval worm that was now thankfully dormant in Guy's downstairs mind. Guy felt his mouth mirrored in Merry's—the kiss was the portal that led them into each other. There they were in the alley: two creatures from the same species tasting each other. They were so alike and so different. Guy could never feel this way about his own reflection. He felt a tiny sherbet firework burst in his scrotum. Blood was seeping into his penis.

"Gee, I'm so wet," murmured Merry into his ear. She followed these words with her tongue, slipping it around this waxy orifice to the singer's delight. Guy slid his left hand under the back of her tights and made his way with it round to the front. His fingers glided through her delicate curls, as soft as baby's tears, till they found her labia in their dark ravine. She was telling the truth.

Their mouths opened to each other again. Merry's fingers had molded themselves around his cock, which was at high noon. They were both primed. The barriers between them were lifting, and the immigration people were waving everybody through. But the stage door alley of the Marsupial Winter Gardens has its limits. It would be much more practical for them to fuck back at her place. Furthermore, Guy's breath was not so good. Merry pulled Guy's hand away, withdrew her own, and disconnected her mouth from his.

"Let's go, huh?"

"Mmmm . . . yeah . . . go."

"Oh, hey," said Merry tactfully. "Want some gum? It's minty, nothing weird . . ."

"Er, yeah—why not?"

Guy stuffed the wrapper into his pocket with one hand while he stuffed the gum into his mouth with the other. He blinked his eyes and started chewing. He was beginning to relax for the first time that evening. Now he just had to de-tumesce for a while. Merry disengaged herself from his embrace and went to the back of the car. She popped the trunk and came back to collect Guy's bag. But even as she was picking it up . . .

"What are you doing?" He grabbed the bag from her rudely and clasped it to his chest like a baby. "No, it's OK—it always rides in the front with me. It's just got, you know, *things* in it"

"Things in a bag! Heavens to Betsy—what is this world coming to?" said Merry. Bag etiquette—how could she forget? For a moment, she stood looking over the roof of the car at Guy. She twisted the beads around on her necklace and smiled at him, her tongue darting deliciously through her lips.

Guy had more or less packed away his erection.

"OK", she said. "Your side's open."

The two of them lowered themselves into the orange car. Guy put his bag on his lap and reached around for a seat belt. There were a few drops of rain on the windshield. It must have rained, then, he thought. In the seat next to him, Merry took some lipstick out of the glove compartment and applied it to her lips in the rearview mirror. Her face was quite flat from sideways on. Her bob adhered to her face, obscuring it even though she was leaning back slightly. She extended her lips over her teeth to aid the probing lipstick. To help her see what she was doing, Guy flicked on the inside light next to the mirror. Her lipstick looked brighter than before.

"Ankff," she said.

Guy settled back in his seat, safety belt already in place, although the engine hadn't yet started.

"Are you still in that place on LaCherité and—what is it—Sixth?"

"Excuse me?" The lips relaxed briefly but the face stayed glued to the lipstick.

"You know, Merry—we were there last time."

"Uh-uh," her head shook slightly, "I never had a place on LaCherité." She turned to face him, crimson lipstick in place.

"I think you've got the wrong girl," said Myra Kwok, her red mouth glistening. "You're mixing me up with somebody."

She twisted her keys in the ignition. There was a David Cassidy key chain attached to them. She looked toward Guy with lifeless eyes.

But the seat belt was undone, the door was open, and Guy and his bag were gone.

Guy ran down the alley, out of the gates, and slewed left down a side road. He heard Myra's car leaving the Marsupial and he ducked into a narrow passageway that ran between two apartment blocks. His breath was quickly deserting him, so he gave up running and, instead, loped crabwise through the dark with his bag slung over his shoulder. The distempered orange sky reflecting the city lights lit his way.

After a few hundred yards, he came out on a walkway that in turn became a bridge over a freeway. As he stooped to get his breath, he saw, in the canyon below him, the orange sports car heading west. When it had passed, Guy sprinted over the bridge. He was just refilling his lungs, leaning against a eucalyptus tree at the bottom of a hill, when he realized he'd left his bag back on the other side of the bridge.

Fuck!

Guy was halfway back across the bridge when he saw the orange car returning, heading east this time. There was no other traffic about. Guy flung himself down and waited. The car hissed along thirty feet below him, but as soon as Guy raised his head to check his situation—as though Myra was likely to slam on her brakes in the middle of a freeway, shimmy up a firemen's ladder, and force herself on him—he saw by the retreating taillights that this wasn't the sports car but a police vehicle. Had Myra already passed?

The bag was waiting at the edge of the bridge, as if hoping to hitch a ride. When Guy crossed the bridge for the third and final time, the police car passed below him going west. Guy gripped the bag and maintained a straight course. He decided that he wouldn't think about what had just happened until he was ready to do so. As his breath came back, he began chewing his gum again.

Soon he was climbing the hill. His pace had slackened, but he still peered cagily out from behind the trees that stood on each street corner. After a few discreet streets of wealthy bungalows, he came to a park. He walked up into it for a while, until the incline of the hill began to peter out. Sitting down beneath the stone outline of a sphinx, he looked out across the city.

The lights of the city seemed to cover everything. The sky was clear now, but there were still far more lights below than there were stars above. Guy smelled eucalyptus on the breeze that was cooling his sweaty skin. Dark areas in the endless fields of lights—they must be the water, thought Guy. He was still panting. The sound of his own breath came into his ears like that of another animal. From the bag, he pulled out the wine and drank. He was hot, and slipped off his jacket. In the pocket, where earlier there had been nothing to smoke, he found a packet containing three cigarettes. Menthol, but cigarettes nonetheless. He retrieved the wrapper from his pocket and took the chewing gum from his dry mouth. Then he carefully replaced the gum in the wrapper and stuffed the little package into his trouser pocket. The Party of One was under way. He lit up, swallowed more wine, and stared at the myriad lights. His upstairs and downstairs minds were merging for the evening. The tension was ebbing away . . .

Guy stood up and dropped the dying cigarette end into the damp grass. He trod it flat and then replaced the cork in the bottle, and placed the bottle in the bag. There was no moon, but tufts of dirty orange cloud hid some of the stars. Guy found himself tramping along a pathway lit by art deco lamps, their glass heads mimicking flames, through an undulating wood. It was as if the surface of the sea had frozen and then trees had begun to grow on it. Then someone had come along and planted the lamps.

The ribbon of pathway and lamps wound on as far as Guy could see. It rose and fell, seeming to lead neither up nor down. The sound of traffic had fallen away, and Guy became aware of the hooting, shrieking, rustling, and scratching noises that filled the night air outside the city. He followed the wavy path with his bag in his right hand and his jacket draped over his left shoulder. His silhouette moved from lamp to lamp like a cartoon figure.

Philosophy was ventilating his mind, which felt all the better for not being walled in by anything but his own skull. Maybe, thought Guy, maybe Harry was right about the demon: perhaps it was Myra Kwok, who had assumed the shape of Merry Kakouli. He had been so sure that it was Merry with him. She had acted, sounded and *tasted* like Merry. Right up until they were in the car. He had never been intimate with Myra Kwok. But then there she was! What was that all about? Perhaps Guy had overreacted a little, but Myra had definitely got in there under false pretences.

He wondered, therefore: could Merry Kakouli and Myra Kwok possibly be one and the same person? They both had the same initials—wasn't that bit of a coincidence? For that matter, had he ever seen them both together in the same room at the same time?

Yes, Guy had, earlier in the evening. In the big room with the kangaroo. Kangaroo? Yes, the room with the kangaroo. They had all been in there: Merry and Myra Kwok and Lord Anchovy and that boy Byron . . . Byron Boy? Boy Byron? Byron Bay? No, it wasn't Byron Bay, it was . . . Byron Bulstrode? Who was that? No, that was Ralph Bulstrode, who had hung himself naked in the cloisters at school. Why did that always make Guy think of salad? Did they even have salad at school in those days, or was it just cabbage? No, it wasn't Byron . . . that poor gray boy at the end of a rope, hanging there like a bell. That was Ralph, surely.

The lamps went by.

Merry and Myra were similar, but one of their similarities was that they were different. Merry was taller, and she had a cute nose. She had wide eyes: not wide apart, just wide. Myra had . . . Guy had always avoided looking at Myra. He had no idea what kind of nose she had. She deflected his gaze as if the Real her was standing three feet to one side of the Physical her. Like Due North as opposed to Magnetic North. Perhaps that was why Easy Chapman always looked to one side of you when he talked to you: he'd grown up surrounded by people like Myra Kwok. But was she a demon?

Guy considered their voices, the way the two women talked. Merry sounded like a foghorn with most of the lower-midrange frequencies taken out of it. You couldn't miss a word she said, even if you couldn't always make it out. On the other hand, Myra hardly seemed to open her mouth: her words appeared like subtitles at the base of your vision. Again, that seemed like something a demon would conjure up.

Guy's feet were taking him somewhere. He unexpectedly left the wavy path of lamps and turned down some steps that he hadn't been aware of until a second before. Here there were no lamps, but the sky was clear and swarming with stars. He was descending a gentle path that was flanked with what looked, in outline, like cypress trees. The air was becoming more humid. Guy heard the needle whine of a mosquito and felt it land on the rim of his right ear. He stopped to put down his bag and jacket. Then he flicked his ear and clapped his hands together beside it, hoping to kill the insect. But the whining sound grew stronger, and Guy realized that it was coming from somewhere near the bottom of the steps.

As he craned his hearing through the blood-warm air, Guy realized that he was listening to the drone of pipes, not a mosquito. It wasn't a bagpipe sound; it was more like the reedy skirl of an oboe, but Guy's ear detected a sustained note underpinning it. The music was modal and backward-sounding. The notes would swell and end abruptly. Guy pictured the music as a graph, lightning blue, writing itself on the air as the pitch rose and fell.

As the path approached the source of the sound, it became more labyrinthine, often doubling back on itself. A scent of jasmine caressed Guy's nostrils and tickled the back of his throat. The steps that he walked on gave way to plain ground. The pipes held their circular pattern in the aromatic air; the music reminded Guy of something that Lord Anchovy played during the soundchecks. Guy would have removed his T-shirt but for the mosquitoes. He was getting thirsty for real water. The path felt spongy, almost fleshy, to his feet. The cypress trees loomed against the stars.

Had that really been Myra Kwok? A feeling of doubt spread

through Guy as the air and the music grew close around him. If only he had looked more closely, might he have seen that it was Merry after all? It had seemed like Merry in the beginning. He had been tired and very unsober: so had he been mistaken? Indeed, wasn't that Merry's car? As for what happened in the car: that had been chilling, but maybe Merry had acted like Myra just to freak him out. If she was capable of hiding in his wardrobe, she was certainly capable of posing as Myra Kwok.

In which case, she had succeeded. Now Guy began to torture himself with visions of himself and Merry arriving at her apartment, stripping off their clothes, and enjoying each other. Guy had to stop and light a cigarette to chase these visions away.

Then, without warning, the path came out at the edge of a small lake. Guy gasped. A sliver of bone yellow moon hung low over the water and was reflected in its unruffled surface. The lake was circular, maybe twenty yards across, with a stone rim running all the way around it.

On the right-hand edge, a statue of a naked man stood about twelve feet tall. It peered down into the unfathomable darkness (of course, thought Guy, for all he knew, the water was only six inches deep) as if it were contemplating jumping in. The statue was lit from below by green and white lights that shone up from the stone pedestal on which it stood. The lights enhanced the delicate sinews of the stone youth. Guy could see where its paunch would be if the time ever came when the statue could grow it.

Directly across the lake, Guy discovered the source of the music. In a wooden coffee stall, bathed in red and purple light, a life-sized mechanical piper mimed to the sound, its fingers lifting and descending one by one like sausages onto the instrument. This was a Middle Eastern horn, something between a crumhorn and a sha-hanai. The piper's head swiveled from side to side. It seemed to be made of papier-mâché—or glass fiber, possibly—and crowned with a fez. Its shiny surface reflected the red and purple lights that played on it. The eyes were demurely lowered, and the head rotated in an arc that was narrow enough for the mouthpiece always to remain connected with the mouth. The music was indeed a tape playing backward, Guy realized; the mechanical piper raised and lowered his horn as if baiting the cool, self-absorbed statue across the lake.

Guy noticed a small round table in front of him by the lake's edge. On it was a glass carafe, like the one that had held the roses from Merry. There was a small slatted wooden chair poised by the table, so Guy sat down in it. He took the carafe between forefinger and thumb and squinted at the statue through it. The carafe was full of a clear liquid. Guy sniffed at the neck of the delicate vessel—it smelled of nothing. Must be water, thought Guy.

A wineglass with a fluted stem and a bulbous head also stood on the table. Guy filled it from the carafe. He raised it to his lips and drained it at once; the water was cold and delicious. As he drank, the music died away to nothing. The piper's horn came to rest level with the horizon, pointing at the statue opposite. The piper seemed to be waiting for a coin to be pushed into a slot in its back. Guy fished the wine bottle out of his bag and replenished his glass.

His attention turned to the statue. It stood ominously above the dark lake. Its spoiled mouth and downcast eyes were fixed, not on the surface of the water, but on something beneath it. It radiated a powerful lack of interest in everything around it, so that Guy, who was only half its height, felt in no way overlooked. The statue was mirrored to perfection in the lake. Guy lit his last cigarette and blew smoke toward the white figure. There was one word carved in Roman capitals on the plinth below it. Guy could guess what it spelled:

NARCISSVS

He rose from his seat and edged along the rim of the lake to confirm it. He paused as soon as he was in reading distance. Narcissus, indeed: his namesake! The young man who fell in love with his own reflection in a pool and drowned when he tried to embrace it.

Guy raised his glass to the statue, which continued to gaze down at itself in a morose, pouting trance. How could you fall for anyone as self-centered as that? Guy wondered, showing a healthy misunderstanding of his own appeal. But he proposed a toast anyway.

"You and me, boy."

He stood by the lakeside, aping the statue with one hand on his hip, his right knee pushed rakishly forward. Instead of a fig leaf, Narcissus had a miniature elephant's head over his crotch, from which the trunk dangled like an uncurling phallus. As Guy watched, the trunk seemed to shift slightly.

Guy felt sleepy. He was about to throw his cigarette butt into the pool but, thinking better of it, returned to sit at the table. He noticed that the glass he had but lately drained had been filled again. Feeling thirsty, he drank it down. It did taste like water. The air was close and fetid, as if a bubble of decay were about to burst. It had a savor both putrid and appetizing, but he couldn't tell whether it was animal or vegetable. Only that it was unwashed.

There was a mechanical vibration around the pool. Ripples spread from the edge of the water and collided in the middle. On the surface, the image of Narcissus was disturbed. Guy could feel gears shifting beneath the lake and its environs. He heard a grinding sound and looked up to see that the statue was itself an automaton. Its twin red eyes flickered on like lasers in its head, which turned stiffly on its stone shoulders to train its gaze on Guy. Down below, the elephant's trunk elevated itself into an elegant crane shape.

"Boy howdy," thought Guy.

Fascinated though he was, Guy knew that his own reserves were almost drained. The red light in him was about to be extinguished. It had been a long night and now it was over for him. He picked up the carafe, but it slipped out of his hand and shattered on the ground. The breaking glass echoed around the lakeside and was gone. For a brief moment, the horn player in the fez reactivated, but the sound died away after a couple of bars. The statue of Narcissus trained its pinpoint gaze back across the lake to the artificial musician: then its eyes, too, went out.

Guy put his hands together on his faithful bag and then lowered his head onto it. It had been a great gig. Tomorrow he would enjoy it all in retrospect. They mostly were great gigs. It was a great band. He must tell the guys how well they played, mustn't take them for . . . for whatever. Byron Hunter! That was the guy's name. He was a good . . . something or other. And Merry Kakouli was a great woman . . . unless, of course, she was Myra Kwok. There had been something in the water he just drank. Guy looked up at his namesake, halted midway through his auto-erotic paces. Hope he doesn't pollute the lake, he thought. Hope he doesn't . . .

• • •

It seemed as though only a few moments had passed, but now it was bitterly cold. Guy woke as though from an anesthetic to find his head practically frozen to the bag. His ears were pink and tender. He opened his eyes to see snowflakes twirling down above him, white against the blue of dawn. To his side, the iced-over lake was dusted with snow. The coffee booth was closed and draped with a tarpaulin, which was rapidly whitening as the flakes poured from the sky. Guy raised his head and saw that the statue had lost its own head in the night: a patina of snow now lodged between its shoulders. Pathetically, it had both hands clutched together over its groin, as if to protect the genitals from whatever had happened to the head. Of which there was no sign.

Guy stood up and unzipped his bag. Where his head had lain, there was still a grain of warmth. A fried dryness inflamed the center of his skull. He was stiff from cold sleep. Inside the bag, beneath his already-moldering stage gear and a couple of CDs given to him by Dickie Bollo, was a polo-necked sweater. It was neither warm nor dry, but it would be one more layer between Guy and the weather. He pulled it over his snow-peppered dark green locks and then pushed his arms through it. He brushed the snow off his jacket, which had hung all night on the back of the chair, and put that on, too. The sleeves were stiff with frost. The wine bottle had survived the night on the table, and Guy scooped it up and laid it in his bag without wiping the snow off it.

His feet had chilled in their sweaty socks, and Guy had to stamp back and forth by the lake to get some warm blood into them.

He picked up the bag and followed the shoreline, giving the statue a wide berth. He didn't notice the dusting of snow on its buttocks and calves. Twenty yards or so beyond the lake, Guy came to a red-brick garden wall with fig trees pinned along it. This had escaped his attention the night before. A few gray leaves remained curling from the fig branches. Set in the wall was a pale green door, newly painted. Guy pushed this open and walked through. When he had gone a dozen paces, he returned and closed it but didn't bother with a last look at the lakeside scene.

The sky was whitening. A flock of crows swarmed against it like a giant fingerprint. Ahead of Guy was an open field. The furrows were all emphasized by the snow, which continued to drift down over the dark outline of Guy and the bag as they proceeded around the edge of the field. But when he climbed over the stile at the end and passed the coppice of oak trees with their browning leaves, the snow became sleet. He heard a pheasant honk like a rusty car horn from the coppice. Ahead of him lay another field, and beyond that, the gray Chateau roosted in its nest of chestnut trees.

Guy was exhausted. He was following an inner map that required no conscious thought, much as he had been doing at the end of the previous evening. This was not the dawning of a new day; it was merely an interval. As soon as he came to rest, he would sleep profoundly. He had only to get home. As his empty mind switched to automatic pilot, he lost all recollection of the night before, save that he had dozed off for a minute. That, and a feeling of regret. In an inexplicable way, Guy felt that he had lost something, or missed some opportunity. An old friend had called, perhaps, and he had missed the visit? But he was too tired to let this feeling overwhelm him.

He made his way around the field, brushing against the brambles that still carried the last sagging blackberries of autumn. The sleet gave way to drizzle and then to nothing. Guy felt the embers of warmth in him fanned by the effort of walking and the milder sky. His blood was really circulating now, thawing him properly. Sex was something he hadn't troubled himself with for years; his appetite had gone when Janine did. But this morning, as the blood traveled around his lanky frame, it triggered a steady pulse in his loins. Could this be connected with his sense of loss? In his dreams, maybe: but Guy was no longer asleep.

Now he was reaching the edge of the field. His bag seemed to skip along by his side, eager to be home. There was no way he was going to undress when he got in. Even the boots could stay on; it was cold enough.

His left hand had been fumbling for some while with a small object in his trouser pocket. As he came to the gate, Guy stopped, put down his bag, and pulled his hand out of his warm pocket. Between his forefinger and thumb was a mangled blob of green paper and gray gum. Guy put it underneath his nose, sniffing it in with the sharp morning air. It smelled of mint, faintly. Guy sniffed again. There was another aroma, weakly underpinning the mint. Maybe it was just his own fingers. Guy made to throw the object away, yet, without thinking, he replaced it in his trouser pocket.

He tried to unlatch the five-bar gate, but it was stuck. Jean-Yves needed to oil it. Or Moose, perhaps. Moose? What was this name that came from his dreams? He mouthed the word to himself—"Mousse . . . Mousse"—then let it pass from his mind. It was a name that belonged only to his dreams. Guy sighed and dropped his bag over the gate. The birds inside cushioned the bottle from the fall.

Then he climbed over the gate and hoisted up the bag one more time. Now there was only the gravel path that led past the chestnuts to the rear of the house. Then that, too, was gone.

Next came the courtyard full of baling machinery, which Jean-Yves had failed to protect with tarpaulins—the cretin! This weather always brought the rust. What did he do with all that time of his? The man didn't even drink. Then came the scullery door. Guy heaved it open and was home.

White flour, dusty sacks, cabbages, rat droppings—a barrage of musty odors, but they smelled like home to Guy. He dropped the bag and unzipped it; yes, there was the bottle, nestling amid the still-warm bodies of the pheasants. He pulled it out and held it up. The glass was too opaque to see through. He shook it: there was still a drop left for breakfast. Well, it would be lunch effectively by the time he was up and about. Le Compte d'Anchoie would not be returning till dusk, which would still give Guy and Jean-Yves the whole afternoon to tidy up.

Carefully, Guy placed the bottle on the flagstones. Then he placed himself next to it on an old Hessian sack. Outside, doves cooed and clucked in the cot on the wall. Before he could even pull another sack over himself, Guy was asleep. What a night—and what dreams, what dreams!

• • •

Merry Kakouli sat in the Aladdin Coffee Shop. She, too, was beat. In the absence of Guy, and against her better judgment, she had gone back to the Unagi with Byron Hunter and Dickie Bollo, where they had drunk beers and talked about records for the rest of the night. Now she felt mildly annoyed with her self; she had specifically gone out to see Guy, not to sup the crumbs from the egos of musicians as they wound down and started repeating themselves.

A morning edition of the *Sun Times* lay in her lap. Noticing this, Merry put on her glasses. In the entertainment section was Eileen Fanshawe's review of last night's show. Below a photograph of Cher dressed as a World War Two fighter pilot was one of Guy Kincaid onstage at the Marsupial. That was quick! Fanshawe had hedged her bets on Frame by Frame, but she thought it was the best Narcissus show since they had played at the Prawn Factory on their first visit. Merry had been at that show, too.

Rather puzzlingly, the review was attributed to someone named "Ben Grasslet," although Eileen Fanshawe was credited at the top of the page. That's writers for you, thought Merry—always overcomplicating shit.

She let her focus dissolve from the paper and allowed it to settle on the wall opposite her table. What was that picture doing there, of an old European castle, a gray castle in an avenue of spindly trees? Everything else in here, down to the fez worn by the waitress, was Middle Eastern. When you looked closely, so many things didn't fit, she thought—as though life were an article written in a hurry by someone who hadn't bothered to do their research properly.

And Guy . . . that was a bummer. Even Myra Kwok, who had maps of the rock gods, and tracked their movements twenty-four hours a day, even Myra Kwok had said that she hadn't seen Guy for hours. Of course, she could have been lying, but Myra probably didn't have the imagination to lie. When Merry had opened the door of Byron's room on her way out, Myra had been standing right there.

"You know," she said when Merry asked if she'd seen Guy, "I, like, totally spaced on him—wasn't he with you?"

Now, in the coffee shop, she was dimly aware of Karl Blight, the guitarist, having an argument with a Scottish guy in the corner.

"Alright, JJ, I take your point, but Moose is gonna tell you the same thing. You can hear it from me or you can hear it from him."

"Karl, man, tha's no what I' m talkin' about. The rest of youse is flyin' home, right? But it's a week's work, aye, a week's work tae drop that bus in Fucksville, Tennessee, and get back tae start wi' the Ventricles in Chicago . . ."

Merry fiddled with her black beads and stared ruefully down into the dregs of her third cup of coffee. It wasn't like Guy to flake out like that.

Or was it? She had, after all, only met him five times before, and always in much the same circumstances. She glanced down at the paper that still lay open in her lap. There was the photo of Narcissus—a.k.a. Guy Kincaid—waving his top hat and grinning. The stage lighting sharpened his bone structure and made him look ageless. He existed. He was in the public arena like Henry Kissinger or Marlon Brando. But the Guy she knew was a bit smelly and felt like a skinny horse. Kissinger and Brando were names and photographs: you would never run into them, and if you did, they would probably be odorless.

Maybe Merry just didn't want to think of Guy as a flake. She'd been sure of his interest last night, sure they'd wind up together. But, she must have been mistaken. As the Aladdin began to fill up for breakfast, Merry was even tantalized by a phantom memory of having collected Guy in her car after the show: but she obviously hadn't. That must have been the last time he was in town. Wishful thinking? Get outta here! She could have checked his hotel room—Narcissus were staying at the Langoustine, right next door, and some of the entourage were even having breakfast here in the Alladin—but it wasn't her style to pursue people. Even the roses and the wardrobe . . . She'd taken the trouble to surprise him, but he'd seemed a bit sniffy. A trifle blasé. Perhaps these days he had a girl in every wardrobe.

• • •

Jean-Yves picked up the bottle. It was almost empty, although the cork had been replaced. He sniffed it, then grimaced as if to an unseen audience and put the bottle back down onto the flagstones, where it clinked again. Still bent down, he unzipped a corner of the hold-all, stuck two fingers inside, paddled them briefly back and forth, then retracted them. He looked satisfied, as though he had completed a cursory medical examination. Jean-Yves rose to his feet, then crept from the scullery back to his bicycle. The man on the sacking continued to snore as the first drops of rain pattered on the atrium roof.

East Side Story

WAYNE KRAMER

BECKER OPENS his eyes slowly. It's much too bright and much too hot to lie in bed for another minute. August in Detroit is like that. His head is splitting.

"Goddamn! Do they have to make so much fucking noise collecting the garbage?"

Of course it's a rhetorical question, but with a hangover like this a hummingbird sounds like a Sherman tank.

"Maybe I'm sensitive. Nothing a cold beer, shot of vodka, and a couple of codeine won't fix. How did last night end anyway?"

Some blurry images of a bar and a late-night coke binge with his roommates flash across his brain.

"Hmmm . . . it'll come to me sooner or later." He wonders how it is that he ends up in these situations over and over again. But the past is passed and today is here and he has a bunch of shit to do. Being a semi-employed misunderstood criminal genius is a lot of work.

Becker begins his day like this a lot. Rolling out at the crack of noon and on the hustle. Head pounding. Things have been spiraling down lately as his dope consumption increases. Funny thing about heroin, it always takes a little more to get that same snap. Funny like a peculiar kind of funny, not "ha-ha" funny.

His room is in what could be called a commune, but flophouse might be more accurate. It's an old wood-frame four-bedroom house his mother owns and has let him take over to live in. He rents out the other bedrooms to a revolving cast of musicians, roadies, and go-go girls. Some nights there's a pretty good party going on.

Not much use in taking a shower as the drain is stopped up and, besides, lately he finds the touch of water on his skin repellent.

Picking out a pair of slacks that don't have too much wear and tear on them, and a semi-clean brown shirt, he heads downstairs to see what's new in this hipster hotel he calls home.

The place is deserted. No one else is there. Good. No one around to interrupt his morning contemplation.

A quick look around the living room reveals two Sony portable color TVs atop a big burned-out console model. Note to self: Call that friend of Frankie's on the East Side and see is he interested in the Sonys. Could be a quick two hundred and fifty bucks. That would keep him right for a few days.

Becker strolls into the kitchen and is greeted by a sinkful of dirty dishes, food wrappers and beer bottles covering every available inch of counter space. A look in the fridge reveals an empty Chinese food container, some ketchup and A-1 steak sauce. A half-full two liter bottle of Sprite will have to do for breakfast. He searches his pockets for the two Tylenol 3s he saved for now and washes them down with the flat soda.

From the porch he sees that the neighbors have not picked up their morning newspaper. A quick dart across the yard, snatch the paper up, and back in the house. He's combing through the seeds and stems to gather up a joint, "a pinner," he likes to call them. He sits down with the joint and the paper and tries to relax while he figures out his day.

In thirty minutes or so the codeine starts to kick in and Becker slowly feels his way back into consciousness. Some days feel good. A good scam, sell a pistol, a color TV, some pills.

"Just trying to get over," he sang to himself. As if he's the hustler in Curtis Mayfield's song "The Pusherman."

"Trying to get over . . ."

Some days the cash rolls in and copping his dope and getting high are a satisfying way to pass the time. Really. It's kinda fun in a romantic way. Other days are not so much fun and he really hates the idea of getting dope sick, the burning freeze of narcotic withdrawal. He *really* hates it and, at this point in his life, he's really *not* going to get sick, no matter what. So hustle he must.

The car horn honking outside snaps him out of his reefer haze and he lumbers down the broad concrete porch that runs the width of the house. Danny Taylor sits waiting in his piece-o'-shit '67 Chevy station wagon.

"What d' ya know, bro? Keeping your head up?" yells Danny through the driver's-side window. "Take a ride with me. I gotta take care of some business and then we'll hook up. Do something right for our heads."

"Lemme lock the house up."

In a couple of minutes they're rolling down Plymouth Road toward downtown Detroit.

"Where we headed?" asks Becker.

"Down to the Dumont Gallery. I got these oriental rugs to sell. The dude is cool. I sell him shit all the time," Danny says with true hustler confidence.

"Where they from?"

"Found them laying in the street, bro, laying right in the street," says Danny.

"It's amazing how folks will leave valuable items unattended," Becker snorts like a wise-ass.

They both laugh and Becker slithers into the opportunity in front of him. "Look, Danny, you're a well-known thief. Let me go to work with you on a couple of these jobs. I can handle it, and I need the money."

"Where in the hell did you hear that?" Danny replies. "My how people talk. I'm hurt, wounded." Danny's tough-guy, fast-talking persona adds to Becker's admiration for his companion's slippery ways.

Becker decided not to repeat himself. Danny caught the message the first time loud and clear.

"Yea, that's true what folks say. I am a thief, but I've been thinking about it and I've come to the conclusion that I'm not a scoundrel, not really. In fact, maybe the next time I'm robbing somebody's place, I'll take some toys and then give them to homeless kids for Christmas or something like that." Danny looks over to Becker, his right arm on the steering wheel, "You know what I mean, bro?"

Becker finds it hard to keep from busting out laughing at the absurdity of this but he has his own agenda.

"So, what do you think, Danny?" repeats Becker. "We rob and then we split the profits, OK?" He's laid it out.

"Yea, well, sure, but after expenses come off the top right?" asks Danny.

"Expenses? What fucking expenses? We drive out to the suburbs, break into some houses, steal their TVs 'n' shit, and sell the stuff. What expenses?"

"Gas, upkeep on my car, there's a lot of expenses: maintenance, insurance . . ."

"Whatever." Becker will say anything right now in order to get let into the game.

After a short drive downtown listening to WCHB-FM, "The Soul of Detroit," they pull into an alley off Jefferson Ave. The sign out front reads: The Dumont Gallery—Home of Fine Furnishings since 1923. Danny backs the wagon up to the loading dock. "Stay right here," he says. "I'll go set it up."

He reappears at the loading dock door and they haul the rugs up onto the dock and into the elevator. Danny motions Becker to follow him and all three hundred pounds of Aristotle Dumont into the elevator and up to a fifth floor open loft space. The big man smells like garlic and is constantly sucking his teeth.

As they step out into the room, Becker whispers to Danny, "This dude needs to learn to floss."

They're met by Dumont's helpers, an older black man he calls "Slim" and his partner, "Junior." Have they done this before? Becker, Danny, and Aristotle step out of the way to let the two workers carry the rugs into the loft. They unroll the rugs at Aristotle's feet. Real beauties, deeply rich in color and design. Very plush and obviously very expensive.

Aristotle steps onto the rugs to have a closer look at them. His foot kicks something hard and transparent. The object slides across the rug and into the concrete floor, making a noise. Everybody turns and looks. Glass castors. A half-dozen of them still in place on the rug where, surely, they had been placed to protect the rug from furniture legs. Seems the rugs had been rolled up in a hurry.

A smirk from Slim and Junior didn't help. Slim's obviously a see-no-evil type; loyal from the first day Aristotle told him he'd pay him in cash to keep the "referrals" coming. That was going on eighteen years ago this Christmas and Slim hasn't missed a rent payment yet.

"Where did you say these rugs came from, boys?" Dumont asked.

"They were my grandma's. She died," Danny quips without missing a beat. The big man grunts and looks over the top rug, then motions for the next to be unrolled, and then the next. He made some calculations on a notepad and showed Danny the figure.

"Nine hundred," Danny whispers to Becker as he walks to the back office to square up with the big man.

Becker takes the stairs down to the first floor and wanders around the main showroom while waiting for Danny to come out of the office with the cash.

"Hmmm . . ." He checked the price of an oriental rug on display. "Twenty-two hundred bucks! Let's see. We just sold him three rugs at nine, three hundred each. He can resell them for . . ." The math was too much for Becker to face.

Danny bounds out of the back with an envelope in hand, trying to stuff it inconspicuously into his leather jacket's inside pocket. "Let's went. My motherfucking man Tyrone on the East Side has the bomb. Had a taste this morning and it's the shiznit."

The Chevy groans as they peel out of the alley and head to Tyrone's.

The next two months are spent working the upper-class neighborhoods in northern Detroit and on the West Side. Sometimes two or three nights a week they work it, depending on the cash flow.

Becker finds there's a lot of fringe benefits besides the cash that's paid for stolen guns, antiques, jewelry and TVs. Like, rich people keep frozen steaks in their freezers and expensive booze on their shelves. He even stopped once to fix a sandwich and have a cold beer in the middle of a job. Another time he used the bathroom to have a bowel movement, too. Robbing kind of upsets the stomach.

Danny soon proves to be a less than honorable thief. There's always something funny about the split. Things never seem to be worth what they should be. Becker's share always turns out to be less than he figured on. Not to mention the nightly drama of actually breaking into a home not knowing if the owner is waiting on the other side of the door with a shotgun. Or the dreaded fear of him coming home as they're loading his precious belongings out the back door.

But then, there's always the trip to Tyrone's and the relief that it brings.

Becker reminds himself that residential burglary is a high-stress occupation and if it weren't for the guaranteed promise of withdrawal that came with running out of cash, he probably wouldn't keep doing it.

Oh well, I gotta go meet Tyrone.

By the end of September, Becker starts to phase out the residential burglary business and into a nice steady pill connection he found in Livonia. He has a young roadie type who sells the pills in the park to stoners and he really doesn't have to do much work except cop the pills and collect the profit. And go see Tyrone.

It seems like another fine fall day in the Motor City. The summer heat is gone and the leaves on the trees are starting to turn beautiful shades of gold, red, and brown. There's something nice about living in this part of the country. Becker makes a mental note to buy a camera and shoot some photos. He always thought of himself as an artist.

"Yea, I'll get that camera on the way back from Tyrone's."

He knows better, but gives himself over to these fantasies a lot. As he steps up to his porch he glances down the street and notices a marked Detroit police cruiser rolling up the block. His eye is drawn to another behind that one then another one, then a couple more.

"Damn, someone's in the shit," he says to himself.

As the phalanx rolls up to him, he sees an unmarked car with what looks to be two detectives in the front seat. There's a sheepish-looking Danny in the backseat giving him the peace sign with hand-cuffs on. Another marked cruiser is bringing up the rear. They stop in front of his house. Cops are rushing toward Becker from all directions with guns drawn. A skinny detective is holding a piece of paper saying, "Are you Becker Edwards? I have a warrant for your arrest."

Becker's head is spinning as the detective keeps talking. "We know who you are, Becker. We don't think you're a bad guy. We only want to recover the property. Can we look in your house, Becker?"

Becker is totally flummoxed, everything is happening in slow motion. He can't think straight. "What the hell is happening? I'm being busted. What's Danny doing with the cops? What do they mean, 'recover the property'?"

"Yea. Sure. No! I mean, I'm not sure," he says, trying to remember if there's anything hot in the house.

"Work with us, Becker. We don't want to see a nice young guy like you go to prison."

Becker finally gets his mind clear and says flat out, "No, you can't go into my house." But it's too late now. Cops are carrying antique candelabras and color TVs straight from his living room to the trunk of their cruisers.

The cops have all they need on him and tell him so.

"Cop humor is a fascinating thing," Becker thinks to himself as he's mirandized and handcuffed.

He overhears an older detective brag to a young uniformed officer. "Now watch a professional investigator handle this case, kid," the older detective says.

"Fightin' crime," Becker says to himself under his breath.

After a brief interview at the stationhouse, Becker, in mock code-of-the-underworld fashion says only, "I'm sorry, I need to speak to my attorney." He's led to the lockup. Coming down the row of holding cells, Becker comes face to face with Danny in the cell across the range.

Danny looks at Becker with his best, "Oh my God! They got you, too!" look and starts to plead with the officer.

"Hey officer, can we go to the hospital now? I'm sick, real sick," he whines. "The detective promised he would take me to the hospital. Whaddaya think?"

The uniformed cop ignores him as he turns the key to lock Becker into his cell.

Danny directs his attention to Becker. "I didn't tell on you, bro. Really, I mean it. I know stealing was not really your thing so I took your roommate Gary with me on a few jobs."

"The cops were waiting for me and Gary when we came out of this old mansion in Berkley. We scored these great antique music boxes and there they were, spotlights, guns, bullhorns blaring," Danny yells at the top of his lungs now. He's crying and coughing the cough of dope sickness. "So the kid spilled his guts about everything and everyone. Man, I'm so sick. You believe me, don't you bro?"

Becker knows this has to be an Academy Award-winning performance, but he is compelled to answer back. He just can't control himself.

"Little Gary? Why the fuck did you do that, Danny? Gary's just a kid. He was cracking on me about joining us and I told him I didn't know what he was talking about. I knew he was flaky. You can't trust him."

"But he kept bugging me," Danny explodes. "He said he'd been watching us and needed the money. He said he did B&Es before."

Becker knew this was probably true, but he also knew none of it mattered. What was done was done and now the chips were gonna fall where they may. No more of those movie tough-guy fantasies about revenge and the criminal code. We're all a bunch of liars, hustlers, and junkies and we're getting what's coming to us. It's inevitable.

Becker sits down on the concrete bunk and waits for his own sickness to come on.

In the morning the judge is completely bored as he sets Becker's bond at twenty thousand dollars and ships him off to the Oakland County Jail.

O.C.J. Not his first visit here. Funny, but Becker really doesn't mind the County that much. The hard-guy pecking order can be a little annoying to endure, but they seem to keep it to themselves. After a few days his dope sickness passes and he actually doesn't mind the routine. It's a simple life and it's temporary.

It was two weeks of hanging with the homies, living on bologna sandwiches and listening to endless stories of crime and bravado before Becker's court-appointed attorney gets his bond dropped to personal recognizance.

Becker goes home, if you can call it that. His house is stripped clean of anything of value. The TV, stereo, electric guitar, and leather jackets are all gone. Angie, one of the roommates, a nice big-breasted go-go girl, says she thought his "friends" had come to collect his stuff for safekeeping while he was away.

That's nice. Safekeeping.

"Angie, can you spot me fifty bucks to get back on my feet?"

"Sure, sweetie."

Off to the East Side to meet Tyrone.

A Eulogy of Sorts

from DOGHOUSE ROSES

STEVE EARLE

HAROLD MILLS died last night, alone in his seventy-five-dollar-a-week room at the Drake Motel, and I'm probably the only motherfucker on Murfreesboro Road that misses him. Hell, I'm the only one that knows he's gone. I just happened to pull up in front of his room just as the EMTs carried him out with a sheet over his face. I had intended to use his place to shoot a couple of pills and cook up an eightball of coke I'd just bought, but I guess I was a little late. On another night he probably would've laid there in the bathroom floor for days until the smell alerted the manager. As it was, the couple next door was interrupted in mid-stroke by a loud bang, which as it turns out, was Harold's big ol' head smashing into the tub as he went down. The crushing blow to the back of his skull alone could've easily killed him, but I'd be willing to bet Harold was dead before he hit the floor.

Junkies die down here everyday. Most of the time nobody notices but other junkies, and they perceive only a brief interruption in the food chain. Nobody down here is really capable of mourning in the normal sense. Oh, we suffer the inconvenience of losing a connection, or a safe place to get high, or scam a new set of works, or maybe crash for a few hours, but that's about it. As unnerving as life in this neighborhood may appear to the uninitiated, we, the wraiths who inhabit its darkest corners, find each day even more numbingly boring than the one before. But that's cool. We hate surprises. Any break in the tedium makes us uncomfortable. You see, all junkies travel in ever-narrowing concentric circles until the day they find themselves running for their lives with one foot nailed to the floor, as the Beast bears down on them. Grieving over another dope fiend finally, inevitably running out of luck is simply a luxury nobody on the pike can afford, because all of us know that but for the grace of God . . . well hell, there ain't no grace down here. It's just a matter of time.

So when Harold's time finally ran out, I wasn't there. Not that I could've saved him anyway. Harold didn't die of an overdose per se. He most likely had a heart attack that was coming anyway, no matter what the coroner's report says. Ol' Harold merely expedited matters with one long, final pull on his meticulously maintained glass pipe. The pathologist on duty probably never looked any further than the painfully thin, needle-scarred arms before rendering Harold's entire life down into homogeneous statistic.

When I first met Harold Mills he was a real player, the biggest Dilaudid dealer in South Nashville. Dilaudid is the trade name for hydromorphone hydrochloride, a pharmaceutical narcotic typically prescribed only for terminal cancer patients. Nashville, located smack-dab in the middle of the most landlocked state in the Union, has never enjoyed a particularly dependable heroin supply. Then in the seventies two brothers by the name of Mitchell from North Nashville's middle-class black community began to bring in Dilaudid, misappropriated from drug wholesalers in Detroit and Chicago. A good supply of relatively cheap, strong heroin kept the price of the pharmaceutical drug low in major northern cities, but in Nashville the tiny yellow pills brought between forty and sixty dollars each on the street. In a market where an addict could spend nearly that amount on a bag of highly diluted, low-grade Mexican heroin, "D's" were an instant hit. Harold, being related by marriage to the Mitchell brothers, was in on the ground floor.

The first time I saw Harold he was slow draggin' Lewis Street in a sky blue 1978 Cadillac sedan DeVille. He was dressed sharp in an old-school, super-fly, dope-dealer-with-a-heart-of-gold-and-a-tooth-to-match kind of way. He draped his slight six feet two frame across the entire front seat as he leaned across to eye me suspiciously through the passenger-side window. I was being introduced by a coke dealer named Clarence Brown. Make no mistake, South Nashville was *about* cocaine. By this point in my career as a lifelong dope fiend, I had taken to smoking several hundred dollars' worth of rock cocaine everyday. Coke was a drug I had never particularly cared for. By this time, however, my tolerance for opiates had become prohibitively high, so I took up the practice of "speedballing," that is, adding a little coke to my frequent injections of Dilaudid for a little extra kick. Exposing myself to cocaine opened the door for freebasing—mixing the deadly white powder with baking soda and cooking it down into smokable "rock" (or "crack" on the East Coast). One hit, crossing my eyes to watch the opaque white smoke billow and expand in the glass bowl and then disappear like a flirtatious genie as I removed my finger from the carburetor and inhaled deeply, and it was a wrap.

No drug had ever grabbed a hold of me as quickly or held me as tightly in its grip. I became conditioned, like some space race laboratory monkey, to keep pushing that button, too far gone to give a fuck whether I received a banana-flavored pellet or a 110-volt shock. I'd drive to the projects in East Nashville every morning and buy a pill or two, and as soon as I was straight, head down south to Clarence's to smoke. By five or six in the evening, I was getting sick again, so I'd slide back across the river to cop a few more pills, then back across the bridge and—what did the directions say? Repeat if necessary? Well, it was always necessary as a motherfucker. Clarence had only recently given up on trying to "help" me kick Dilaudid. He saw my other habit as a waste of money I could be spending on coke, his personal drug of choice. When he finally got it through his head that

that wasn't ever going to happen, he introduced me to Harold Mills, the only hustler down South who regularly traded in Dilaudid. To Clarence this was simply a means to an end: keeping one of his best customers on his side of the river where he could keep his eye on me. Harold listened while Clarence vouched for me, looked me over one more time and then there was a sudden flash as he bared that big, gold front tooth in an ear-to-ear grin. "I heard about you. I heard you spend money."

He sold me a pill (at ten dollars less than I was paying for singles out East) and scribbled his beeper number on the dismembered top of a hard pack of Kools, promising to cut me a better price when I bought more than one.

I began seeing Harold twice a day, every day, once in the morning and once just before dark. I knew better than to try and procure a whole day's supply of dope in one run. That kind of thinking only led to a bigger, even more expensive habit, and God knows I was capable of shooting as many pills at one sitting as I could buy. At first I'd just beep him and he'd meet me somewhere up on the pike. After he got to know me better, he gave me his home number, and I would call to make sure he was home before driving to his apartment in the projects where he lived with his wife Keena and their three boys, ages three, four, and seven. I'd do my wake-up shot right there in Harold's bathroom, and then we'd sit around for a while, watching Oprah and shit on the tube and play with the kids. Harold taught his oldest boy, Courtney, to call me Uncle Honky. He thought that shit was hilarious. In the course of those long dreamlike mornings I found out what I should have already known: Harold sold Dilaudid because Harold shot Dilaudid—lots of it. I was a good customer. Most addicts couldn't afford the kind of volume I bought everyday. Harold was beginning to get "hot" on the street, which meant that every time he rolled out on the pike he ran the risk of being stopped on sight by one of the neighborhood patrol cars or even the vice squad. My business meant Harold could support his own habit without taking so many chances.

We quickly fell into a daily routine of getting high together and solving all the world's problems by the time Keena got home from work. We'd engage in long animated discussions on politics (Harold styled himself a Democrat but he reckoned I was probably a communist), music (we both loved the old Memphis stuff but I knew more about hip-hop than he did, which he didn't care for anymore than "that hillbilly shit ya'll listen to"), even the existence of God (I didn't believe in God, Harold did; he just figured that God didn't mess with junkies one way or the other). Never mind that neither of us had voted, bought records, nor been to church in years. Oh yeah, we knew we were addicts. We even referred to ourselves and each other as "junkies." "You a junkie motherfucker." "Well you a junkie, too." Then we'd laugh our asses off. But God forbid a "citizen" ever calls us that. "Junkie" is a funny word like that. It's kind of like "nigger," I guess.

Harold, like me, was a fairly nontypical dope fiend. He still had a family, a place to live, a car, food to eat. Our common ground, it turned out, was that most of the catastrophes that punctuate "those other" junkies' lives hadn't happened to us . . . yet. You see, we were both smart enough to know our luck couldn't hold out forever, so I guess we had just decided to stick together for a while and wait for the other shoe to drop.

And drop it did. I finally lost touch with Harold a few years later when I migrated to Los Angeles in my never-ending quest for stronger and cheaper dope. In the shape I was in, it didn't take me very long to wear out my welcome in L.A., and eighteen months later, I was back on the pike asking around about Harold Mills. Some folks said he was locked up. "Naw, he out East living with his auntie." There was even a story that Harold had AIDS.

When I finally tracked him down, I immediately saw where the

AIDS rumors came from. Harold was always thin, but now he was nothing but sallow, translucent skin, stretched taut over brittle bone. He was wearing a faded, threadbare sweat suit and run-over Kmart sneakers, shit he would never have been caught dead in a year earlier. His usually close-cropped hair was grown out and matted from months of scuffling up and down the pike, hustling for hits. When he recognized me, he smiled, revealing that even the trademark gold tooth was missing along with several of his own. But it wasn't AIDS that had taken Harold down through there. It was rock cocaine.

In all the time I'd known him, I'd never seen Harold Mills touch crack. I use to have to listen to him and Clarence, the coke man, one in one ear and one in the other, like those little guys that sit on a motherfucker's shoulders in the cartoons, one admonishing him to do the right thing and one leading him astray. Only, in my cartoon they were both devils. Harold used to say, "That shit was sent by Satan his self to finish the dope fiends off." Now the Beast had him by the balls, and he knew it. On top of that, his heart had been weakened by endocarditis, an infection of the bloodstream common to IV drug users. Harold's deterioration in such a short amount of time was especially unsettling to me. After all, he was the same kind of junkie I was. Seeing him like this was too much like looking in a mirror and being confronted by my own death staring back at me through hollow sockets. But, after an awkward instant we exchanged dope fiend pleasantries, drove across the river, bought six pills at an exorbitant price, and retired to the Drake Motel to get high. I rented Harold a room there, where he lived for the rest of his life . . . about seven months.

Harold Mills will be buried tomorrow in Greenwood Cemetery in South Nashville. The funeral will cost his grandmother, who raised him, her entire life savings. She rarely saw Harold the last few years of his life. He'd appear on her doorstep now and then, and she'd give him twenty dollars and watch helplessly as he faded back into the night. Then she'd cry herself to sleep. She never once turned him away, even though she knew what he did with the money. She was just thankful that he loved her enough not to come around too often.

Harold will go down to Greenwood decked out in a new blue suit and surrounded by his wife, his kids, and several relatives, mostly older, who haven't seen him since he was a child. Good, solid, working folks who never knew the hustler, the junkie, the derelict. Never saw him sitting in the backseat of a police car in handcuffs or led into a courtroom dressed in a blaze-orange jumpsuit. Never had to watch in horror as he mined scar tissue-armored veins for the nearly always empty promise of blood commingling with morphine, just before he pushed it back into his ravaged body and waited for the rush that never quite lived up to that sacred memory of his very first hit.

Most of these folks never knew that Harold Mills. They'll come to Greenwood to bury a husband, a daddy, a grandson, and a little boy who used to ride his tricycle through their flower beds.

I won't be there to say goodbye. None of us, the creatures that knew Harold out here on the pike, will be there, because funerals, they say, are for the living . . . and we're already dead. We're just waiting our turn.

See you when I get there, brother.

Mom Comes Home

Ann Magnuson

MICK JAGGER is making a solo rock video. He's covering B. J. Thomas's "Hooked on a Feeling" and he's hooked on this retro Seventies concept that features him dancing in front of these giant blowup photos of Andy Warhol's silk-screened flowers. The half dozen or so set pieces have one large stylized daisy painted on each panel and Mick runs back and forth between them, then stops and sings in front of each one, gyrating and gesticulating wildly in his signature histrionic bantam rooster fashion.

I think he looks perfectly ridiculous. Not only is he too old to be doing this Seventies retro thing, but this Seventies retro thing is too old to be doing.

My mother, looking young, shapely, and snappy in one of her favorite early-Seventies paisley sheaths, is producing the video from her headquarters—the wood-paneled kitchen in the house I grew up in.

"What am I going to do?" Mom asks (somewhat despondently) as she drops some fresh corn on the cob into the boiling pot usually reserved for spaghetti. "He doesn't want to change it!"

Mom has brought me on board as director but, frankly, I am at a loss.

"How can we save this thing?" I wonder. "He's so stuck on this goofy dancing and this el-lamo retro bullshit that we'll never get this project near anything even remotely hip!"

"I know," Mom sighs as she starts beating the hamburger meat into patties. "Remember we had this same problem with Bowie during his Trent Reznor period?"

"Yeah," I remember, "and he wouldn't believe that those flash cuts were tired even then."

"Goodness, yes," Mom says, placing one of the patties into the sizzling frying pan. "Even I thought that Damien Hirst animal carcass imagery was overdone."

"Just don't overdo those hamburgers" I cautioned. "You know the crew likes their meat practically raw."

But I couldn't think about the crew right now. I had to figure out how to save our production company's reputation. In this business, one bad video can ruin you.

I surveyed my surroundings. Adjacent to my mother's kitchen was a gigantic prop warehouse that extended from the door near the refrigerator, past the neighbor's house, and all the way to the end of our tree-lined street. It looked a lot like Charles Foster Kane's storage unit that appears at the end of *Citizen Kane,* except this warehouse was kinda empty.

But I think I see something way down at the end in the far corner. Yeah, there's some twinkling lights down there. So I go to investigate, walking toward the far west end, where I come upon a fantastical swimming pool. It was about the size of your average Beverly Hills backyard pool except this one looked like something Captain Nemo owned; something out of H. G. Wells; a Victorian sci-fi vision of Atlantean splendor.

There was no water in the pool so I could really get a good look at the dazzling gold and lapis lazuli tilework that glistened under the gas-lit chandelier hanging overhead. Inlaid every few feet along the perimeter of the pool were large crystal balls made from amethyst and amber, each one hanging over the side of the pool and held in place with ornate ironwork fashioned to resemble an eagle's talon.

It really was a sight to behold.

Now we're cooking with gas, I think to myself.

I take a closer look around and notice the entire west wing of the building is decorated in Belle Epoch splendor. There is a massive mahogany staircase to the left of the pool that looks like a Gaudi-style waterfall. Florid Art Noveau wallpaper covers the walls and all the windows are Cubist designed stained glass. Tiffany lamps with dragonfly motifs sit on the various Federalist end tables and beautiful antique Persian rugs cover the floor.

"Okay, okay" I think out loud. "This could work."

I look around me and begin to envision Mick as a Miss Hav-isham/Norma Desmond-type character. Stuck in the past but des-perate to keep up with the present. And a combination of the two attitudes creates a strange new kind of future.

Now hear me out.

Okay, like Captain Nemo, Mick is a victim of his own genius, a victim of his own creation, a delusional one-time innovator who has retreated into the safety of his myth, trapped in his own—if you will—legendary iconography and, like that old grandfather clock standing in the foyer over there, he needs to be wound up daily by a dutiful butler/bodyguard named Max in order to keep up with the times; because he, Mick, has been forgotten, discarded by a youth-obsessed world gone digital.

Yes! We'll film the whole thing in letterbox! Emphasize the epic proportions of the story! Maybe even throw in some subtitles.

Oh my God, do you think we could get Anita Pallenberg to play Mrs. Bates, the withered, apple-doll corpse sitting in her old rocker in the basement, eerily lit by a bare light bulb swinging back and forth in the stale, fetid air?

Wait a minute, is Anita Pallenberg still alive?

It doesn't matter. This could work. It really could work!

I go running back to the kitchen, where Mom is hard at work cranking the salad spinner.

"Mom! Mom! Did you hear what I said?" I ask, out of breath from my run.

"Of course I did, honey" she said, not so much annoyed as bemused. "I can hear everything."

"Well, don't you think it will work? And we'll let Mick keep his dumb-ass daisy dancing. That'll just emphasize his *madness*."

I emit a maniacal cackle just to emphasize my point, then run up the circular stairway outside the kitchen, up to the third floor landing and look out the big picture window. There is a gorgeous orange-pink sun setting over a magnificent mountain range in the distance.

"Wow!" I gasp, then call to my mom. "HEY MOM! What mountain range is this? The Alps? Or is it the Himalayas?"

I don't wait for her response.

"They're great!" I yell. "Let's work them in!"

I pull out my viewfinder from my backpack and start setting up shots, talking to myself but assuming the whole time that my mother can hear.

"The mighty mountain that stands in mockery against time. That's our wrinkled star."

"Oooooh," I gasp, looking at the beautiful desert that stretches out to the south of the mountain range. "We'll do a David Lean thing here—a 360° pan that rests on Mick's haggard face as he looks out toward the horizon at . . . at . . . ."

"At what?" my mom asks from the bottom of the stairs, beating some eggs for her famous coconut cake, the one she always made for my birthday. "*What* is he staring at?"

I'm momentarily lost in a reverie.

"It doesn't matter" I reply, quickly snapping out of it. "The audience will project their own dreams and/or disappointments onto him—just like they did onto Garbo's face at the end of *Queen Christina*."

"And what about a girl?" Mom asks knowingly as she walks back to the kitchen, emphasizing the word 'girl' with just a soupçon of acidity. "There has to be a *girl*."

"Yeah, you're right," I say with a pout. "The record company will insist on it. And she has to be in her twenties, right? Maybe even a teenager? She has to be at least forty years younger than Mick . . ."

Oh brother! This part always makes me sick to my stomach.

"But wait . . . okay, okay,that's all right. Because she's the object of his affection but she's not real . . . she's . . . she's . . .

" . . . she's a *ghost!* An apparition! A sexy ghost babe wandering the hallways of his lonely mansion and he can never quite capture her . . . except . . . except . . .

". . . except as a *painting* that hangs over the huge marble fireplace. That's it! It is her! The beautiful Angelique. She of heaving bosom and blond bouffant. A Carnaby Street bird cast in a Hammer vampire film! Barely out of her teens. His first love! The one that left him all those years ago for Bryan Ferry and broke his heart.

He's *hooked* on her! Get it? "Hooked on a Feeling"? And he's doomed for eternity to try to recapture that feeling! To recapture his lost youth by dancing himself into a orgiastic stupor in front of these tired seventies Warholian flower silkscreens—because THEY represent the time in his life when he was young! Young, sexy, and happy! The time in his life when he had HER!"

"It's got a little *Veritgo* thing going on too doesn't it?" Mom asks as she pours the cake batter into a greased bundt pan. "We can cast a young Kim Novak"

"Oh yeah! Yeah!" I say. "Maybe we'll have her ghost entice him to the top of the belltower, where she falls, then, since she's a ghost, disappears, leaving him alone to gaze at the mountains in the west, where the sun sets—and that would be him, of course, the Setting Sun. '*Sunrise/ Sunset/ Swiftly go the years,*' you know."

Mom hums a few bars.

The sun sinks behind the snow-covered peaks and it grows dark. Mick lights a candelabra and then turns from the turret atop his haunted house and begins to make his way down the stairs until his— and our—attention is drawn to a small door at the end of the hallway.

The door is rattling on its hinges. Someone—or some*thing*—is back there.

He removes a key from his nineteenth-century waistcoat pocket and, with sweat building on his stiff upper puffy lip, he puts the key into the keyhole and turns it.

He opens the door.

Then THRUSTS the candelabra inside. The light scares the creature! The creature jumps back!

Mick taunts the creature with the flames. The creature is taunted. He taunts! It is taunted! He taunts! It is taunted! He taunts! Taunted! Taunts! Taunted!

TAUNTS!

And as the flames flare into the lens we quickly dolly in to see . . . what? The object of his sadistic taunting.

What is it? Why it is . . . it is . . .

Her!

HER!

The object of his longing.

But she is not the same. True, it is the woman in the painting or, rather, was. For now she is . . . oh sweet mother of God . . . she is . . . old! *Old*, I tell you!

She is . . . gasp . . . his age!!!!

Her straggly hair and wrinkly face cannot disguise it. She is a middle-aged woman and is no longer of any use!

And there can be no denying it—she *was* his wife! She was the first Mrs. Rochester! She did not die in the fire but was imprisoned—imprisoned to spare her master the shame.

And why is he ashamed of her? *Because.*

Because she is "old"!

Old! Old! Old!

OLD!!!

"Brilliant! Cut! Print! It's a Wrap!" sez Mom.

• • •

"I have to admit," my mother says to me as everyone packs up the equipment and loads it into the trucks, "I wasn't so sure about this one. But you pulled it off, as always."

"I had to," I tell her, feigning coolness. "It's Mick Jagger after all—he's an icon. We have to protect our icons."

"I never really followed him," Mom tells me as she politely hands each crew member their well-earned twelve-pack of Bud. "To tell you the truth," she continues. "I was more aware of the Beatles. You know, I always blamed them and Timothy Leary for getting you and Bobby into drugs."

Everyone has a big laugh over that remark, including me—even though I've heard it over and over again.

Before you know it, the crew is gone, well on their way home, and it's just me and Mom left to clean up the mess.

"You relax, Mom" I say taking the dirty cake pan out of her hands. "I'll do the dishes tonight! It's the least I can do for the best producer a director ever had."

Mom kicks off her heels and lays down on our plush, burnt-sienna sofa while I load up the dishwasher.

It was a good feeling. I never did the dishes growing up. I mean, dads and kids don't do dishes, right? That's something moms do.

I think that's one of the big reasons my mother had an affair with that creep from the local community theater and then left my dad, my brother and me. She hated being a housewife. She hated doing dishes.

But after her second husband moved her out to California, where he promptly dumped her for a younger woman (and convieniently took advantage of the community property laws), my mother eventually stopped crying into her Valium-stained pillow, rolled up her sleeves, got back to work, and now she's one of the top rock-video producers in the world.

"Hey, Ann," Mom says from her perch. "What do you say we get out of this video thing and launch our own Internet start-up? I still think there's money to be made on the World Wide Web."

"Sounds good," I say, handing her a cup of Celestial Seasonings Vanilla Honeynut tea. "Except the bubble pretty much burst on that baby. Unless you're into porn."

"Well, then maybe we get into something completely different?" she says while blowing on the hot hippie brew. "You always liked animals. Remember when you wanted to become a veterinarian?"

I did and smiled at the prospect of working with kittens and cute little bunny rabbits. Except I wondered if I could handle medical school—especially after a life in show business.

"It's never too late," Mom nudged. "And I could go back to journalism. Or run a bookstore. Or, better yet, a food bank! Something with a real future in it."

"Yeah," I mused. "Besides, this racket is a young person's game."

"And let's face it," she continued, getting up off the sofa and making her way to the stairs, "this rock video stuff is so 'over.' I don't know about you, but I don't wanna be stuck without a pot to piss in when I'm older, pardon my French."

"Ditto," I tell her, switching off the lights and following her to the top of the stairs, where I kissed her goodnight, then disappeared into my psychedelic black-lit bedroom—happy that Mom had finally come back home.

The Cracks

WILLIE NILE

If THESE walls could talk . . . indeed . . . The cracks are screaming at me.

Sitting in the front room of my downtown New York apartment, I'm staring at the weatherbeaten, timeworn, fresco wannabes of this old Italian-immigrant building, contemplating whether or not to plaster them over before the painting is to begin.

It began as a few whispers, building to a scream . . . The cracks are screaming at me.

Shut-up, I say unto you. Leave me in piece. The piano beckons. But no, they will not listen. They will speak. They will be heard.

Then rave on ye mighty oracles, rave on. I will but listen . . .

One crack tells the story of Theresa, the small, beautiful, elderly widow and all her years living in the rear apartment on the third floor, where the hot Sicilian sun swirled in the stairwell on the day her only brother passed away.

"Tony die! Tony die!" She whispered softly in her broken English, in disbelief. "Tony die! Tony die!" The words reeling from her pale, white, eggshell face. It was all she could say, handkerchief in hand, damp from red-eyes weeping. Sweet Theresa. Gentle Theresa.

Another crack spoke of Dream Eagle, the jolly playwright on the sixth floor, singing opera in his nightgown on Sunday mornings, and the howls of laughter coming through the walls in the wee hours as he watched his beloved Charlie Chaplin.

There was the story of Angry Anne, better know as "Moleface," screaming bloody murder at her fragile eighty-two-year-old mother again and again, for no apparent reason, like a needle in the eye on the third Sunday in Lent. The piercing shrieks could be heard a lifetime away. The poor old woman spoke no English whatsoever and never left the building for as far back as anyone could remember. You could see her face from the street from time to time as she peered out the window at the goings-on below. No one ever knew what became of her or why fate cast that sad shadow of a daughter over her. If the meek do inherit the earth at some point, I reckon her to be a plantation owner in Sardinia with Angry Anne's leather heart laid out as a welcome mat.

They spoke of Rickie, the young grandson of the super, and that Fourth of July years ago when twenty-five dollars' worth of firecrackers accidentally went off while still in his pants pocket. He ended up in St. Vincent's for two weeks with burns on his crotch and up and down his ten-year-old legs.

He survived worse than that in the years to come and wound up marrying the village beauty and having two children of his own, who, hopefully, will have better luck on Independence Day than he did.

One crevice told the tale of Dora's husband Leo, Rickie's father, just back from a year in California doing time for dealing drugs, being gunned down on Minetta Lane by men in a passing car while on his way back from the gym. He was buried in the tears and the killers were never caught.

The cracks open and close at will . . . their will. When a friend stops by there are no screams, no stories, only silence. They sit and wait, these storyvores. Sometimes they're all yelling, or speaking, or murmuring at once and it's utter chaos. Other times it's your basic lone wolf doing his version of Hamlet in the pre-dawn hours.

I do enjoy history though. The building is old, the walls dry, the paint peeled, but the building is alive, living and breathing, like some immigrant ghost ship docked for a pale century on the broken streets of New York. So, indeed, the piano beckons, but the stories intrigue me. I would hear more . . . so, carry on, my dear plaster-challenged carnivores, carry on. You are all mouth. I am all ears.

Poe had his telltale heart. I have my tattletale wall. Bleed on . . .

Raoul, apparently a man fond of his Jack Daniels and Lucky Strikes, used to sit outside the front door on the stoop, like some wayward, red-faced bodyguard for the Wizard of Oz, regaling all who would enter with a smile and a yarn, bobbing up and down for an apple of conversation. He was especially talkative with the young females passing by, most not appreciating the attention and certainly not biting.

One extremely hot and humid August night, he fell drunk down the cement cellar stairs, ending upside down with his feet sticking straight up in the air against the wall and his head pressed against the bottom stair, like some black swan who couldn't swim diving for pearls in the wrong ocean. There he lay till his body was found two days later, heat wave still intact.

It took another day for the overly busy crew from the city morgue to come for his remains, as the ninety-five-plus-degree fervor was taking its toll on the children of paradise. The perfume of grief filled the air with flies.

His daughter, Mercy, accused the Arab neighbors on the block, with whom he didn't get along, of pushing him down the stairs and murdering him.

He was buried in a brown coffin, with a bottle of Jack in his suit-coat pocket and a carton of Lucky Strikes by his side.

One of the cracks began shouting about Carlos, the scar-faced boyfriend of Louise. After being spurned and thrown out for physical abuse, he followed one of the residents into the building and set a mattress in the hall on fire to voice his displeasure. The fire was quickly put out and his voice wasn't loud enough to get him back into the good graces of Louise. He moved to the East Side and was never seen again.

A gentler fissure gushed about the young child Serena and the two baby ducks she received from her father one spring. At barely two years of age she would carry them, one under each arm, walking around the small apartment playing with them constantly. She would put them in her drawers and play hide-and-seek and dress them up for a night on the town. She would take them for a swim, putting them first in the kitchen sink and then, as they grew larger, in the bathtub, where they would swim to their heart's content.

As summer approached, their constant quacking in the middle of the night threatened to disturb the neighbors and they were taken to a convent in the country for safekeeping.

On hearing this, one of the larger cracks told the fissure to shut the hell up as the story was making him gag. He then proceeded to tell the story of Third Floor Anthony and the Bones of Arizona.

It appears there was a family that lived directly across the street on the third floor. The family consisted of Anthony, a six-foot-four-inch, two-hundred-and-fifty-pound hairy mob enforcer; his wife Emily; and their three young boys, all under the age of five.

In the summertime, Anthony would lean on the windowsill in his wife-beater T-shirt, muscles bulging—although he wasn't one to beat on his wife—and watch the world go by. He didn't seem to have a job with normal hours, as he was around for weeks at a time. Every now and then he would go away for a week or two to who knows where and come back and sit by the window, beer in hand and usually one or two of the boys on his lap. You would often see Emily pulling the boys in a wagon on their way to the park to play in the sand. Occasionally, Anthony would join them. They seemed to be a close and relatively happy family.

One winter, Anthony disappeared. Apparently, he was arrested by the police for some nefarious offense and decided that being an informant was better than spending ten years of his life in some hapless penitentiary. Besides, the boys were growing and needed a father to help guide them through the iron and steel of the big town.

After a couple of months and still no Anthony, a large black Lincoln Continental could be seen regularly parked outside the front entrance to the building across the street.

It appears that Tommy "No Socks" Carrera, the head of the local crime family, had taken a personal interest in helping out Emily and the boys and would visit her a few days every week bringing money, food, and gifts for the family. He would encourage her to ask Anthony to come back home, assuring her that no harm would come to him or the family if he came back and that all was forgiven and there would be a job for him when he returned.

This went on for a couple of months until one day the visits suddenly stopped. No more big black Lincoln parked cozily by the curb. No more money. No more food. No more gifts for the boys. No more sweet talk. No more nothin'. Just silence.

A few more months passed.

One day, the word came down that they found Anthony's bones in a desert out in Arizona.

Emily and the boys moved away shortly after that, never to return.

So I look up at these walls and these cracks and I wonder. Should I patch them up? Should I plaster them over before painting?

No. I don't think so. Can't do it. They speak to me. I love the stories they tell. Sometimes they just get a little loud, is all.

As it is, the piano beckons. I feel a story coming on.

Again the Last Plane Out?

MICK FARREN

EVEN THOUGH gasoline now cost more than gin, an olive-drab GM truck, belching smoke and spattered with mud the color of dried blood, pulled up in the main square, outside the bar, and government soldiers in World War II vintage helmets, and ragged, sweat-stained fatigues, with the striped shoulder flashes of the Simba Division, began unloading a few thousand red, green, and yellow loyalist flags. The flags were small; just paper triangles on little sticks, the kind handed out to crowds at political rallies. They were left in an untidy heap of open disorganized boxes, stacked against the plinth of the repeatedly torn-down and then replaced statue of the city's supposed founder. As the truck pulled away to the grinding of a dying gearbox, a twitchy teenager with an M16 was left behind to guard the boxes of flags. For some reason, the occurrence outraged Lenny the Addict. "Now what dumb shit is this? Who the fuck needs flags? Jesus fucking Christ, half these fuckers don't have food or paper to wipe their asses on. Flags?"

Although the question wasn't actually rhetorical, Lenny the Addict didn't require an answer from anyone in particular, just a general rustle of agreement. While heat vied with humidity as the primary cause of discomfort, he could hardly expect any more animated response from the patrons of the bar at the Hotel Europa. It was hot and the civil war dragged on. Lenny the Addict was drinking the local squeezings, probably the cheapest high in the hemisphere, husbanding his hard currency against the remote possibility that a connection yet to be named might sell him some morphine syrettes. And when Lenny the Addict was drunk—as opposed to stoned—he talked. Yancey Slide, who was drinking maybe the only good scotch in the city, slowly turned his head, looked at the flags, but declined to speak, making instead a sound somewhere between a sigh and a snarl. Yancey Slide was nearing his threshold of intolerance for Lenny the Addict. Okay, so at least one token junkie was needed at the downfall of any city, but Slide couldn't understand why Lenny the Addict needed to keep him company. It wasn't as though Slide could be of any use to the skinny degenerate.

Dolores Haze was a different matter. Slide could always tolerate her company. In fact he would privately admit to an indolent and largely theoretical attraction to the woman with the complex and highly unconventional history. She looked over the top of her heart-shaped sunglasses at the arrival of the flags, and then shook her hair loose, creating a sudden waft of unexpected perfume. This week her hair was the most plausible ash-blond that could be created with the limited resources still available in the Capital. Her lipgloss and nail polish were a dark magenta. Slide respected Dolores Haze for two things. She was always able to discover cosmetics no matter how dangerously unstable the political situation, and she was always plugged in close to the heart of the prevailing rumor mill. "The latest is that the Simbas flip-flopped and now the functional majority of the Army is supporting Zidika, whatever that might mean. I guess our new President is planning a rally for the CNN cameras."

Jorges the one-eyed bartender, who looked a lot like a heavyweight, eyepatched version of the Artist Formerly Known as Prince, maintained his own totalitarian regime in the bar at the Hotel Europa, deciding absolutely how many drinks a customer could expect in return for a Rolex or a DVD player. He kept the TV above the bar tuned to CNN. Right now, a report on the situation in the capital was being aired. A tall, attractive, and, above all, dry reporter stood in front of the burned-out Opera House. The setting was familiar, but the story the woman with the hair-job and the radio mike was telling to the world bore no resemblance to the situation as observed from what was left of the bar at the Hotel Europa.

Dolores Haze pinned the credibility problem in an instant. "That CNN bitch isn't sweating. Three minutes of exposure to any reality in this place, and you're sweating like James Brown. I'll bet good money she hasn't ventured out of The Internationale since she got here."

Dolores Haze was absolutely right. Only The International—or, as it was more usually called, the Time-Warner embassy—had air-conditioning. Everyone else in the Capital was sweating. The Hotel Europa's AC had been dead for almost a month. It had gone when the building had been hit at ground level by a stray anti-tank rocket during the street fighting when Tetsu's people had pulled back to the North Side. The air had gone, as had an entire plate glass wall. That they had intermittent electricity to run the TV and watch the disinformation hit the airwaves amounted to a blessed mercy.

"I mean, shit, if you aren't in the relevant temperature, how the fuck are you going to understand anything?"

As Dolores Haze castigated the TV a bead of sweat ran down the inside of her right breast. Slide was drunk enough to happily watch the beads of sweat run down the insides of Dolores's breasts for hours. Her white cotton dress was damp and all but transparent. Slide didn't know what to call the garment. He wasn't hep to couture. To him it looked retro-Fifties, like the one Marilyn Monroe wore in *The Seven Year Itch*. That movie had been set in a New York City heat wave. Marilyn kept her panties in the icebox. High-August New York heat waves were bad, but nothing compared to the capital in a change of regime. Slide allowed himself a short whiskey fantasy. He and Haze were making slick night-heat liquid love on the creaking bed in his room in the middle of an air raid. Desperation and damp sheets sheltered them as explosions blossomed, sirens howled, searchlights probed, and a blast three blocks away blew the windows in, covering the two of them with diamonds of broken glass. It was unlikely to become reality, however. Not that Haze wouldn't be willing, but air raids appeared to be a thing of the past. All factions in the civil war had run out of even antique warplanes, and the Hueys-for-hire had mostly headed back to the coast, knowing they were unlikely to be paid.

Lenny the Addict interrupted Slide's voyeur daydream by deciding Dolores's information was a personal affront. "So the Army's backing Zidika? So what? What the fuck does the Army mean anymore? Like, where's that junkie Major who was selling me my fucking morphine now that I need him? Most of the bastards who haven't deserted are in business on their own account, and some, as I'm learning to my cost, can't even take care of business. All that signifies now is the AK Youth."

In this Lenny the Addict was absolutely right. Everyone knew all real power lay with the kids, the AK Youth, as they'd come to be called. The fifteen-, fourteen-, twelve-, and eleven-year-olds; the killer children with the Dracula eyes, and time-release caps of a complicated descendant of Ritalin actually sown into the flesh of their arms. These were the children who detonated Semtex like it was firecrackers at Chinese New Year, and took pride in hacking off the right arms of surrendering prisoners with machetes and pangas. Here in the Capital the very stars in their courses were directed by whether the baby machine gunners had been smoking heroin, or crack, geezing meth, or drinking needle beer, and the rattle of their AK47s was so unpredictably random, Slide figured it gave both unpredictable and random a bad name. Their reasons for slaughter exceeded all in the murky and unfathomable night, and when they drummed and chanted, rhyming in contemporary dementia, they raised dark and ancient gods to sanctify and offer sacrifice. They even seemed to speak their own unique language, as though traditional tongues were too slow and too linear for their wired and tweaking speech centers. All childhood had been lost in the ebb and flow of apparently perpetual warfare. Some of the mercs claimed that on an especially holy day, the AK machine gun kids would eat their own wounded.

"And anyway, who the fuck is going to show up for a rally to honor Zidika, for chrissakes? Who'd dare?"

Yancey Slide didn't move. He didn't want to move. He'd been at the bar so long, he had his hunch curled to perfection; elbows precisely rooted, and boot heels hooked into the crosspieces of the barstool just so. He preyed over his Johnny Black on the rocks like a ravaged vulture guarding his own. He had two more bottles stashed in an arrangement with Jorges. That was Yancey Slide for you. Where everyone else was drinking Tikky, or squeezings, or some leftover abomination from the dusty bottom of the bar like bubblegum schnapps, Slide had Johnny Black. Some claimed he wasn't human except in the most superficial sense, and if it was said to his face, he never argued.

"They'll Shanghai a bunch of kids from out of the bush. Hand them the fucking flags, and tell them if they cheer loud enough, and wave the flags hard enough, they'll feed them, and, if they don't, they'll kill them."

"And then?"

"What then? For those kids there is no then. The concept of now is pretty fucking precarious. They'll turn them loose in the city with the rest of the scavengers, or they'll draft them, or they kill them anyway."

"All for a thirty-second image on CNN?"

"The one things there's plenty of is people. You could say the bottom's dropped clean out of the people market."

Dolores Haze made the flat and obvious statement. "It's time we took the hint and got out of here."

Lenny the Addict nodded. "We gotta get out of here."

Although Lenny declaring he had to get out of there sounded straightforward enough, it was more complex than many might imagine. Lenny the Addict not only had to get out, but he had to choose a destination with some care. If he wound up in some Hottentot burg where he couldn't cop opiates within the first few hours of leaving the airport, he would find himself sick, shaking and royally fucked. Slide knew this had to be one of the primary churning conundrums in Lenny's loop-the-loop, squirrel cage brain. Not that Slide could spare much sympathy for Lenny the Addict. Now that even the Russians were narco-players, dope was pretty much every place that could boast an airport capable of bringing in a 747, and the life of the globe-trotting dope fiend was a hell of a lot easier than it had been a few years earlier.

Lenny turned to face Slide directly. "How long do you think planes will still be coming in and out?"

Yancey Slide shrugged. What the fuck did he know? "Three, four days, maybe a week."

Dolores Haze had been fucking the door gunner of a freelance Huey crew who'd been looking for a doomed romance before pulling out. He'd given her the inside scoop on the state of Patrice Lumumba Memorial Airport. "The e-vac vultures are lining up on the taxiway. Everything from antique DC3s to piece-of-shit Gulfstreams creaking from hundreds of over-the-limit air miles. They've moved everything from cocaine and rock bands to Chinese software pirates. Right now, they'll take anyone at a price. The real trick is getting out there. There's checkpoints and roadblocks all the way, HIV-positive regular Army looking for a shakedown, technicals who finally ran out of gas, AK kids using passing cars for target practice, or laying mines just to see shit blow up. The highway to the airport is decidedly hairy any way you look at it."

Slide gestured to Jorges to pour him another Scotch. All the gin joints in all the third world seemed to be haunted by the same ghosts when the veneer civilization really began to peel. The white mercs had staked out their turf in the far back of the bar, where a boom box was playing death metal. The mercs were mainly Eastern European; Ukrainians and Serbian Chetniks, plus some Libyan-trained Irishmen. The thrill seekers and psycho killers with their Street Sweepers, matched Suomis, and CZ 25s had long been shredded to history. The Soldier of Fortune amateurs with the Death or Glory tattoos never had what it took. They held on to grenades too long, stepped on landmines, were speared by bamboo pongee sticks, painted themselves into impossible tactical corners, or, in some of the more extreme cases, were fragged from this mortal coil by their own comrades.

Slide was surprised Hertz the German had survived so long, and was still one among the slumped figures in camouflage fatigues, scuffed jump boots propped up on tables, trying to drink away the thousand-yard stare. With the mutant Doberman that was always at his side, he was an extremely unpleasant showboat even by Yancey Slide's expansively lax standards. Slide found conversation with the German close to impossible. He had a habit of sexually juvenile non sequiturs. Out of the blue he'd make remarks like "The sound of the cane on taut rubber is singularly distinctive, nicht war?" According to fairly reliable rumor, Hertz had this game he played with his women of simulated necrophilia. First inducing insulin coma and then, as he put it in his thick stormtrooper accent, "bringing the bitch back with a sucrose shot."

Right at this moment Hertz was turning his blonde-beast, Nazi charm on the stranded script girl from the French documentary film crew who had arrived in the capital a week earlier. As parlor ex-Marxists they thought they could shoot footage of the AK Youth, but had been quickly set straight and, luckily for them, without too much loss of life. While they were packing to go, the script girl had engaged in a screaming Gallic fight with the director, and a prolonged pouting sulk had resulted in her losing her ride out, and now she was thrown to the wolves of her own resources and survival skills. From where

Slide sat, she didn't seem to have many of either, except for a passing resemblance to a dark-haired version of the young Brigitte Bardot. Would she get the insulin treatment from the German? Would that be her supposed ticket to comparative safety? Slide wondered if a single cc of the drug remained in all of the city, unless, of course, the German carried his own stash. Slide didn't doubt, even without the drug, Hertz had plenty more unnatural tricks up his abominable khaki sleeve.

The dark-haired Bardot, as she laughed with the German, head to head, lips close to lips, had no clue what she was really getting into, but, in this she was not so unique. What the fuck did any of those assembled imagine they were doing there or really getting into? Some had the excuse they were only doing their job, plying their trade, or following their avowed calling. The mercs would maintain the atrocities just went with the job description. The journalists would likewise deny all accusations of advanced auto-wreck voyeurism, and claim they were simply relaying the story to a concerned world, or recording all for posterity. Lenny the Addict would blame his presence there on some disastrous counter-syncronicity of wrong turns and missed connections because Lenny, a perpetual victim of fate, was never responsible for his actions, and his being in the Capital was at least a huge and hideous misunderstanding, if not an actual conspiracy.

In the area of conspiracy, James Jesus Valentine, the Europa's CIA spook in residence, had more than once copped the tired plea that he was only in the Capital obeying orders, protecting the vital interests of the United States. Slide was at something of a loss to figure how exactly the vitals of the US were being protected by Valentine's current and lopsided conversation with Misty Mona, a bizarre, popeyed, drag-queen homage to the post-Supremes Diana Ross. He couldn't see what concern there might be at Langley, the State Department or the White House with Mona's whacked-out-on-Tikky-and-Benzedrine reflections on the cosmetic advantage of using Lee Press-On

Nails on her toes when wearing open-toed sandals. Valentine was, however, famous throughout the Capital as a master of plausible deniability, and having an answer for everything. If challenged he would coolly respond that he was preparing a report on how the rules of entropy dictated no city could fall without a quorum of drag-queen adventurers in attendance.

Slide had Jorges pour him another shot from his private stash. He hoped the booze would take him past the stage of seeking explanations for what, in truth, completely defied explanation. Back in the Seventies, legend told how a couple of New York cops had found a dead gorilla in the South Bronx. They hadn't even tried to offer reasons or theories, and Slide knew that was ultimately the best way. If he searched for reasons for too long, he would eventually wind up asking himself why he was there in the capital, and that was a question he knew he shouldn't even consider from a distance, let alone approach.

In general terms, Slide figured the material paradoxes were a part of the attraction. All in the Europa Bar were, to one degree or another, vultures picking over the carcass of an imploded nation-state. A Harry Lime romance of uncut diamonds and tainted penicillin. Just before everything ran out, crude economic law dictated a sudden rush of exotic consumer variables would hit the darkest strata of the black market. An abrupt plethora would occur: Cuban cigars; Beluga caviar; A-list celebrity porn; Durban Poison; Napoleon Brandy; primo flake; cut price gold and gems; and lately, in the modern world, deep-frozen body parts, as the elite of the ancien regime freed up their terminally hoarded goodies to pay the freight up the political gravity well. In the Capital this was happening with a vengeance. Word was Zidika himself had personally purchased—from a strange individual who dealt in such things—a pair of genuine of French government colonial-issue guillotines, cherry-perfect down to the tall polished oak-beam frame, the steel blade, and the rubbed brass hardware. Formal public executions, with full and bloody pomp and circumstance, could start anytime, and anyone even tenuously connected with Tetsu and the PRP had an unseen, unwritten, but wholly tangible death warrant hung round their necks and they just hadda, hadda, hadda, get away.

Flesh would also need to be factored into the equation. A byproduct of any local apocalypse was always a hot and cold human buffet fit for the imagination of the Marquis de Sade. In the ad hoc culture of collapse, where torture and murder were merely items in the tool kit of maintaining power, the strangest of the passionately strange were able to indulge whims previously unimagined. Just two nights earlier a human being had run through the square and past the bar, blazing like a gasoline torch, and everyone had assumed it was the work of the lone and secretive Iraqi, late of the Republican Guard, who liked setting fire to women and teenage boys, supposedly fire-cleansing them for Allah or Zoroaster. Slide's best theory, though, was that it really had very little to do with either sex or plunder. When order and structure collapsed, a form of energy was released, and this was really what drew them, and on what they all fed.

On television the sweatless and sanitary CNN reporter was explaining how troops loyal to President Zidika were rapidly restoring order in the major cities. This prompted a former SAS man to mutter "Bollocks" in a thick Scottish accent, but then even he fell silent as all eyes turned away from the TV to the missing window, and the square beyond. Slide groaned inwardly, and swallowed his shot of scotch, as five ominous figures followed their shadows across the threshold and into the bar. Lenny the Addict let out a short fearful breath.

"Oh shit."

One of the new arrivals was a regular army captain in a reasonable clean and complete uniform. Simba division again. He led a hand-cuffed and badly beaten prisoner by a short length of rope tied around his neck. The prisoner's head was covered with a flour sack. Two eyeholes had been cut for the unfortunate to see out; the traditional and accepted mask of the informer. Clearly the hooded one's life was being spared for at least as long as he could be led round the bars and cafés to identify his former colleagues and comrades. The captain and his prisoner, however, were not the primary reason the interior of the Europa had lapsed into such deathly silence, and Jorges had even used his remote stealthily to turn down CNN's audio. The captain and his prisoner had an escort of three young AK kids, the eldest of whom couldn't have been more than twelve. The tallest and most senior, despite the heat, wore a black PI trenchcoat over VC shorts, and a Marilyn Manson T-shirt. His Air Jordans looked practically new, as did the Mac11 held down by his side. The gun seemed to have only recently come out of its Cosmolene. Some motherfucker was shipping in new matériel despite the embargo. His two companions were less sharp in T-shirts and ultra-baggy fatigue pants. One had jump boots and the other was barefoot, although the barefoot one did sport an old A3 flying jacket, and a red bandanna wrapped around his head. Both were armed with battle-scarred but totally serviceable Kalashnikovs.

Taking advantage of the distraction and human silence, a jade-green lizard made its way down the crumbling plaster of the wall behind the bar. As the informer studied the assembled faces, seeking candidates for Zidika's new guillotines, Slide couldn't help but make a move of minor defiance. He took one of Dolores's cigarettes, and lit it with his Zippo, the one with the Jack Daniels logo that had traveled with him over more than half the planet. Doombeam eyes from the black trenchcoat swiveled and focused, but Slide was not about to be stared down by any twelve-year-old, no matter how homicidal. He met them squarely. The youngest began to raise his AK, but the trenchcoated leader made a cool-it gesture, and psycho-speared deep into Slide's eyes, letting the beam carry its message. This was no child. The kid in the black trenchcoat was as old as Attila the Hun. In his world survival itself was a near-insupportable luxury, and all that remained was feral calculation and random death. Look at me, old-timer, then marvel and fear. You are history, and I am the face of the new millennium. I am primal, but you scream. We are here now, in this sorry city, but how long do you think it will be before you see these eyes in Paris, London, or Paterson, New Jersey?

The hooded informer broke the spell by pointing to a frightened individual with pomaded hair and a Little Richard mustache sitting two stools down from Lenny the Addict. He had once been number three in the hierarchy of Tetsu's Office of Public Order, but now he was just a fragment of the past, fit only for speedy disposal. The man froze as he was identified. A fly landed on his left hand, but he didn't appear to notice. As the captain beckoned him to his feet, his bladder gave way, staining the leg of his linen suit, and leaving a moisture trail on the barroom floor as he was led away. Slide let cigarette smoke drift from his nostrils as everyone in the Europa uniformly exhaled. Even the mercs in their paramilitary bravado knew they only lived because the three kids hadn't been in a mood for massacre.

Dolores Haze turned to Slide. "I think it's high time we braved the road to the airport."

"Again the last plane out?"

"You want to stay and see what happens next?"

"It had occurred to me."

"Are you even human, Slide?"

"Are any of us human, my dear Dolores? Aren't we just a pack of twentieth-century ghosts gazing aghast at the inevitable future."

Summer Vacation

Mary Lee Kortes

My MOTHER used to get drunk and take me in the car for long drives. She'd speed along the hilly backroads connecting the small Wisconsin towns that were home to me and my family. I would get in the backseat and try to go to sleep because I didn't want to be awake when I died. I didn't die though. I just buried parts of myself.

No sympathy required. Some things can grow on their own, unattended. Or just wait with their full potential eternally eager to realize itself. That's how I felt for a long time, like I was pregnant with myself.

Early traumas can lead to a great capacity for imagining the best. I was only five when I asked my mother, "When I die will I be born again?" I just couldn't imagine not existing. It seems like I was always looking for God.

There were no black, brown, or Jewish people where I grew up. Just white Christians. So when a new family moved into town from India, I was sure it signaled the arrival of true spiritual guidance, perhaps all for me. Some kind of customized divine intervention.

The grandfather of the family was an extremely tall man and used to walk past our house every day to the two blocks we called downtown. I spent the summer days on the front porch, waiting and watching. Here he comes again. My very own holy man, direct from India! After weeks of studying his slow, steady gait, I gathered the courage to approach him. I longed to ask him what wisdom he'd come to share, what could he tell me about life and its meaning, what was my destiny. I could see from the self-possessed way he moved that he carried this knowledge with him everywhere, light as breath. It just coexisted with him.

I crossed the street to meet up with him. "Hello," I said, in my eleven-year-old voice. He looked into my eyes, smiled a knowing smile, reached his hand gently around my neck, pulled me toward him, and planted a large wet kiss on my lips. I was shocked and deeply uncomfortable but thought it must just be the way of the gods. He kept his arm around my shoulder and turned me around to walk with him. We started down the sidewalk, past the neighbors' houses. His hand gradually, deliberately made its way down my left shoulder to my nipple. That same smile still spread across his face. In my mind, I began to question this man. How holy is he, really? Is this how it's done over there? It just didn't seem right.

So I respectfully said goodbye and sprinted all the way home. A great sense of confusion masked my even greater sense of embarrassment, one that would visit me again and again as I crossed more sidewalks pursuing other outsiders offering strange detours from the path laid clearly inside me.

One summer afternoon my mother had a bridge party on our front porch. She and her girlfriends drank vodka tonics (I think that's what they were) and shuffled their cards. They laughed high, melodic laughs for several hours. It was like a foreign language to me as I entertained myself in the yard, but somewhere in my soul I understood it, even liked it, and knew I would be speaking it one day too. After her friends left, we were there alone, her drunk, me quiet and shaking invisibly. She was angry because she had to drive the twenty-six miles to Sunfield. She was saddled with having to go and open one of my dad's two movie theaters for business that night. The last thing she wanted to do. "I just can't face those people," she said as she was driving us a bit too freely on the empty roads. I grew especially nervous knowing we were approaching my favorite hill. I had always liked to go fast over the top because it made my stomach tickle. "Here comes the hill, Louise! Mom's going to speed up for you." "No, not this time!" I wanted to scream from the backseat. But I had learned not to disagree.

Somehow we made it, but by the time we arrived in this even smaller town, the alcohol had settled in well enough that she got lost. Delusional is more like it. She decided to stop in to see her parents before going to the theater. When we got to their street she turned right instead of left. The right turn took us immediately into the town cemetery. She couldn't find their house anywhere. The warning bells were screaming inside me. "Get out! Get out!" I jumped from the car and tore down the gravel road. I almost made it back to the street but she caught up with me in the car. I'll never forget the sight as I looked over my shoulder and saw that navy blue Buick speeding toward me. It seemed like it must be going a hundred miles an hour inside the cemetery. Another incongruous image for my mental scrap book.

She screamed at me to get back in the car and we drove directly down the street to her parents' house. We both knew they weren't home. They were up at the lake. But she got out nonetheless and went inside. My golden opportunity.

I ran again, but this time I took a path the car couldn't follow—through their backyard and across the backyards of the neighboring houses. These were wide blocks and I knew my mom probably couldn't see me from the street. I finally made it to my father's parents' house. I knew they weren't home either but I tried their door anyway. Like mother like daughter. Then I ran to my aunt Marian's, two blocks away.

I'll never forget the shock on my aunt's and uncle's faces when I burst in, thoroughly terrorized and trying to swallow my tears. They could have filled in the blanks all by themselves, but I told them how Mom was going to come looking for me and I had to hide. I feel like they saved my life that day. She showed up, screaming, "Where's

Louise?" They said they hadn't seen me and sent her staggering away. That was before MADD.

The weather was perfect those next few days. The summer sun was out in style. The smell of fresh-cut grass complemented the taste of my aunt's fresh lemonade. My cousin Sarah was going to day camp and took me along that week. We made sock puppets. Mine was white with a big yellow mouth and black eyes. We had dinner together every night—my aunt and uncle and Sarah and me. Afterward, Sarah and I would go outside and play for a while till my aunt made popcorn at about eight-thirty. It was a perfect life but I was just visiting.

And so this darkly glorious summer vacation had to end. My father came to get me after four days. The ride home was long and still. I was glad when he didn't speed up over the hills. When we got home, I wore my sock puppet to show my mom what I'd made. I went to hug her, hoping she wouldn't be mad at me for running away from her. She was startled by the white thing on my arm, like she thought I'd been hurt. Maybe she thought it was something she'd done but couldn't remember. I'll never know. A year later, the path inside her led her away forever.

No sympathy required. Some things can grow on their own, unattended.

Looked a Lot like Che Guevara

STEVE WYNN

I HAVE had some of my best conversations in parking lots long after clubs have closed and this particular night in Hollywood seemed like it would be no exception. Having strummed my last chords of the evening, watched the headlining band play their last encore, gulped down my last beer, and, as always, been the last person to walk through the club's exit, I found myself in the parking lot with my friend Sindre, who seemed ready to challenge me to be the last man to leave the premises.

No problem there. Sindre and I have had many such late-night bull sessions and the combination of the late hour, the simmering buzz of Hollywood, and the lingering effects of the third Bud Light (hey, they were free) seemed to indicate that we were ready to solve the world's problems, if not our own. We struck the pose of Guys Killing Time in a Parking Lot Late at Night that has been developed through the ages. Hands in pockets, shoulders slightly slouched, kicking imaginary artifacts across the asphalt.

At the far end of the lot a group of kids stood around a Ford Explorer, sipping from plastic cups and falling into various stages of amorous behavior. I think I heard Jay-Z coming from inside their SUV but I'm not always so good at determining songs from the bass line alone. They seemed wrapped up in their own activities, and even though I knew that Hollywood had long since surpassed my new hometown New York City in terms of sleaziness and unpredictability, my finely honed radar didn't pick up on any cause for alarm. At six-foot-four, Sindre was enough of a deterrent for anyone wanting to hassle us, or, even worse, to pick one of us out as an easy mark.

Don't get me wrong. I'm not afraid of much, I enjoy the chance to use guile, rhetoric, and whatever menace I can muster to escape a bad situation. It's just that I hate the idea that anyone would mistake me for an easy mark. It's always bugged me.

Our conversation had turned from Wall Street scandals to the National League East pennant race when she walked over. What was it that Bowie said? Looked a lot like Che Guevara? Yeah, that was it except without the facial hair and beret. And she was twenty. And very much alive.

"Are you guys musicians?"

Oh, here we go. The first sign of mark-making. Facile and obviously pointless conversation based on an obvious observation. I leaned into my guitar case and said 'Yeah.' Nothing else.

She wasn't looking for a dissertation. I waited for the inevitable hustle. What was it? Money? Booze? Didn't matter—I was on guard.

"That's so cool. I would love to be a musician. I'm twenty and I don't know what I want to do with my life. Isn't that terrible? I'm not in school and I don't have a job and I don't even know what I want to do. And I'm twenty. What do you think I should do?"

She really said all this. As my defense and suspicion turned to confusion and curiosity I decided to throw her whatever could pass for wisdom as well as a hopefully graceful exit. "You should read as many books as possible. And travel. And don't worry about a job. You're really young. Plenty of time, don't worry about careers." Expecting gratitude, a hasty retreat, and maybe even boredom at my answer I turned to Sindre and resumed my analysis of the Mets pitching staff.

But she wasn't finished. "And I don't have kids. I'm twenty and I don't have kids. Everybody I know has kids except me. I don't even have a boyfriend."

What did I look like? Ann Landers? Dr. Ruth? The Dalai Lama? "Hey, most people I know are twice your age," I replied, "and don't have kids. Consider it a blessing. You can do anything and go anywhere and then when you're ready you'll have them." Oh man, was I really saying these things? I'd gone from the fear of being an easy mark to the disgusting realization that I was . . . SOUNDING LIKE A GROWN-UP. But she held on to my every word as though no one had ever given her such advice before. This obviously wouldn't end easily, at least without some greater distraction.

That's what came next. A woman came strutting across the parking lot, looking very concerned. She was about as tall as Sindre and her mini-skirt ended at somewhere near my upper torso. Suddenly we were a quartet.

"Do you know if the club is still open? Is there anyone still in there?" Sindre, who had begun to look bored as I was playing Mr. Chips to my new disciple, perked up as this was more to his liking. "They've locked the doors but I think there are still some people in there closing up." "Good," she replied. "I think my friend was working tonight. Can you come with me? I want to bang on the door and see if they'll answer." Don't know why she needed help banging on the door but I was still deep in the throes of career placement and family planning. Sindre and his leggy companion left for the other end of the parking lot.

I didn't feel so good about being alone with my little runaway. "Where do you live?" she asked. "New York," I answered and she oohed and aahed and told me that she had always wanted to go there. She told me she was born in El Salvador and grew up in Mexico, places I had never been and had always wanted to visit. But she wanted to talk about New York. "How can I get there? Can I take a bus?" I was about to change from guidance counselor to travel agent when Sindre returned. "Hey, look. I guess I'm gonna go. Uh, it was good to see you. I'll talk to you later." I figured some kind of exchange with his friend had transpired in a way to his liking and couldn't really blame him for wanting to make a quick getaway. I'd see him again soon and he'd hopefully have a damn good story.

But that left me alone with my inquisitive friend. And with her friends still across the parking lot I felt a little less sure of the situation. My car was a block away and, while my guitar was pretty much worthless and I had almost no money in my pocket I also wasn't up for a confrontation. I decided it was time to close shop and end the session of night school. "Well, good luck," I told the young girl. "I'm sure you'll do fine."

"Wait. Don't you want to go out for coffee or something?"

"Uh, thanks and everything but I have some friends waiting for me and it's getting late."

"Is it because I'm twenty? Is that why you don't want to go out with me?"

"Yes," I answered. "And because I have a girlfriend. And my friends really are waiting for me. But really, you're going to be fine."

"Can I have your phone number."

"No. Look maybe we'll meet again. It's a funny world."

"I just can't believe I'll never see you again. I really like you."

Well, this was ridiculous. And I was confused about the motivation. I still couldn't figure out why she was so insistent and why she didn't want me to leave. But I couldn't figure out her game. She hadn't asked me for money and her friends seemed oblivious to our conversation. And I began to think that I was in danger of passing up a situation that would make for a good story or at least a good memory. I wasn't attracted to her but I was curious, a little bored, and my friends actually weren't waiting for me. I had nowhere to go.

"Okay, let's go get a cup of coffee."

Her face lit up and next thing I knew we were at the Denny's on Sunset and she was telling me all about her life. How she had run away from juvenile hall when she was younger and had lived on the streets ever since. She had worried that she would be arrested at some point and might have to serve some time for running away but had been lucky so far. She had become good at staying on the right side of the law and really did want to make something better for herself. Maybe move to another state, go to school, get a job. Something. And she said my advice had really helped her.

I don't know at what point I decided that it would be a good idea to invite her to spend the night but that's what happened. And as we drove along Sunset to Beverly Drive and turned right into Beverly Hills she must have thanked me a hundred times. "You're so nice. I really appreciate it."

When we pulled up to the sprawling estate, I hit the high-beams and asked her to get out and get the key. "It's under that potted plant. They leave it here for me when I'm in town."

She quickly found the key and let us into the house. "Wow, it's beautiful," she said as she wandered around, touching everything in her path and picking up objects as if they would disappear unless she personally verified that they actually occupied some physical space.

"Yeah, look. I just want to go to bed. Are you coming?"

And, to be honest, I hadn't intended to have sex with her. Jeez, she was young enough to be my daughter. But these things do happen and I certainly wasn't surprised when I woke up the next morning and she was gone. Yeah, she was gone along with many of the items that had lined the various counters and tables the night before. Jewelry and clocks and things that glittered like gold. They were gone. She was gone.

And I was glad that I had remembered a casual friend pointing out the house where he had done construction the year before. And the story that the owners always leave for the winter for ski trips. And that they always leave the key under the potted plant beside the door. Always figured that information would come in handy. And, of course, when the cops came they would find her fingerprints, not mine, on everything inside the house. I figured that they would have those very prints on file somewhere. Me, I grabbed a few knickknacks and made my way out the door. An adventure, a good story and even a few souvenirs.

I am definitely NOT a mark.

Why I Ate My Wife

from THE CONSUMER

M. GIRA

EVERYTHING MERGES eventually—everything is organic. It's impossible to distinguish one thing from another thing. When your mind is emptied of selfishness, it crumbles and dissolves in the water. If I cut at my body and concentrate correctly, I won't feel it. Each time my heart beats, it jerks violently and whips my spine loose, tugging at the base of my brain. Memories move through the clotted and rotting forest inside my head and crush the present beneath them. My memories don't belong to me. They're as unknowable as a centipede fluttering its legs in the dark corner beneath the sink. When an image moves through my nervous system, it's with the predatory greed of an intruder. My body's laid open, transparent, defenseless. Each second of time is an individual insect feeding on my blood.

When my wife and I joined our bodies together, I fell into her body and wore her skin like a rubber sheath. She protected me from the outside. Because she's dead now, I'm certain to be eaten soon. I'm a skinless body, my muscles drying in the sun. I feel myself shrinking.

I used her as a process, a system through which we could blend with matter beyond our selfish thoughts. When her hand stroked my leg, when her mouth wet my skin, the arousal I experienced was the first wave of a current which would ultimately erase us both. I love her more than I need my own identity. Though her body lies here on the table before me, I don't need to open my eyes to see it in detail, to feel it physically saturate my senses. Love allows microbes and viruses to pass through my body without resistance. In loving her, I lose the will to live. If I eat her body now, I'll take her back into myself. But with each mouthful I swallow, I'll remove a commensurate amount of myself.

Her fragrance lifts up shimmering above her in a mist and flavors the air with honey. Her breasts have now begun to slide down the hill of her ribs, rotting, no longer firm with arrogance or inflated with the promise of fertility. The nipples I once took into my mouth and sucked and chewed, stand straight as if in defiance against the retreat of the body of her breast down her side. Gravity is pulling her down into itself like quicksand. Her belly is shifting, emitting obscure demonic incantations from inside its depths as it breeds gas while decomposing. Looking down at her open mouth, I can still remember the taste, the slightly caramel flavor of her saliva, and feel the rubbery resistance of her tongue slipping into my mouth, circling across my teeth, wrapping itself around my tongue. But now, an open cave in her face displays the dead thick leather tongue like the cadaver of a beached sea mammal, crawled into the dark space of her mouth to hide from the sun and the swarming flies. Her lips, which were once a rare fruit I sucked for juice, are now shriveled and cracked like a dried apricot. Her eyes stare back up at me, searing my face with corrosive acid. My tears drain slowly down the corners of my eyes, thick as mineral oil.

Seven days ago, she stood secretly in the doorway of our bedroom watching me, curled in the bed reading, unaware of her presence, until she had silently approached and breathed warm breath against the back of my neck. Now her flesh lies here devoid of gesture or empathy, reduced down to a process, like yeast reacting to water. The molecules that comprise her body are moving, detaching from one another, rearranging and dissipating into the surrounding chemical stew of biology, no longer held together by the adhesive material of her individual will. I feel my own body churning with particles, genetic material, atoms, parasites. . . .

The smell of her sex crawls into the womb inside my brain where it gestates, forming a perfect memory, a hard red core of impossible lust that glows and warms my thoughts. I bend down to her for a last futile kiss. The inside of her mouth excretes a sticky white glue that smells as if it came from a place deep in the earth—a cache of animal compost hidden in a lightless tomb. I take a serrated kitchen knife and remove her fingers carefully, catching the draining fluids on a white bath towel. I eat these possessed fragments of her soul with empirical care, transfixed by her unblinking eyes. I'm intoxicated with the finality of her memory and the transmission of her taste, odor, and texture into my mind and body.

As weeks pass, each day brings the ingestion of another piece of her essence. As the substance of her being enters me, I'm transformed into an entity beyond myself, and beyond her too. This evolution is just the first step in my own slow decomposition, as I blend with the infinite organisms that will in turn feed on me, ultimately mixing me with the atmosphere . . .

The Lady of the Valley

RAY MANZAREK

THE SUMMER heat had finally come to the valley. It descended like a great weight, pressing down on the head and the chest, making a man unable to think and barely able to breathe.

Esteban sat in the shade of the California bay trees and Fremont cottonwoods and big leaf maples and valley oaks that followed the banks of the river. It was cool in the shade of those trees that lived with the river. It was called a river, but in the heat of August in the Napa Valley it was little more than a trickle. Everything was dry. The land, the trees, the river, the grasses, and especially Esteban's throat. Everything except the grapes. They loved the heat. They were already fat, and now they were beginning to create their sweetness. In another month or so they would be ready to harvest.

But until the crush began—that was what they called the harvesting and the pressing of the grapes—there was nothing for Esteban to do. He should have been in the San Joaquin Valley working the stone fruit: the peaches, apricots, and nectarines. There was always work in the San Joaquin, and every year he worked the stone fruit and the melons until the crush came in the Napa Valley.

But this year was different. This year Esteban just wanted to be in Napa. He felt connected to something when he was there. He felt there was a purpose to things and a reason for a man to be alive.

He loved the small valley—it was only about three miles wide and no more than thirty miles long running north to south—whereas the

San Joaquin was overwhelming, as big as one of those small states on the Atlantic Ocean.

Esteban had never been to the East Coast. There was no work for a Mexican field man in those little states. And he would not work as a cleanup man in a restaurant as many of his countrymen did. He would not work as an unloader of trucks, or a sweeper of offices in the giant glass buildings in the bad-smelling cities, or stand and wait at the paint stores with all the other men, waiting to be hired to paint the walls of the houses of those bad-smelling cities, or a grease man under cars in some garage, fixing the very things that made the cities smell so bad.

He had to work outside, in the air. Where a man could breathe and feel the sun on his shoulders and put his hands into the earth. He needed the soil beneath his feet and under his fingernails. When he saw the black line at the tip of each finger he knew that his hands had done a good day's work. He felt alive then, not like so many of his countrymen all across the *Estados Unidos.* The millions of men who worked the hard and dirty jobs that the white men did not want— nor the black men, either. Those men, his countrymen, kept everything running. Without them, everything would fall apart. The Mexican men knew this; Esteban thought that probably everyone in America knew this, but they could not say it aloud.

And so he sat in the shade, waiting for the crush, and just dreaming in the heat of the valley. He wished he could stay there and work year-round but there was little chance of that. Very few Mexican men were needed after the grapes were harvested. And the ones who did stay and work for the owners of the vineyards, doing all the little tasks that needed to be done in the winter and early spring, were all legal. They had their green cards and many were even citizens. They had families and little homes and Esteban envied them. He knew them, and they liked him. Some had even tried to help him become a citizen, but the reading for the tests was too much for Esteban. The words on the page made his head feel as if the heat of the valley had descended on him.

He felt thick and lethargic and lost all motivation. The names of the presidents and the dates and the Constitution and the branches of government were meaningless to him. Sometimes they would swim about on the page and lose their order in the lines of words, becoming random shapes that Esteban thought looked like the flowers on the stone fruit trees in the springtime in the San Joaquin. And sometimes he could only concentrate on the white spaces at the end of each sentence and where they fell on the page. He would see patterns in those spaces and feel as if there were secrets hiding in those white holes, those blank spaces. And he became more interested in the secrets of the white than the meaning of the black letters.

And so he sat in the shade, waiting for the crush and knowing he probably never would become a citizen. But it didn't matter. He was happy with his life. He had friends in the valleys, a little money in a bank in the town of Napa, Friday and Saturday nights for drinking and a woman when he felt the need for one, and Sundays for the church and for nursing his hangover.

Although lately, Esteban had stopped going to church. He still thought of the little Christ child at Christmas time, and His rising from the dead on Easter—he really didn't know how Jesus had done that—but other than those two days, Esteban had little time for the mysteries of the church. They didn't seem to matter to him anymore. He was more interested in the mysteries behind those white spaces on the page and the many questions those spaces raised in his mind.

But it was too hot even for thinking on that August day. The entire valley seemed to be sleeping in an afternoon haze. Nothing was moving. Only the stream that trickled along over the stones on the river bottom. But then, Esteban thought, the water always moved. It had to, that was its life task. It came down from Mount St. Helena, through the valley, out to the Carneros plain, and finally into the bay of San Pablo, coming to rest only when it merged with the waters of the Pacific Ocean just beyond the Golden Gate Bridge. And then it was gone. It no longer existed. It had become all water, the ocean that encircles the planet. The great ocean that is the same water everywhere, winding continuously around the globe, touching all the land, everywhere.

But where Esteban sat, the water was just a little trickle, and the sound of it moving over the stones was very pleasant, soft and somehow comforting. And the light shinning on the wet stones was bright and glistening and always changing. Esteban felt very good with himself. And so, it seemed, did the valley. It was the kind of day in which even the soil was content with itself, knowing that it was doing its life work. Everything was suspended in a light and heat that made the entire valley seem radiant and untroubled.

Esteban had closed his eyes only for a moment when he heard a woman's voice calling to him. He turned to look up the stream and there she was, standing barefoot in the water, smiling at him.

"How are you, Esteban?" she said. "It's so hot, isn't it? I had to put my feet in the stream." And then she laughed. "Or what little there is left of it. But it is enough, don't you think?"

"Yes," said Esteban. "Enough to cool your feet. But how do you know me?"

"I've always known you."

Now Esteban laughed. "Only my mother has always known me . . . and, *por favor*, you are not my mother."

She smiled and spoke with the sound of birds. "But perhaps I am."

Now Esteban was puzzled. Who was this woman that was standing in front of him, in the little stream, in the heat of this August day, in the middle of the Napa Valley? Was she one of those people who were not all there in the head? One of those wandering, homeless people that always talked to themselves and never seemed to know who they were, or where they were? Or was she one of the drunks that used to always be around the area of the courthouse in the city of Napa? Until, that is, they started to, as they say, gentrify the downtown, bringing back to life the old shops and buildings and offices and even the old, abandoned opera house. Cleaning and painting and restoring everything until a *boracho* had no place to hide anymore. No shadows to disappear into. No cheap bars in which to waste away a life. Was this woman one of those alkys who had been driven out of her sanctuary and was now just wandering in the valley until eventually moving on to the cheap bars in downtown Sacramento? Or had she escaped from the old Napa State Hospital? The hospital that had been there seemingly forever and was, back when it was first built, called The Napa Asylum for the Insane. Was she actually a madwoman?

But none of these possibilities made sense to Esteban. This woman had a beautiful smile and the sound of birds in her voice and her hair was clean. She wore a delicate dress of a beautiful blue cloth, a blue almost like the sky, with little flecks of gold woven into the fabric. The dress softly draped itself over her lithe body—she seemed to be about forty years of age—down to her ankles. If she were one of those others she would have been dirty, with matted hair, and a strange look in her eyes. Instead, Esteban felt an uncommon peace coming from this woman. And yet she said she had always known him and he knew she was not his mother. Esteban, however, had not seen his mother since his last visit—almost five years ago, now—to his home in the little town of Charapan in the hills of Michoacan.

"I'm sorry, ma'am," he said. "But I know you are not my mother."

The woman only laughed and splashed a little water with her feet. It glistened like a spray of diamonds. "Ohh, that feels good," she said. "I was beginning to think I would never cool off.

And then there came a silence and nothing seemed to move, not even the water. The lady looked at Esteban, into his eyes, and then through them, into his core. He felt her gaze enter into him and he felt that she knew everything about him. She knew his joys, his desires, his deepest secrets; and in that instant he knew that he could hide nothing from her. And he also knew that she was the Lady of the Valley and that she had always been there, and she was the heart of everything in the valley, and, perhaps, the heart of everything in the world. In that instant Esteban knew this. And he felt her love for the valley—for the hot waters of Calistoga, the heights of Atlas Peak and the Mayacamas Mountains, for the broad sweep of the Carneros, for the horned owls and blue jays and the mule deer and the black-tailed jackrabbits, for the tiny grapes that hung on the vines that were everywhere on the valley floor, for the Lombardy poplars and the Gingko trees that turned so yellow in the autumn, and the Chinese pistachio that made a riot of colors with its leaves in October. And her love was as great as all things.

"And I love the people, too, Esteban," she said, knowing his thoughts. "That is why I have come to you. For your help."

Now the clarity left Esteban's mind. "I do not understand," he said, feeling very insignificant in her presence. "How can I possibly help you? I am just a harvester of your fruit. I can do nothing but cut the clusters of grapes off the vine. That is all I know. And I am not even legal in this country."

The lady laughed again and little bells sounded in the air. "If you are here . . . you belong here. And you know when the grapes are ready, don't you?"

"Yes, my lady. I know when the sugar is right, and I know when it is time for them to come off the vines. I know how to treat them. You have to be gentle with them when they are ready. They are like a woman about to give birth, filled with ripeness and sweetness."

"And you love those grapes, don't you, Esteban?"

He paused for a moment, reflecting. "When I am working in the vines, once in a while I will take an entire bunch and hold it up in the air, tilt my head back, squeeze the grapes as hard as I can and let the juice pour into my mouth, down my throat, down into me. The taste is so good, so deep and so sweet that I forget myself, and I become the juice. I become the sweetness of the grapes . . . and then, sometimes I think, I *am* the grapes.

He smiled at the lady. "Or they are me. I can't be sure which is which. All I know is that it happens when the sun is bright and hot on me."

"I want you to do something for me, Esteban," the lady said. "I need someone to talk to the people. Someone like themselves, whom they will not be afraid of or think of as an outsider. Someone who understands."

"Understands what?" Esteban asked.

"What you have just spoken of," the lady said.

"But I have only spoken of the grapes. Everybody already knows everything about them. There is nothing I can tell anybody about growing grapes and making wine that they do not already know."

The lady nodded. "I know, but I want you to tell them other things. And I want you to go into the San Joaquin Valley, to Modesto and Merced and Fresno, and down to Bakersfield and tell them. They don't love the San Joaquin like we love our little valley. They need to be reminded more than anyone here in Napa."

"Reminded of what, my lady?"

She splashed the water again and more diamonds rose from the stream, took on a solidity, danced in the air for a moment, sparkling, and then fell back into their original element. Water into water. "Do you remember the story of Adam and Eve in the Bible?" she asked Esteban.

"Everyone does. God was very angry at them."

The lady smiled. "Well, what if He wasn't?"

"Then why did He throw them out of the Garden? He told them not to eat the fruit, and when they did, He got angry at their sin and threw them out into the world, to suffer forever. And we are their children."

"But I'm telling you, Esteban, He didn't get angry," the lady said.

"Then why do we have to suffer for their sins?"

"Who's suffering?"

"We are all suffering," Esteban said. "All mankind."

"Are *you*, Esteban?"

"Well, not right now. Not on a day like this." He spread his arms out and looked up at the sun. "This is a beautiful day." Then he turned his gaze back to the woman in the stream. "But sometimes I suffer. Yes, sometimes I do."

"And how do you suffer?"

He had to think about that. He actually could not remember suffering like the Bible spoke of, but he gave it a good effort, just to be accommodating. "Well . . . sometimes I get cold and wet. In the winter, when the rains come, I feel soaked to my bones and I shiver with the freezing cold. I hate that, my lady."

"Of course you do. No one likes to be cold. But isn't it wonderful when the rain finally stops and the warm sun shines down on everything? Doesn't that feel good?"

"Yes, my lady. Nothing could feel better."

"Esteban, do you suppose our sun is the same sun that warmed the Garden of Eden?"

"I don't know. Is it possible?"

"Yes, it *is* possible."

Esteban could not even imagine such a thing. He looked up at the sun—perhaps the same sun that had shone down on Adam and Eve—up through the leaves of the cottonwoods and the laurel trees, the valley oaks and the big leaf maples that lived along the water's edge. And the leaves of the trees broke up the direct sunlight, scattering the rays of light into dancing patterns that played on everything around Esteban and the lady. Beyond the trees the light was straight and hot, but where the two were, on the banks of the Napa river, everything was diffused and soft.

Esteban held his head up to the sun—just as he did when he squeezed the juice of the grapes into his mouth—and drank in the dancing light, feeling it play over his face. It felt comforting and good, like it did when he was a child in Michoacan and would lie under a tree in the summertime when there was no work to be done and it was too hot for games. He remembered how he stared up through the branches and leaves at the passing clouds and felt almost as if he could fly up into the midst of them. As if he could rise up off the earth and just float away into the sky.

And now, as a man, he was feeling it again. Being in the valley on that hot summer day, in the presence of the lady, with the sun shinning down from the clear sky and its light dazzling his eyes, Esteban began to feel as if he could float off the earth. He felt as if he could rise up like a bird and take flight into that sun. Up, and out into the blueness. Up, into the clean air, into the light of the sun. Held aloft by the energy of the light. Floating on the rays of the sun. In light. In the air. A child again, with no fear.

He turned his head to his companion. "My lady, I feel like I did when I was a boy back in Michoacan." There was wonder in his voice. "I swear I could fly if I wanted to, into that sun!"

The lady smiled at Esteban. "Now you know what the Christ child was talking about when he became a man. 'You must become like a child again to enter the kingdom of heaven,' he said. He remembered what it was like to feel the peace of childhood and to be cradled in the arms of his father, the sun, just like you are. You are feeling the same thing he did."

Esteban sat there, almost in a trance. Then he realized what the lady had said. "I am feeling the same thing that Jesus felt? But how can that be? I am just a man."

"So was he," the lady said.

"But he was God, my lady. Everyone knows that."

"Did he walk on this planet, Esteban? Did he sit in the shade of a tree when he told his stories to the people? Just like you are sitting in the shade, right here, right now. Did he eat and drink, did he sleep, did he laugh? Was he born of the flesh, born of a woman, did he live . . . and did he die?"

Esteban nodded. "Yes, he did all of those things."

"Then he was a man," the lady said. "Those are the things a man does. Gods do not eat and drink and laugh. Gods do not walk on the earth. Men and women, they walk on the earth. They make love and give birth to their children. They laugh and live and die. Just like you, Esteban. Just like Jesus."

"He didn't make love, my lady. Jesus would not make love to a woman."

"Why not? Didn't he talk about love? Wasn't that his whole mission? To have people love each other? He wanted everyone to love God and, as he said, 'love thy neighbor as thyself.' He wanted people to be in love . . . with everything!" She stretched her arms out as if to encompass the whole valley and laughed little pearls out into the air. "With *everything*, Esteban."

Her laughter seemed to enter Esteban's heart. It hit him in the chest and vibrated into the core of energy behind his ribs. Then it spread quickly through his body, tickling him from his toes to the top of his head. And it was not unlike sex.

The feeling in the nerve ends of his entire body was sweet and exquisite. So sweet that Esteban had to laugh out loud. "Oh, my lady. I feel so good! Between the warmth of the sun and your laughter in my heart . . . I have never felt . . . so happy!"

"And that is how the Christ child felt," the lady said. "The sun was the same for him as it is this day for you. As it is for everyone on our planet." Then she raised her arms to the sky, cupping her hands together as if to contain the energy of the sun, as if it were water from the stream.

"The sun is for all of us," she said. It is our great love and our joy. It spreads over the entire earth, giving life to all the things that live on the earth. All the plants and animals and people. We are all the children of the sun. He is our father."

"And you . . ." Esteban looked at the lady standing barefoot in the little stream with her arms extended up to the sky and her hands cupped together as if to catch a liquid sunbeam. "You are our mother, aren't you?"

The lady brought her arms down out of the sky, down to her sides, and smiled at Esteban, deeply.

"Then we," he went on. "We are *your* children, too."

"Yes, Esteban," she said. "You are."

Now it was his turn to smile at the lady. "And if we are your children, you must have made love to somebody to give birth to us. Am I right?"

The lady turned her gaze away from Esteban demurely, almost shyly, like a young girl. "Yes, Esteban."

In that moment, with that gesture, he realized that he loved her. It was a love of a surprising tenderness that Esteban had never felt before, and he knew he would do anything to protect her. "You made love to the sun, didn't you, my lady."

She nodded her affirmation.

"He is not your father. He is your lover."

Time was suspended again. Everything seemed to stop, waiting for the lady's reply.

"Yes, Esteban. He is my lover." And she turned back to him, her eyes sparkling. "But without him, I would not exist. So he is my father, too."

"But without you . . . we would not exist. Am I right, my lady? There cannot be only a man. There must be a woman, too. The woman gives birth to life. Without you, nothing could live on this planet. I would not be here, this valley would not be here, if it were not for you."

"Yes, Esteban. I have given birth to you, and the energy of the sun sustains you. As it sustains me, and all of us. Without the light nothing of the flesh exists. Without the light there would be nothing but the darkness, waiting for existence to begin. Waiting for the sun to begin the creation of the world. The darkness is the respite for our days of life in the light. And in that light we are alive."

"And it is always there, isn't it? For all of us," Esteban said.

"Yes, it is always the same. The warmth and the energy never change. In the the time of ancient Egypt there was once a pharaoh who loved the sun. The same sun you sit under, Esteban. And he spoke of his love for the light to all his people, the people of Egypt."

As she spoke, the lady stepped out of the stream and sat down softly in the shade across the stream from Esteban. She faced the Mayacamas Mountains to the west as Esteban looked east to the Silverado Trail and beyond to Atlas Peak. And she continued:

" 'Look at your father in the sky,' the pharaoh said to them. 'Look how the good sun rises in the east, the horizon of his dawning. He is the morning light calling forth all his creation from the darkness. All his children from their sleep. All his birds of the air and his beasts of the fields and even his fishes of the sea. He calls them all to life. And he loves everything, from the least of his creatures to his greatest creation . . . *you*, my people. And he only wants you to sing and dance in his light. He calls you forth in the morning to go again into the world and live your lives, fully and joyously, delighting in all the pleasures of the earth.' "

The lady paused for a moment, as if to catch her breath in the rush of words.

" 'And at the noon time,' the pharaoh said to his people, 'your father wants you to sit in the shade of his trees and enjoy your lunch with him. To drink a little wine from his grapes as you eat your bread from his fields and your cheese from his cows and goats. He wants you to rest from your morning's labors and refresh yourself. And to think about how good it is to be alive in his light, alive on our glorious earth.'

"The pharoah went on to tell his people of the joys of our planet, Esteban. All the joys of our days. He said to them: 'And your father in the heavens wants you to go forth and complete your day's task. He wants you to love one another as he loves you. He wants your families to come together at eventide and give a word of thanks to him and to eat your evening meal with each other in love and peace, enjoying the fruits of your labors. And he wants you to sing and play music around your fires at night, enjoying the great canopy of stars he has placed over our heads. The stars that we will all become when we leave our bodies behind on this earth and enter into the light with him. Rejoining him in the energy, the oneness!' " And then the lady stopped. She raised her head to the light and rested in her thoughts, smiling to herself as though at some ancient memory.

"My lady, he did love the sun, didn't he," Esteban said as he turned to the light. "That pharaoh felt the same life that we are feeling now." He raised his arm to the sky and opened his hand to cup the sun as if he were cupping a woman's breast, softly and with great tenderness.

He sat there, feeling the radiance in his fingertips and in his palm, and it was warm and had a life of its own. It was a life that could give life to the earth and sustain all things, and it carried with it all the answers to the questions that the white spaces on the printed pages had created in Esteban's mind.

"I understand, my lady. I think I know the answer now. It's all so easy," he said as he turned his outstretched hand in the air, caressing the sunlight as it warmed his palm. "Lately I had been wondering about things."

The leaves of the valley oaks and the big leaf maples and the arroyo willows and the California buckeyes danced a veil of shadows across the lady's face. "What kind of things, Esteban?"

"Ohh . . . about being alive, I suppose. Why are we alive? There must be some reason. After all, why should I even exist? Me, Esteban Morelos . . . what right do I have? I am nothing but a simple man. The earth does not need me. It wouldn't matter if I was ever here or not."

"But you love the soil, don't you, Esteban? You love this valley and everything in it, yes?"

"You know I do, my lady."

"Then the earth *does* need you. It needs to be loved. The earth will perish, it will wither and die if people do not love it. The earth needs the love of its people to continue its existence. Our energy is like the energy of the sun. We nourish everything. The plants and the trees and all the animals can feel our love, if we give it, and the resonance of our love can heal them and make them more abundant."

"But how is that, my lady?"

The lady of the valley smiled at Esteban, across the trickling little stream. "Simply because they feel good, Esteban. They feel happy and secure being with us, if we love them. They have no words to express themselves—or confuse themselves, as we do—they have only their feelings, which are much more acute than those of humans. Consequently, they thrive or die away with our love of them, or our mistreatment of them."

"I think the earth can get along without people, my lady," Esteban said, "but the people cannot get along without everything you have created for them."

"That is true, Esteban. But now that people exist, the earth is dependent on them. Before there was human conciousness, the earth went about its business of being the home for all the plants and animals and fishes and birds. But then the humans came into existence, and the earth was over-joyed at their ability to understand the mysteries of life. The earth was delighted that these new creatures could understand and appreciate what, exactly, the earth was. Only the humans knew that our home was a globe, spinning around the sun, in the vastness of an infinite universe. Only the humans knew how all life was connected and lived together in depend-ency, on all the land and in all the oceans. And the earth was proud that these new creatures could understand the great dwelling place that the earth actually is. And then the earth fell in love with the humans. And it felt good to the earth to be in love. And now the earth needs that love. It cannot survive without that love, that energy."

Esteban smiled at the lady. "And that energy, for all humans, is the sun, isn't it? The sun loves us the way the earth loves us, and we, the people, must love the earth the way the sun loves us. With the same warmth and beautiful energy. Is that it, my lady?"

The veil of light and shadow danced across the lady's face, partly hiding her smile. "Yes, Esteban. That is it."

Esteban rose to his feet and extended both arms to the sky, up into the light as far as they could go. "Then the sun is the answer, my lady. It's why I am here. To feel its warmth on my face, on my hands, all over my entire body." He smiled up into the light. "To feel . . . how good it feels. And inside of me, too." He brought his hands out of the sky and held them to his chest, over his heart, pressing his strong, callused hands against his ribs. "In here, my lady. I can feel the warmth in my heart."

Then Esteban became silent for a moment, his eyes closed, his head turned up to the sun, his hands clasped together over his heart. He seemed to be transported, beyond himself, in a kind of enchantment. And the lady of the valley looked lovingly at him. She knew what he was feeling. This was what she had come for. Esteban was now ready to understand. She knew he was a good man. She knew he did not harbor any of the resentments in his heart that were destroying the joy of the people of the earth. She knew that greed and lust and anger and envy had not eaten into and permanently attached themselves to Esteban. She knew the light of the father in the sky would warm Esteban's heart and burn away any evil and any fear. And so she smiled at Esteban as he stood there in his rapture.

Finally, Esteban spoke. His voice was calm and peaceful. "The energy is like . . . it is like, everything. We come from that energy . . . we *are* that energy . . . and then we dance and sing in the light of that energy. Here, on earth! We live in the light and we are the light. And that energy will support us. We do not have to be afraid. As long as that sun is in the sky, as long as our *father* is in the sky . . . there is nothing to fear. There is no reason to kill each other. There is no reason to go crazy with anger . . . and kill another man."

He continued in his revelation, speaking with a new assurance. "We have to trust in the energy. I can feel it, my lady. It will take care of us. It will support us in all things, because . . . because it *is* us. And *we* are the energy. And the light of the sun is the purest energy there is. And it is where we have all come from." He took his hands from his heart, stretched his arms out to the valley and turned in a circle. A circle of enchantment. "It is where *everything* has come from! And it is where we will all go . . . someday."

Esteban turned to the lady, away from the Mayacamas, where the sun would set behind the mountain range and eventually into the Pacific Ocean. "I know it is true, my lady. I can feel it in my heart. This is why I am here, this feeling . . . inside of me. *This* is the truth." And he placed his left hand over his heart. *"Mi corazon."*

"Yes, Esteban. I knew you would understand. It is the light, the fire in your heart. And once it begins to burn, the flame will never go out. It is in you now . . . forever. It will always be with you, to support you in all the things you do. To be your warmth in even the coldest, darkest times. You will never have to be afraid ever again. You can live your life the way it is supposed to be lived, in joy and delight and ecstasy. Because you know who you are."

Esteban bent down and reached his hands into the stream and splashed cool water onto his face. The beads glistened on his skin as he smiled at the lady of the valley. "I am everything! I am the sun, the moon, the air, and this water." He rose up and kicked at the water, the little stream that the Napa River had become, and diamonds once again flew up into the air. "I am all of it, my lady . . . and so is *everyone*. But I think they have forgotten."

"They have," the lady said. "And that is what I need you for, Esteban. To remind them. Can you do this for me? Can you tell them of what they have forgotten?"

"Have we always known these things?" Esteban asked in turn. "I have a feeling that somehow I have always understood, you know, somewhere inside of me, perhaps in . . . I'm not sure. Have we, my lady?"

"Yes, Esteban. We all know the answers. Deep inside ourselves, we know. Because when each of us is in our mother's womb, we know all the secrets, all the answers, all the reasons. We know everything in the womb. And then at the moment we come out of the water and into the air . . . we forget everything. It all goes out of our heads at the moment we take our first breath. And then we are innocent babes, knowing nothing, with everything ahead of us. Our entire lives ahead of us . . . the great adventure of our lives on earth. Everything yet to come. Our entire destiny yet to come. And that is the way of life, Esteban."

Esteban laughed with elation, for he recognized a great truth, and it pleased him. "Then how simple it is, my lady. The answers to all our problems have always been with us. All we have to do is remember them."

"The answers are all in our hearts, Esteban," said the lady. "But they are locked in by our fears. And do you know what the key is, Esteban? The key to unlock ourselves?"

"Yes, my lady. *Now* I do!" Esteban said, almost shouting his joy into the air.

The lady of the valley smiled at his outburst of delight. "Then tell me, my son."

"The *light* is the key. The light of the sun, shining down on us, into our bodies and into our hearts! Warming us all over! I am free, now. My heart is alive again. I feel so good, my lady, like a child again. And what I felt in the womb of my mother . . . I now feel in the warmth of my father. I am the light of my father. I am alive, my lady."

"As you always have been and always will be, my son," the lady said.

Esteban brought his hands to his chest, over his heart, and looked up into the sun, enchanted. And for a moment everything was suspended again. The valley seemed to draw in its breath and hold it for an instant as one of its children ascended into the sky. Into the light, aloft, in the arms of his father.

And the lady of the valley was glad in her heart, for Esteban had come home to his mother and his father. Now he understood. And so she stepped behind one of the valley oaks on the bank of the little stream that ran down the center of the Napa Valley, her valley, and was gone.

Esteban stood with his eyes closed, his face to the light as the sun began to approach the ridge of the Mayacamas Mountains. "This is the light of the Garden of Eden, my lady. It is the same sun that gave light every day to Adam and Eve."

He opened his eyes ever so slightly and looked at the sun through his lashes as the light danced over his face. "Our sun is the same sun that was there at the beginning. It hasn't changed."

Then an idea came to Esteban. "My lady, if this is the same sun that was shining down on the Garden of Eden . . . why couldn't this still be the Garden of Eden? If God was not angry at Adam and Eve, perhaps He never threw them out of the Garden. Perhaps they only forgot . . . like children just out of their mother's wombs, they forgot. They ate the fruit, gained the knowledge of good and evil, life and death, and became so caught up with trying to preserve their lives that they forgot they were living in the Garden of Eden."

Esteban took a deep breath, filling his lungs with the sweet air of the Napa Valley. "I know what you want me to do, my lady. To remind everyone that this is *still* the Garden of Eden. We never lost it. It is still here. We only have to remember it." He turned to the lady of the valley. "Isn't that it, my lady? And he saw that she was gone. "My lady?"

But there was no answer. Only the sound of the trickling stream, a sound like the high laughter of children, and the chattering of the birds as they began preparations for their twilight concert, and the faint buzzing of the flying insects as they darted about, glistening their iridescence in the rays of the setting sun. And then a breeze began to blow, rustling the leaves in the trees, cooling the afternoon heat of the Napa Valley and carrying the good sweet smell of the ripening grapes to Esteban's nostrils. He loved that smell of the grapes and he knew their time was near. And he knew that the abundance around him was the abudance of the Garden of Eden. And he knew his father was in the sky and his mother was the very earth itself. And he knew he was alive!

And this is what he would tell the people, as the lady of the valley had asked him.

Author Biographies

ERIC BURDON was the driving force of the grittiest British Invasion band, the Animals, pioneered the San Francisco psychedelic rock scene as Eric Burdon and the New Animals, fronted WAR, the biggest funk band of the seventies, and continues to tour relentlessly with new incarnations of the Animals. He is the author of two memoirs, *I Used to Be an Animal, But I'm All Right Now* and *Don't Let Me Be Misunderstood*, written with J. Marshall Craig. In 1995 Eric was inducted into the Rock and Roll Hall of Fame.

JIM CARROLL is a poet, musician, and diarist from New York City. As frontman for the Jim Carroll Band, he recorded three albums for Atlantic Records: *Catholic Boy*, *Dry Dreams*, and *I Write Your Name*. His autobiography, *The Basketball Diaries*, which recounts his youth as a troubled basketball star at Trinity High School, became a national best-seller and feature film. Carroll's books include *Living at the Movies, Fear of Dreaming, The Book of Nods, Forced Entries,* and *Void of Course*. His writing has also appeared in *Rolling Stone, Poetry,* and the *Paris Review*.

EXENE CERVENKA was the co-lead singer and songwriter of the Los Angeles punk group X. Her new band, Original Sinners, recently released their first LP. She has contributed to several books, including *Forming: The Early Days of Punk* and *Adulterers Anonymous*. Her own collection of poetry, *Virtual Unreality*, was released in 1996.

RAY DAVIES was the driving force behind the influential British Invasion band The Kinks. As lead singer, songwriter, and rhythm guitarist with the Kinks, Davies recorded thirty albums and penned the hit singles "Lola" and "You Really Got Me." Following his time with the Kinks, Davies went on to become somewhat of a renaissance man, recording two solo albums, including the soundtrack for the film *Return to Waterloo*, which he wrote and directed, as well as authoring four books, including three collections of short stories, and his autobiography, *X-Ray*.

PAMELA DES BARRES is the author of three books *I'm with the Band: Confessions of a Groupie, Rock Bottom: Dark Moments in Music Babylon,* and *Take Another Little Piece of My Heart: A Groupie Grows Up.* She was a member of the legendary GTOs (Girls Together Outrageously), the "groupie group," whose 1969 album *Permanent Damage* was produced by Frank Zappa.

STEVE EARLE is a country-blues guitarist and songwriter. He has released over fifteen albums, the most recent of which, *Jerusalem,* came out in 2002. Earle is also the author of *Doghouse Roses,* a collection of short stories.

JOHN ENTWISTLE was the bassist for the Who and often considered one of the most influential bassists in rock history. Entwistle's career with the Who, as well as with various solo and side projects, and most recently with the John Entwistle Band, produced dozens of albums. He was also a noted songwriter whose credits include the Who's "Boris the Spider." Entwistle died in 2002 at the age of fifty-seven.

MICK FARREN is best known as the lead singer of the Deviants and is one of the driving forces in Europe's underground rock movement. In his four decades of creative output, Mick has released twenty-three novels, eleven nonfiction books, and nearly twenty albums. His latest novel is *Underland.*

KINKY FRIEDMAN is perhaps best known for his groundbreaking and provocatively titled band Kinky Friedman and His Texas Jewboys. With their unique brand of satirical country songs, Kinky and the Jewboys enjoyed enormous success, touring with the likes of Bob Dylan. Kinky has enjoyed a successful writing career, having written more than a dozen books including, *Meanwhile, Back at the Ranch* and the forthcoming *Kill Two Birds and Get Stoned.*

M. GIRA is a founding member of the seminal New York avant-garde band Swans, who have released over fifteen albums to date. Gira has also enjoyed a prominent solo and collaborative recording career as well as having authored *The Consumer and Other Stories,* a collection of short stories and prose, which was lauded by Dennis Cooper as "one of the purest, scariest, and most beautiful books I've read in years."

RICHARD HELL helped launch the punk revolution with the Neon Boys and later the Heartbreakers. He formed the Voidoids in 1976, and released *Blank Generation*, an album whose title song remains a defining anthem of punk sensibility. He is the author of several books, including *Go Now* and *Hot and Cold*.

ROBYN HITCHCOCK launched his career with the Soft Boys, a not-quite punk band. After the Soft Boys disbanded in the early Eighties, Hitchcock embarked on a remarkable solo career, producing albums like *I Often Dream of Trains* and *Jewels for Sophia*. With his second band, the Egyptions, Hitchcock released *Element of Light, Globe of Light*, and *Perspex Island*. The Soft Boys have recently reunited, released a new record *Nextdoorland*, and resumed touring.

JOAN JETT'S musical career began with the monumental all-girl band the Runaways in the late 1970s. After the band's breakup, Jett went on to become one of the most successful female rockers of the Eighties, releasing her first solo album, the classic *Bad Reputation*, in 1981. Shortly thereafter, she formed the Blackhearts, releasing such chart-topping classics as *I Love Rock 'N' Roll, Album, Glorious Results of a Misspent Youth, Up Your Alley*, and *Fetish*.

GREG KIHN had a slew of hit records in the Eighties (including the international number one "Jeopardy" and "The Breakup Song"), published four novels in the Nineties (*Horror Show* was nominated for the Bram Stoker Award for best first novel), and now hosts the morning show on 98.5 KFOX radio in San Jose, California (currently number one in the ratings). He has toured the world and played with virtually every major rock band of his generation, including the Rolling Stones. He is now working on *Rubber Soul*, a Beatles novel. He lives in northern California and likes tomato juice.

LARRY KIRWAN has released ten records as the leader of the Irish-American rock band Black 47 and is the author of a collection of plays titled *Mad Angels*. His first novel, *Liverpool Fantasy*, is scheduled for release in 2003.

MARY LEE KORTES is the lead singer and songwriter of the critically acclaimed New York-based band Mary Lee's Corvette. Their album *True Lovers of Adventure* was rated "the best album of 1999" by *Billboard Magazine*.

USA Today praised her "wide-ranging musical intelligence matched by smart lyrics," while *Entertainment Weekly* applauded her "lovely, nuanced voice and deft storytelling." The band's most recent album is a live cover of Bob Dylan's *Blood on the Tracks.* In addition to writing for Mary Lee's Corvette, Kortes has penned hit singles for Amy Grant and Once Blue. As a singer, she has recorded with a wide range of artists, from Placido Domingo to Billy Joel.

WAYNE KRAMER: Ex-MC5. Ex-convict. Ex-substance abuser. Extremely happy fellow. Plays guitar. Writes songs. Makes records. Produces bands. Runs record company. Sings. Dances.

MARC LAIDLAW is the author of six books: *Dad's Nuke, The Orchid Eaters, Kalifornia, The Third Force,* and *The 37th Mandala.*

LYDIA LUNCH is a musician, author, actress, and photographer. Her musical career began with Teenage Jesus and the Jerks and has seen success with several solo albums including *Queen of Siam* and *Widowspeak,* as well as collaborative efforts with the likes of the Birthday Party and Einstürzende Neubauten. Her books include *Incriminating Evidence* and *Adulterers Anonymous,* written with Exene Cervenka.

ANN MAGNUSON is an actress, singer, writer, and part-time performance artist. She has performed Off-Broadway and in theaters, galleries, and nightclubs around the globe as well as at the Serious Fun! Festival at Lincoln Center and the Museum of Modern Art. She appeared in the films *Making Mr. Right, Clear and Present Danger,* and *Panic Room,* as well as in numerous independent features. She was the lead singer and lyricist for the band Bongwater and released a solo album, *The Luv Show,* for Geffen Records. She pens a monthly column "L.A. Woman" for *PAPER* magazine. Get on the electronic mailing list via www.annmagnuson.com.

RAY MANZAREK is best known as a founding member and keyboardist for The Doors. He has also released two solo albums, *Golden Scarab* and *Carmina Burana.* In addition to being a musician, Manzarek is the author of the autobiographical *Light My Fire,* detailing his experiences with the Doors and his life after leaving the group, as well as a novel, *The Poet in Exile: A Journey Into the Mystic.*

WILLIE NILE has been hailed by the *New York Times* as "the most gifted songwriter to emerge from the New York scene in some time." *Beautiful Wreck of the World*, the most recent album from the highly acclaimed Buffalo, New York-born singer, was chosen as one of the top ten Albums of the Year by critics at *Billboard* magazine, the *Village Voice*, and *Stereo Review*, also reaching the finals of the Independent Music Awards for best rock album of the year. Lucinda Williams called "On the Road to Calvary," the song Nile wrote about Jeff Buckley, "One of the most beautiful songs I've ever heard." Nile, who currently lives in New York City, is working on a new album for a spring 2003 release. More information about Willie Nile is available at www.willienile.com.

GRAHAM PARKER first rose to prominence in the 1970s with his band the Rumour, who released such new wave classics as *Howlin' Wind*, *Heat Treatment*, *Stick to Me*, and *Squeezing Out Sparks*. Beginning in the 1980s, Parker embarked on a solo career that has produced a number of successful albums including *The Mona Lisa's Sister*, *Human Soul*, *Struck by Lightning*, *Burning Questions*, and *12 Haunted Episodes*. His most recent album is *Deepcut to Nowhere*. His first book, *Carp Fishing on Valium: And Other Tales of the Stranger Road Traveled* was released in 2000.

SUZZY ROCHE helped pioneer the girl band movement in the late seventies as the youngest sister in the aptly named group, the Roches. Their albums include *We Three Kings*, *The Roches*, and *Will You Be My Friend?* With the Roches, Suzzy has performed on *The Tonight Show*, *David Letterman*, and *Saturday Night Live*.

JOHN SHIRLEY is a true renaissance man—screenwriter, punk musician, lyricist, novelist, essayist, and short story writer. He released *Red Star* with the Panther Moderns, and provided many of the lyrics for Blue Oyster Cult's *Curse of the Hidden Mirror* and *Heaven Forbid*. John has written a number of science fiction novels, including *City Come-Walkin'*, *Transmaniacon*, and *Eclipse*, as well as numerous thrillers including *A Splendid Chaos* and *Three-Ring Psychus*. His screenwriting credits include *The Crow*, *Deep Space Nine*, *VR5*, and *Poltergeist*.

JOHNNY STRIKE began his musical career on lead guitar and vocals for Crime. Billed as San Francisco's first and only rock and roll band, the group is widely credited with founding the city's punk scene. Strike now performs with TVH, whose album *Night Raid on Lisbon Street* was released in 2002. His writing has been previously published in a number of journals including *Headpress* and *Ambit*. His first novel, *Ports of Hell*, will be published by Diagonal in the fall of 2003.

PETE TOWNSHEND is the guitarist, synthesisist, composer, and co-founder of the Who. He has also released a number of solo albums, including *Empty Glass, All the Best Cowboys Have Chinese Eyes*, and *Psychoderelict*. His literary interest sparked the creation of the Magic Bus Bookstore, a small publishing company called Eel Pie Press, and his first collection of short stories, *Horse's Neck*.

STEVE WYNN is acknowledged as one of the great cult artists in rock music. Novelist George Pelecanos calls Wynn's songs "the aural equivalent of noir literature." The founder and lead singer of the Dream Syndicate, with whom he released four albums, Wynn has also released seven solo albums and two with the indie supergroup Gutterball. His latest album is *Here Comes the Miracles*.

Credits